THE
COMING PRINCE

THE
COMING PRINCE

by
Sir Robert Anderson

Biographical Sketch
by
Warren W. Wiersbe

KREGEL PUBLICATIONS
Grand Rapids, Michigan 49501

The Coming Prince by Sir Robert Anderson.
Reprinted 1957 and copyrighted ©1984 by Kregel
Publications, a division of Kregel, Inc. All rights
reserved.

Kregel Reprint of the Tenth edition 1957
Reprinted 1963, 1967, 1969, 1972, 1975, 1977,
1980, 1982, 1983, 1984, 1986

(Sir Robert Anderson Library)

Library of Congress Catalog Card Number 63-11464
ISBN 0-8254-2115-2

Printed in the United States of America

CONTENTS

v

APPENDICES

To assist the reader's understanding, the publisher now offers additional facts and developments since this work was first published.

When you are reading you'll come across some small numbers in the text (1, 2, 3 etc.). Numbers corresponding to these numbers are listed in Appendix 4 found on pages 305, 306, 307, which contain this updated information.

PREFACE TO THE TENTH EDITION

THE COMING PRINCE has been out of print
for more than a year; for it seemed inadvisable
to reissue it during the War.[1] But the War has
apparently created an increased interest in the
prophecies of Daniel; and as this book is therefore
in demand, it has been decided to publish a new
edition without further delay. Not that these pages
contain any sensational "Armageddon" theories. For
"a place called in the Hebrew tongue Armageddon"
is situated neither in France nor in Flanders, but in
Palestine; and the future of the land and people of
the covenant will be a main issue in the great battle
which is yet to be fought on that historic plain.

Prophetic students are apt to become adherents of
one or other of two rival schools of interpretation.
The teaching of the "futurists" suggests that this
Christian dispensation is altogether a blank in the
Divine scheme of prophecy. And the "historicists"
discredit Scripture by frittering away the meaning
of plain words in order to find the fulfilment of
them in history. Avoiding the errors of both these
schools, this volume is written in the spirit of Lord

---

1 See Appendix 4, p. 305 note 1

Bacon's dictum, that " Divine prophecies have springing and germinant accomplishment throughout many
ages, though the height or fulness of them may belong
to some one age." And this world war is no doubt
within the scope of prophecy, though it be not the
fulfilment of any special Scripture.

Very many years ago my attention was directed
to a volume of sermons by a devout Jewish Rabbi of
the London Synagogue, in which he sought to discredit the Christian interpretation of certain Messianic
prophecies. And in dealing with Daniel ix., he
accused Christian expositors of tampering, not only
with chronology, but with Scripture, in their efforts
to apply the prophecy of the Seventy Weeks to the
Nazarene. My indignation at such a charge gave
place to distress when the course of study to which it
led me brought proof that it was by no means a baseless libel. My faith in the Book of Daniel, already
disturbed by the German infidel crusade of " the
Higher Criticism," was thus further undermined.
And I decided to take up the study of the subject
with a fixed determination to accept without reserve
not only the language of Scripture, but the standard
dates of history as settled by our best modern
chronologists.*

---

* As regards the regnal years of Jewish Kings, however,
Fynes Clinton's month dates are here modified in accordance
with the Hebrew *Mishna*, which was a sealed book to English

The following is a brief summary of the results of my inquiry as regards the great prophecy of the "Seventy Weeks." I began with the assumption, based on the perusal of many standard works, that the era in question had reference to the seventy years of the Captivity of Judah, and that it was to end with the Coming of Messiah. But I soon made the startling discovery that this was quite erroneous. For the Captivity lasted only sixty-two years; and the seventy weeks related to the wholly different judgment of the Desolations of Jerusalem. And further, the period "unto Messiah the Prince," as Daniel ix. 25 so plainly states, was not seventy weeks, but $7+62$ weeks.

The failure to distinguish between the several judgments of the Servitude, the Captivity and the Desolations, is a fruitful source of error in the study of Daniel and the historical books of Scripture. And it is strange that the distinction should be ignored not only by the Critics, but by Christians. Because of national sin, Judah was brought under servitude to Babylon for seventy years, this was in the third year of King Jehoiakim (B.C. 606). But the people continued obdurate; and in B.C. 598 the far severer judgment of the Captivity fell on them. On the

readers when the *Fasti Hellenici* was written. With reference to one date of cardinal importance I am specially indebted to the late Canon Rawlinson and the late Sir George Airey.

former capture of Jerusalem, Nebuchadnezzar left the city and people undisturbed, his only prisoners being Daniel and other cadets of the royal house. But on this second occasion he deported the mass of the inhabitants to Chaldea. The Jews still remained impenitent, however, in spite of Divine warnings by the mouth of Jeremiah in Jerusalem and Ezekiel among the exiles ; and after the lapse of another nine years, God brought upon them the terrible judgment of " The Desolations," which was decreed to last for seventy years. Accordingly in B.C. 589, the Babylonian armies again invaded Judea, and the city was devastated and burned.

Now both the " Servitude" and the " Captivity," ended with the decree of Cyrus in B.C. 536, permitting the return of the exiles. But as the language of Daniel ix. 2 so plainly states, it was the seventy years of " The Desolations " that were the basis of the prophecy of the seventy weeks. And the epoch of that seventy years was the day on which Jerusalem was invested—the tenth Tebeth in the ninth year of Zedekiah—a day that has ever since been observed as a fast by the Jews in every land. (2 Kings xxv. 1.) Daniel and Revelation definitely indicate that the prophetic year is one of 360 days. Such moreover was the sacred year of the Jewish calendar ; and, as is well known, such was the ancient year of Eastern nations. (See p. 68, *post.*) Now seventy years of 360 days contains exactly 25,200 days; and as the Jewish New Year's day depended on the equinoctial moon, we can assign the 13th December as "the Julian date" of tenth Tebeth 589. And 25,200 days measured from that date ended on the 17th December 520, which was the twenty-fourth day of the ninth month in the second year of Darius of Persia—the very day on which the foundation of the second Temple was laid. (Haggai ii. 18, 19. See p. 70, *post*.)

Here is something to set both critics and Christians thinking. A decree of a Persian king was deemed to be divine, and any attempt to thwart it was usually met by prompt and drastic punishment; and yet the decree directing the rebuilding of the Temple, issued by King Cyrus in the zenith of his power, was thwarted for seventeen years by petty local governors. How was this? The explanation is that until the very last day of the seventy years of "the Desolations" had expired, God would not permit one stone to be laid upon another on Mount Moriah.

Dismissing from our minds, therefore, all mere *theories* on this subject, we arrive at the following definitely ascertained *facts* :—

I. The epoch of the Seventy Weeks was the issuing of a decree to restore and build Jerusalem. (Dan. ix. 25.)

2. There never was but one decree for the rebuilding of Jerusalem. (See p. 59, *post*.)

3. That decree was issued by Artaxerxes, King of Persia, in the month Nisan in the 20th year of his reign, *i.e.* B.C. 445. (See pp. 60–63, *post*.)

4. The city was actually built in pursuance of that decree.

5. The Julian date of 1st Nisan 445 was the 14th March. (See p. 123, *post*.)

6. Sixty-nine weeks of years—*i.e.* 173,880 days—reckoned from the 14th March B.C. 445, ended on the 6th April A.D. 32. (See p. 127, *post*.)

7. That day, on which the sixty-nine weeks ended, was the fateful day on which the Lord Jesus rode into Jerusalem in fulfilment of the prophecy of Zechariah ix. 9 ; when, for the first and only occasion in all His earthly sojourn, He was acclaimed as "Messiah the Prince, the King, the Son of David." (See p. 126, *post*.)

And here again we must keep to Scripture. Though God has nowhere recorded the Bethlehem birthdate of Christ, no date in history, sacred or profane, is fixed with greater definiteness than that of the year in which the Lord began His public ministry. I refer of course to Luke iii. 1, 2. (See pp. 95, 96, *post*.) I say this emphatically, because Christian expositors have persistently sought to set up a fictitious date for the reign of Tiberias. The first Passover of the Lord's ministry, therefore, was in Nisan A.D. 29 ; and we can fix the date of the Passion with absolute certainty as Nisan A.D. 32. If Jewish or infidel writers set themselves to confuse and corrupt the chronology of these periods, we would not be surprised. But it is to Christian expositors that we owe this evil work. Happily, however, we can appeal to the labours of secular historians and chronologists for proofs of the divine accuracy of Holy Scripture.

The general attack upon the Book of Daniel, briefly discussed in the "Preface to the Fifth Edition," is dealt with more fully in the 1902 reissue of *Daniel in the Critics' Den*. The reader will there find an answer to the attack of the Higher Criticism on Daniel, based on philology and history ; and he will find also that the Critics are refuted by their own admissions respecting the Canon of the Old Testament.

Most of the "historical errors" in Daniel, which Professor Driver copied from Bertholdt's work of a century ago,[2] have been disposed of by the erudition and research of our own day. But, when writing on the subject, I recognised that the identity of Darius the Mede was still a difficulty. Since then, however, I have found a solution of that difficulty in a verse in Ezra, hitherto used only by Voltaire and others to discredit Scripture.

Ezra v. tells us that in the reign of Darius Hystaspis

---

[2] See Appendix 4, p. 305 note 2.

the Jews petitioned the throne, appealing to the decree by which Cyrus had authorised the rebuilding of the Temple. The wording of the petition clearly indicates that, to the knowledge of the Jewish leaders, that decree had been filed in the house of the archives in Babylon. But the search there made for it proved fruitless, and it was ultimately found at Ecbatana (or Achmetha : Ezra vi. 2). How then could such a State paper have been transferred to the Median capital ?

The only reasonable explanation of this extraordinary fact completes the circle of proof that the vassal king whom Daniel calls Darius the Mede was Gobryas (or Gubaru), who led the army of Cyrus to Babylon. As various writers have noticed, the testimony of the inscriptions points to that conclusion. For example, the Annalistic tablet of Cyrus records that, after the taking of the city, it was Gobryas who appointed the governors or prefects ; which appointments Daniel states were made by Darius. The fact that he was a prince of the royal house of Media, and presumably well known to Cyrus, who had resided at the Median Court, would account for his being held in such high honour. He it was who governed Media as Viceroy when that country was reduced to the status of a province ; and to any one accustomed to deal with evidence, the inference will seem natural that, for some reason or other, he was sent back to his provincial throne, and that, in returning to Ecbatana he carried with him the archives of his brief reign in Babylon. In the interval between the accession of Cyrus and that of Darius Hystaspis, the Temple decree may well have been forgotten by all but the Jews themselves. And although it was a serious matter to thwart the execution of an order issued by the king of Persia (Ezra vi. 11), yet in this instance, as already noticed, a Divine decree overruled the decree of Cyrus, and vetoed their taking action upon it.

The elucidation of the vision of the Seventy Weeks, as unfolded in the following pages, is my personal contribution to the Daniel controversy. And as the searching criticism to which it has been subjected has failed to detect in it an error or a flaw,* it may

------

* One point may be worth notice in a footnote. The R.V. reading of Acts xiii. 20 seems to dispose of my solution of the perplexing problem of the 480 years of 1 Kings vi. 1 (see pp. 81-83, *post*). But here, in accordance with their usual practice, and in neglect of the principles by which experts are guided in dealing with conflicting evidence, the Revisers slavishly followed certain of the oldest MSS. And the effect on this passage is disastrous. For it is certain that neither the Apostle said, nor the Evangelist wrote, that Israel's enjoyment of the land was limited to 450 years, or that 450 years elapsed *before* the era of the Judges. The text adopted by the Revisers is, therefore, clearly wrong. Dean Alford regards it "as an attempt at correcting the difficult chronology of the verse" ; and, he adds, "taking the words as they stand, *no other sense* can be given to them than that the time of the Judges lasted 450 years." That is, as he goes on to explain,

now be accepted without hesitation or reserve. The only disparaging comment which Professor Driver could offer upon it in his *Book of Daniel* was that it is "a revival in a slightly modified form" of the scheme of Julius Africanus, and that it leaves the seventieth week "unexplained." But surely the fact that my scheme is on the same lines as that of "the father of Christian Chronologists" creates a very strong presumption in its favour. And so far from leaving the seventieth week unexplained, I have dealt with it in accordance with the beliefs of the early Fathers. For they regarded that week as future, seeing that they looked for the Antichrist of Scripture —"an individual person, the incarnation and concentration of sin." *

R. A.

---

the era within which occurred the rule of the Judges. It is not that the Judges ruled for 450 years—in which case the accusative would be used, as in verse 18—but, as the use of the dative implies, that the period until Saul, characterised by the rule of the Judges, lasted 450 years.

I need scarcely notice the objection that at p. 83 I fail to take account of the servitude mentioned in Judges x. 7, 8. That servitude affected only the tribes beyond Jordan.

* Alford's Greek Test., Prol. to 2 Thess. § 5.

PREFACE TO THE FIFTH EDITION

A DEFENCE OF THE BOOK OF DANIEL AGAINST THE "HIGHER CRITICISM."

THIS volume has been disparaged in some quarters because, it is alleged, it ignores the destructive criticism which is supposed to have led "all people of discernment" to abandon belief in the visions of Daniel.

The charge is not altogether just. Not only are some of the chief objections of the critics answered in these pages, but in proving the genuineness of the great central prophecy of the book, the authenticity of the whole is established. And the absence of a special chapter upon the subject may be explained. The practice, too common in religious controversy, of giving an *ex parte* representation of the views of opponents, instead of accepting their own statement of them, is never satisfactory, and seldom fair. And no treatise was available on the critics' side, concise enough to afford the basis of a brief excursus, and yet sufficiently full and authoritative to warrant its being accepted as adequate.

This want, however, has since been supplied by Professor Driver's *Introduction to the Literature of the Old Testament*,* a work which embodies the results of the so-called " Higher Criticism," as accepted by the sober judgment of the author. While avoiding the malignant extravagance of the German rationalists and their English imitators, he omits nothing which erudition can with fairness urge against the authenticity of the Book of Daniel. And if the hostile arguments he adduces can be shown to be faulty and inconclusive, the reader may fearlessly accept the result as an " end of controversy" upon the subject.†

---

* *An Introduction to the Literature of the Old Testament*, by S. R. Driver, D.D., Regius Professor of Hebrew, and Canon of Christ Church, Oxford. Third edition. (T. & T. Clark, 1892.) I wish here to acknowledge Professor Driver's courtesy in replying to various inquiries I have ventured to address to him.

† In accordance with the plan of the work, Chapter XI. opens with a *précis* of the contents of Daniel, together with exegetical notes. With these notes I am not concerned, though they seem designed to prepare the reader for the sequel. I will dismiss them with two remarks. First, in his criticisms upon chap. ix. 24-27 he ignores the scheme of interpretation which I have followed, albeit it is adopted by some writers of more eminence than several of those he quotes ; and the four points he enumerates against the "commonly understood" Messianic interpretation are amply dealt with in these pages. And secondly, his comment on

Here is the thesis which the author sets himself to establish :—

"In face of the facts presented by the Book of Daniel, the opinion that it is the work of Daniel himself cannot be sustained. Internal evidence shows, with a cogency that cannot be resisted, that it must have been written not earlier than *c.* 300 B.C., and in Palestine ; and it is at least probable that it was composed under the persecution of Antiochus Epiphanes, B.C. 168 or 167."

Professor Driver marshals his proofs under three heads : (1) facts of a historical nature ; (2) the evidence of the *language* of Daniel ; and (3) the *theology* of the Book.

Under (1) he enumerates the following points :—

(*a*) "The position of the Book in the Jewish Canon, not among the prophets, but in the miscellaneous collection of writings called the *Hagiographa*, and among the latest of these, in proximity to Esther. Though little definite is known respecting the formation of the Canon, the division known as the 'Prophets' was doubtless formed prior to the Hagiographa; and had the Book of Daniel existed at the time, it is reasonable to suppose that it would have ranked as the work of a prophet, and have been included among the former."

(*b*) "Jesus, the son of Sirach (writing *c.* 200 B.C.), in his

chap. xi., that "it can hardly be legitimate, in a *continuous* description, with no apparent change of subject, to refer part to the type and part to the antitype," disposes with extraordinary *naïveté* of a canon of prophetic interpretation accepted almost universally from the days of the post-Apostolic Fathers down to the present hour!

enumeration of Israelitish worthies, *c.* 44-50, though he mentions Isaiah, Jeremiah, Ezekiel, and (collectively) the Twelve Minor Prophets, is silent as to Daniel."

(*c*) "That Nebuchadnezzar besieged Jerusalem and carried away some of the sacred vessels in 'the *third* year of Jehoiakim' (Dan. i. 1 f.), though it cannot, strictly speaking, be disproved, is highly improbable : not only is the Book of Kings silent, but Jeremiah, *in the following year* (chap. xxv., etc.), speaks of the Chaldæans in a manner which appears distinctly to imply that their arms had not yet been seen in Judah."

(*d*) " The ' Chaldæans' are synonymous in Daniel with the caste of wise men. This sense 'is unknown to the Assyro-Babylonian language, has, wherever it occurs, formed itself after the end of the Babylonian empire, and is thus an indication of the post-exilic composition of the Book' (Schrader)." . . .

(*e*) " Belshazzar is represented as *King* of Babylon ; and Nebuchadnezzar is spoken of throughout chap. v. (vv. 2, 11, 13, 18, 22) as his father." . . .

(*f*) " Darius, son of Ahasuerus, a *Mede*, after the death of Belshazzar, is ' made king over the realm of the Chaldæans.' There seems to be no room for such a ruler. According to all other authorities, Cyrus is the immediate successor of Nabu-nahid, and the ruler of the entire Persian empire." . . .

(*g*) " In ix. 2 it is stated that Daniel 'understood by the books' the number of years for which, according to Jeremiah, Jerusalem should lie waste. The expression used implies that the prophecies of Jeremiah formed part of a *collection* of sacred books, which nevertheless it may be safely affirmed, was not formed in 536 B.C."

(*h*) "Other indications adduced to show that the Book is not the work of a contemporary, are such as the following": The points are the improbability, first, that a strict Jew would have entered the class of the " wise men," or that he would have been admitted by the wise men themselves; second, Nebuchadnezzar's insanity and edict; third, the absolute terms in which he and Darius recognise God, while retaining their idolatry.

I dismiss (*f*) and (*h*) at once, for the author himself, with his usual fairness, declines to press them. " They should," he admits, " be used with reserve.' The mention of " Darius the Mede " is perhaps the greatest difficulty which confronts the student of Daniel, and the problem it involves still awaits solution.[3] The unqualified rejection of the narrative by many eminent writers only proves the incapacity even of scholars of repute to suspend their judgment upon questions of the kind. The history of that age is too uncertain and confused to justify dogmatism, and, as Professor Driver justly remarks, "a cautious criticism will not build too much on the silence of the inscriptions, where many certainly remain to be brought to light" (p. 469). In Mr. Sayce's recent work * this caution is neglected. He accepts, moreover, with a faith which is unduly simple, all that Cyrus says about himself. It was obviously his interest to represent the acquisition of

---

* *The Higher Criticism and the Verdict of the Monuments*, by the Rev. A. H. Sayce. [3] Now solved. See pp. xv and 305.

Babylonia as a peaceful revolution, and not a military conquest. But the Book of Daniel does not conflict with either hypothesis. Mr. Sayce here " reads into it," as is so constantly done, what it in no way states or even implies. There is not a word about a siege or a capture. Belshazzar was " slain," and Darius " received " the kingdom ; but how these events came about we must learn from other sources. Professor Driver here admits in express terms " that ' Darius the Mede ' may prove, after all, to have been a historical character ";* and this is enough for our present purpose.

The remaining points I proceed to discuss *seriatim.*

---

* Page 479, *note.* But the author's appeal under (f) to " all other authorities " is scarcely fair, as Daniel is the only contemporary historian, and the exploration of the ruins of Babylon has yet to be accomplished.

And as regards (h) but little need be said. Professor Driver candidly owns that " there are good reasons for supposing that Nebuchadnezzar's lycanthropy rests upon a basis of fact." No student of human nature will find anything strange in the recorded action of these heathen kings when confronted with proofs of the presence and power of God We see its counterpart every day in the conduct of ungodly men when events which they regard as Divine judgments befall them. And no one accustomed to deal with evidence will entertain the suggestion that the story of Daniel's becoming a " Chaldean " would be invented by a Jew trained under the strict ritual of post-exilic days. The suggestion that Daniel would have been refused admission to the college in the face of the great king's order to admit him really deserves no answer.

(a) This is rightly placed first, as being the most important. But its apparent importance grows less and less the more closely it is examined. Our English Bible, following the Vulgate, divides the Old Testament into thirty-nine books. The Jewish Canon reckoned only twenty-four. These were classified under three heads — the *Torah*, the *Neveeim*, and the *Kethuvim* (the Law, the Prophets, and the Other Writings). The first contained the Pentateuch. The second contained eight books, which were again classified in two groups. The first four—viz., Joshua, Judges, Samuel, and Kings—were called the "Former Prophets"; and the second four— viz., Isaiah, Jeremiah, Ezekiel, and "the Twelve" (*i.e.* the minor prophets reckoned as one book)—were called the "Latter Prophets." The third division contained eleven books—viz., Psalms, Proverbs, Job, Song of Songs, Ruth, Lamentations, Ecclesiastes, Esther, Daniel, Ezra and Nehemiah (reckoned as one), and Chronicles. Now, an examination of this list makes either of two conclusions irresistible. Either the Canon was arranged under Divine guidance, or else the classification of the books between the second and third divisions was an arbitrary one. If any one adopts the former alternative, the inclusion of Daniel in the Canon is decisive of the whole question If, on the other hand, it be assumed that the arrangement was human and arbitrary, the fact that Daniel is in the third group proves—not that the book was regarded as of doubtful repute, for in that case it would have been excluded from the Canon, but that the great exile of the Captivity was not regarded as a "prophet."

To the superficial this may seem to be giving up the whole case. But using the word "prophet" in its ordinary acceptation, Daniel has no claim whatever to the title, and but for Matt. xxiv. 15 it would probably never have been applied to him. His visions have their New Testament counterpart, but yet no one speaks of "the prophet John." According to 2 Pet. i. 21 the prophets "spake as they were moved by the Holy Ghost." This characterised the utterances of Isaiah, Jeremiah, Ezekiel, and "the Twelve." They were the words of Jehovah by the mouth of the men who uttered them. The prophets stood apart from the people as witnesses for God; but Daniel's position and ministry were wholly different. "Neither have we hearkened unto Thy servants the prophets which spake in Thy name": such was his humble attitude. Higher criticism may slight the distinction here insisted on; but the question is how it was regarded by the men who settled the Canon; and in their judgment its importance was immense. Daniel contains the record, not of God-breathed words uttered *by* the seer, but of the words spoken *to* him, and of dreams and visions accorded him. And the visions of the latter half of his book were granted him after more than sixty years spent in statecraft —years the record of which would fix his fame in the popular mind as statesman and ruler.

The reader will thus recognise that the position of Daniel in the Canon is precisely where we should expect to find it. The critic speaks of it as being "in the miscellaneous collection of writings called the *Hagiographa*, and among the latest of these, in proximity to Esther." But, in adopting this from earlier writers, the author is guilty of what may be described as unintentional dishonesty. Daniel comes before Ezra, Nehemiah, and Chronicles in a group of books which includes the Psalms—those Psalms than

which no part of their Canon was prized more highly
by the Jews—those Psalms, many of which they rightly
regarded as prophetic in the highest and strictest sense.*
But Daniel, we are told, was placed "in proximity to
Esther." What does the critic mean by this? He cannot
wish to suggest that Esther is held in low repute by the
Jews, for he himself declares that it came to be "ranked
by them as superior both to the writings of the prophets
and to all other parts of the Hagiographa" (p. 452). As to
Esther coming *before* Daniel, he cannot have overlooked
that it is bracketed in the Canon with the four books which
precede it—the *Megilloth.* He cannot mean to imply that
the books of the *Kethuvim* are arranged chronologically;
and he certainly cannot wish to create an ignorant prejudice.
The statement therefore is an enigma, and the discussion
under this head may be closed by the general remark that
(*a*) implies that the Jews esteemed the books in the third
division of their Canon as less sacred than "the prophets."
But this is wholly baseless. In common with the rest, they
were, as Josephus tells us, "justly believed to be Divine, so
that, rather than speak against them, they were ready to
suffer torture, or even death." †

(*b*) But little need be said in answer to this. Canon
Driver admits that the argument is one "which, standing
alone, it would be hazardous to press," and this is precisely
its position if (*a*) be refuted. If it were a question of the

---

* As the Psalms came first in the *Kethuvim* they gave their
name to the whole; as *ex. gr.* when our Lord spoke of "the
Law of Moses, the Prophets, and the Psalms" (Luke **xxiv.** 44)
He meant the entire Scriptures.

† *Against Apion,* i. 8.

omission of Daniel's name from a formal list of the prophets everything above urged would apply here with equal force ; but the reader must not suppose that the son of Sirach gives any list of the kind. The facts are these. The Apocryphal Book of Ecclesiasticus, which is here re-ferred to, ends with a rhapsody in praise of " famous men." This panegyric, it is true, omits the name of Daniel. But in what connection would his name be in-cluded? Daniel was exiled to Babylon in early youth, and never spent a single day of his long life among his people, never was openly associated with them in their struggles or their sorrows. The critic, moreover, fails to notice that the Son of Sirach ignores also not only such worthies as Abel, and Melchisedec, and Job, and Gideon, and Samson, but also Ezra, who, unlike Daniel, played a most prominent part in the national life, and who also gave his name to one of the books of the Canon. Let the reader decide this matter for himself after reading the passage in which the names of Daniel and Ezra ought to appear.* If any one is so mentally constituted that the omission leads him to decide against the authenticity of these two books, no words of mine would influence him.

(*c*) The historical statement with which the Book of Daniel opens is declared to be improbable on two grounds : first, because " the Book of Kings is silent " on the subject ; and, secondly, because Jer. xxv. appears inconsistent with it. The first point is made apparently in error, for 2 Kings xxiv. 1 states explicitly that in Jehoiakim's days

---

* This section of Ecclesiasticus begins with chap. xliv., but the passage here in question is chap. xlix., vv. 6-16.

Nebuchadnezzar came up against Jerusalem, and that the Jewish king became his vassal.*

And the second point is overstated. Jer. xxv. is silent on the subject, and that is all that can be said. Now the weight to be given to the silence of a particular witness or document on any matter is a familiar problem in dealing with evidence. It entirely depends on circumstances whether it counts for much, or little, or nothing. Kings being a historical record, its silence here would count for something. But why should a warning and a prophecy like Jer. xxv. contain the recital of an event of a few months before, an event which no one in Jerusalem could ever possibly forget ? †

But further discussion on these lines is needless, for the accuracy of Daniel's statement can be established on grounds which the critic ignores altogether. I refer to

---

* Possibly the critic means to question whether Jerusalem was actually captured, *i.e.* carried by storm, at this time. I have, I admit, assumed this in these pages. But Scripture nowhere says so. Taking all accounts together, we can only aver that Nebuchadnezzar came up against Jerusalem, and laid siege to it, that, in some way, Jehoiakim fell into his hands and was put in chains to carry him to Babylon, and that Nebuchadnezzar changed his purpose and left him as a vassal king in Judæa. He may have gone out to the Chaldean king, as his son and successor afterwards did (2 Kings xxiv. 12) ; and it is very probable that Jehoiachin's action in this respect was suggested by the leniency shown to his father.

† The words " as it is this day," in ver. 18, appear to be an allusion to the accomplished subjugation of Judæa. According to ver. 19, Egypt was next to fall before Nebuchadnezzar ; and chap. xlvi. 2 records Nebuchadnezzar's victory over the Egyptian army in this same year.

the chronology of the eras of the "servitude" and the "desolations." Both are commonly confounded with the "captivity," which was only in part concurrent with them. These several eras represented three successive judgments upon Judah (see p. 55 *post*). The chronology of these is fully explained in the sequel, and a reference to the excursus at pp. 228-240 *post*, or indeed a glance at the tables which follow (pp. 241-245), will supply proof absolute and complete that the servitude began in the third year of Jehoiakim, precisely as the Book of Daniel avers.

(*d*) I will refer under the second head of the inquiry to the philological question here involved. It is not in any sense a *historical* difficulty.

(*e*) The reader will find this point dealt with at p. 221 *post*. Canon Driver remarks: "It may be admitted as probable that Belsharuzur held command for his father in Babylon; . . . but it is difficult to think that this could entitle him to be spoken of *by a contemporary* as king." If Belshazzar was regent, as the narrative indicates, it is difficult to think that a courtier would speak of him otherwise than as king. To have done so might have cost him his head! Dan. v. 7, 16, 29 affords corroboration here in a manner all the more striking because it is wholly undesigned. Nebuchadnezzar had made Daniel second ruler in the kingdom: why does Belshazzar make him *third* ruler? Presumably because he himself held but the second place. To avoid this the critics, trading upon a possible alternative rendering of the Aramaic (as given in the margin of the Revised Version), conjecture a "Board of three." But assuming that the words used *may* mean a triumvirate in the sense of chap. vi. 2, the question whether this is their actual meaning must be settled by an appeal to history. And history affords not the slightest hint that such a system of government prevailed in the Babylonian Empire. A true exegesis, therefore, must decide in favour of the alternative and more natural view, that Daniel was to rule as third, the absent king being first, and the king-regent second.

But Belshazzar is called the *son* of Nebuchadnezzar. The reader will find this objection fully answered by Dr. Pusey (*Daniel*, pp. 406-408). He justly remarks that " inter-marriage with the family of a conquered monarch, or with a displaced line, is so obviously a way of strengthening the newly acquired throne, that it is *a priori* probable that Nabunahit would so fortify his claim," and Professor Driver himself allows (p. 468) that *possibly* the King may have married a daughter of Nebuchadnezzar, " in which case the latter might be spoken of as Belshazzar's father (= grandfather, by Hebrew usage)." I will only add two remarks : first, the critics forget that even on their own view of Daniel the existence of a tradition is *primâ facie* proof of its truth ; and, secondly, if the usurper chose to be called the son of Nebuchadnezzar, though with no sort of claim to the title, no one in Babylon would dare tc thwart him.

(*g*) Here are the words of Dan. ix. 2 (R.V.): "I Daniel understood by the books the number of the years, whereof the word of the Lord came to Jeremiah the prophet, for the accomplishing of the desolations of Jerusalem, even seventy years." The prophecy here referred to is admittedly Jer. xxv. 11, 12. Now the word *sepher*, rendered "book" in Dan. ix. 2, means simply a scroll. It may denote *a book*, as it often does in Scripture, or merely a letter. See *ex. gr.* Jer. xxix. 1 (the *letter* which Jeremiah wrote to the exiles in Babylon), or Isa. xxxvii. 14 (Sennacherib's *letter* to King Hezekiah). Then, again, Jer. xxxvi. 1, 2 records that in the fourth year of Jehoiakim, the very year in which the prophecy of Jer. xxv. was given, all the prophecies delivered up to that time were recorded in "a book." And in Jer. li. 60, 61 we find that some ten years later a further "book" was written and sent to Babylon. Where, then, is the difficulty? Professor Driver, moreover, himself supplies a complete answer in his own criticism by adopting "the supposition that in some cases Jeremiah's writings were in circulation for a while as single prophecies, or small groups of prophecies" (p. 254). These may have been the scrolls or "books" of Dan. ix.

But suppose, for the sake of argument, we admit that "the books" must mean the sacred writings up to that period, what warrant is there for affirming that no such "collection" existed in 536 B.C.? A more arbitrary assertion was never made, even in the range of controversy. Is it not absolutely incredible that the scrolls of the Law were not kept together? And considering Daniel's intense piety, and the extraordinary resources and means he must have had at his disposal under Nebuchadnezzar, may it not "safely be affirmed" that there was not another man upon earth so likely as himself to have had copies of all the holy writings? *

---

* Professor Bevan's suggestion on this point is, in my opinion, untenable. But I refer to it to show how an advanced exponent of the Higher Criticism can dispose of (*g*). *Commentary on Daniel*, p. 146. I have no doubt whatever that if Leviticus was before Daniel, as well it might be, it was the law of the Sabbatical years he had in view and not xxvi. 18, etc.

I now turn to the critic's second argument, which is based on the *language* of the Book of Daniel. He appeals, first, to the number of *Persian* words it contains ; secondly, to the presence of *Greek* words ; thirdly, to the character of the *Aramaic* in which part of the book is written ; and, lastly, to the character of the *Hebrew*.

Underlying the argument founded on the presence of foreign words is the unexpressed assumption that the Jews were an uncultured tribe who had lived till then in boorish isolation. And yet four centuries before Daniel's time the wisdom and wealth of Solomon were spoken of throughout the then known world. He was a naturalist, a botanist, a philosopher, and a poet. And why not a linguist also? Were all his communications with his many foreign wives carried on through interpreters ? He traded with near and distant nations, and every one knows how language is influenced by commerce. And can we doubt that the fame of Nebuchadnezzar attracted foreigners to Babylon? What his relations were with foreign courts we know not. Why may not Daniel have been a Persian scholar ? The position assigned to him under the Persian rule renders this extremely probable. The number of Persian words in the book, according to Professor Driver, is "probably at least fifteen" ; and here is his comment upon them :—

" That such words should be found in books written after the Persian Empire was organised, and when Persian influences prevailed, is not more than would be expected " (p. 470).

But it was precisely in these circumstances that the Book of Daniel was written. The vision of chap. x. was given five years after the Persian rule had been established, and these visions were the basis of the book. Notes and records the writer doubtless had of the earlier and historical portions of it; but it is a reasonable assumption that the whole was written after the visions were accorded him.

As regards the Aramaic and the Hebrew of Daniel, I can of course express no opinion of my own. But my position will be in no way prejudiced by my incompetency in this respect. In the first place, there is nothing new here. The critic merely gives in a condensed form what the Germans have urged; and the whole ground has been covered by Dr. Pusey and others, who, having examined it with equal erudition and care, have arrived at wholly different conclusions. But, in the second place, it is unnecessary; for the signal fairness with which Professor Driver states the results of his argument enables me to concede all he says in this regard and to dismiss the discussion of it to the sequel. Here are his words :—

"The verdict of the language of Daniel is thus clear.

The *Persian* words presuppose a period after the Persian Empire had been well established ; the Greek words *demand*, the Hebrew *supports*, and the Aramaic *permits*, a date after the conquest of Palestine by Alexander the Great (B.C. 332). With our present knowledge this is as much as the language authorises us definitely to affirm " (p. 476).

May I restate this in other words? The Persian terms raise a presumption that Daniel was written after a certain date. The Hebrew strengthens this presumption, the Aramaic is consistent with it, and the Greek words used establish the truth of it. Problems precisely similar to this claim decision every day in our courts of justice.[4] The whole strength of the case depends on the last point stated. Any number of argumentative presumptions may be rebutted ; but here, it is alleged, we have proof which admits of no answer : the Greek words *demand* a date which destroys the authenticity of Daniel.

Will the reader believe it that the only foundation on which this superstructure rests is the allegation that *two* Greek words are found in the list of musical instruments given in the third chapter ? At a bazaar held some time ago in one of our cathedral towns, under the patronage of the bishop of the diocese, the alarm was given that a thief was at work among the company, and two ladies present had lost their purses. In the excitement which followed, the stolen purses, emptied of course of their contents,

---

[4] See Appendix 4, p. 305 note 4.

were found in the bishop's pocket! The "Higher Criticism" would have handed him over to the police! Perhaps an apology is due for this digression; but, in sober earnestness, surely the inquiry is opportune whether these critics understand the very rudiments of the science of weighing evidence. The presence of the two stolen purses did not "demand" the conviction of the bishop. Neither should the presence of two Greek words decide the fate of Daniel.* The question would still remain, How did they come to be there? According to Professor Sayce, himself a hostile authority, the evidence of the monuments has entirely refuted this argument of the critics.[†] It now appears that there were Greek colonies in Palestine as early as the days of Hezekiah, and that

---

* I speak of two Greek words only, for *kitharos* is practically given up. Dr. Pusey denies that these words are of Greek origin. (*Daniel*, pp. 27-30.) Dr. Driver urges that in the fifth century B.C. "the arts and inventions of civilised life streamed then into Greece from the East, and not from Greece Eastwards." But surely the figure he uses here distorts his judgment. The influences of civilisation do not "stream" in the sense in which water streams. There is and always must be an interchange; and arts and inventions carried from one country to another carry their names with them. I am compelled to pass by these philological questions thus rapidly, but the reader will find them fully discussed by Pusey and others. Dr. Pusey remarks, "Aramaic as well as Aryan words suit his real age," and "his Hebrew is just what one would expect at the age in which he lived" (p. 578).

† *Higher Criticism and the Monuments*, pp. 424 and 494.

there was intercourse between Greece and Canaan at a still earlier period.

But let us admit, for the sake of argument, that the words are really Greek, and that no such words were known in Babylon in the days of the exile. Is the inference based on their presence in the book a legitimate one? While some apologists of Daniel have pressed unduly the hypothesis of a revision, such a hypothesis affords a most reasonable explanation of difficulties of this particular kind. Why should we doubt the truth of the Jewish tradition that "the men of the great synagogue wrote" (that is, *edited*) the Book of Daniel? And if true, these Greek words may be easily accounted for. If in the list of musical instruments, and in the title of the "wise men," the editors found terms which were foreign and strange to them, how natural for them to substitute words which would be familiar to the Jews of Palestine. * How natural, too, to spell such names as Nebuchadnezzar and Abednego in the manner then become usual. These are precisely the sort of changes which they would adopt; changes of no vital moment, but fitted to make the book more suitable for those on whose behalf they were revising it.

The critic's last ground of attack is the theology of

---

* On this subject see the Bishop of Durham's article in Smith's *Bible Dictionary*.

the Book of Daniel. This, he declares, "points to a later age than that of the exile." No charge of *error* is suggested, for Professor Driver is careful at the outset to repudiate what he calls the "exaggerations" of the German rationalists and their English imitators. But his alliance with such men warps his judgment, and betrays him into adopting statements begotten of their mingled ignorance and malice. Let one instance suffice. "It is remarkable also," he says, "that Daniel—so unlike the prophets generally —should display no interest in the welfare or prospects of his contemporaries." Not even in theological controversy could another statement be found more flagrantly baseless and false. In the entire history of the prophets, in the whole range of Scripture, the ninth chapter of Daniel has no parallel for touching, earnest, passionate "interest in the welfare and prospects" of contemporaries.

Now the question here is, not whether the doctrine of the Book be true, for that is not disputed, but whether truth of such an advanced and definite character could have been revealed at so early a period in the scheme of revelation. It is not easy to fix the principles on which such a question should be discussed. And the discussion may be avoided by raising another question, the answer to which will decide the whole matter in dispute. We know the "orthodox view" of the Book of Daniel. What

alternative does the critic propose for our acceptance?
Here he shall speak for himself, and the two quotations following will suffice :—

" Daniel, it cannot be doubted, was a historical person,
one of the Jewish exiles in Babylon, who, with his three
companions, was noted for his staunch adherence to the
principles of his religion, who attained a position of
influence at the Court of Babylon, who interpreted Nebu
chadnezzar's dreams, and foretold as a seer something
of the future fate of the Chaldæan and Persian empires "
(p. 479).

" On the other hand, if the author be a prophet living in
the time of the trouble itself, all the features of the Book
may be consistently explained. He lives in the age in
which he manifests an interest, and which needs the con-
solations which he has to address to it. He does not write
after the persecutions are ended (in which case his
prophecies would be pointless), but at their beginning,
when his message of encouragement would have a value for
the godly Jews in the season of their trial. He thus utters
genuine predictions ; and the advent of the Messianic age
follows closely on the end of Antiochus, just as in Isaiah or
Micah it follows closely on the fall of the Assyrian : in both
cases the future is foreshortened " (p. 478).

The first of these quotations refers to Daniel
himself, the second to the supposed author of the
Book which bears his name. In the first we pass
for a moment out of the mist and cloud of mere
theory and argument into the plain, clear light of
fact. " It cannot be doubted," or, in other words

it is absolutely certain, that Daniel was not only "a historical person," but "a seer"—that is to say, a *prophet*. But plunging back again at once into the gloom, we go on to conjecture the existence of another prophet in the days of Antiochus—a *real* prophet, for "he utters genuine predictions" for the encouragement of "the godly Jews in the season of their trial."

Now the position of the *sceptic* is in a sense unassailable. He is like the obstinate juror who puts his back against the wall and refuses to believe the evidence. But mark what this suggested compromise involves. As already noticed, Daniel had no pretensions to the prophet's mantle in the sense in which Jeremiah and Ezekiel wore it. He himself laid no claim to it (see chap. ix. 10). He, moreover, passed his life in the splendid isolation of the Court of Babylon, while they were central figures among their people—one in the midst of the troubles in Jerusalem, the other among the exiles. It would not be strange therefore if Daniel's name and fame had no such place as theirs in the popular memory. But here we are asked to believe that another prophet, raised up within historic times, whose "message of encouragement" must have been on every man's lips throughout the noble Maccabean struggle, passed clean out of the memory of the nation. The historian of this struggle cannot have been removed from him by more than a single generation, yet he ignores his existence, though he refers in the plainest terms to the Daniel of the Captivity.* The prophet's voice had been silent for centuries ; with what wild and passionate enthusiasm the nation would have hailed the rise of a new seer at such a time ! And when the issue of that fierce struggle set the seal of truth upon his words, his fame would have eclipsed that of the old prophets of earlier days. But in fact not a vestige of his fame or name survived. No writer, sacred or secular, seems to have heard of him. No tradition of him remained. Was there ever a figment more untenable than this ?

No such compromise between faith and unbelief is possible. From either of two alternatives there is no escape. Either the Book of Daniel is what it claims to be, or else it is wholly worthless. "All must be true or all imposture." It is idle to talk of it as being the work of some prophet of a later epoch. It dates from Babylon in the days of the Exile, or else it is a literary fraud, concocted after the time of Antiochus Epiphanes. But how then could it come to be quoted in the Maccabees—quoted, not incidentally, but in one of the most solemn and

---

* 1 Macc. ii. 60 ; see also chap. i. 54. The First Book of Maccabees is a history of the highest repute, and the accuracy of it is universally acknowledged.

striking passages in the entire book, the dying words
of old Mattathias? And how could it come to be
included in the Canon? The critics make much of
its *position* in the Canon : how do they account for
its having a place in it at all?

It is reasonably certain that the first two divisions
of the Canon were settled by the Great Synagogue
long before the days of the Maccabees, and that its
completion was the work of the Great Sanhedrim,
not later than the second century B.C. And we are
asked to suppose that this great College, composed
of the most learned men of the nation, would have
accepted a literary fraud of modern date, or could
have been duped by it. This is one of the wildest
and most reckless hypotheses imaginable. Nor
would this argument be sensibly weakened if the
critics should insist that the Canon may still have
been open for a hundred years after the death of
Antiochus.* If it was thus kept open, the fact would
be a further pledge and proof that the most jealous
and vigilant care must have been unceasingly exercised. The presence of the Book of Daniel in the
Jewish Canon is a fact more weighty than all the
criticisms of the critics.

---

* The Sanhedrim, though scattered during the Maccabean
revolt, was reconstituted at its close. See Dr. Ginsburg's
articles "Sanhedrim" and "Synagogue" in Kitto's *Cyclopædia.*

Thousands there are who cling to the Book of Daniel, and yet dread to face this destructive criticism lest faith should give way under the influence. And yet this is all it has to urge, as formulated by one of its best exponents. Of all these hostile arguments there is not so much as one which may not be refuted at any moment by the discovery of further inscriptions. In presence of some newly found cylinder from the as yet unexplored ruins of Babylon,* all this theorising about improbabilities and peddling over words might be silenced in a day. And this being so, it is obvious to any one in whom the judicial faculty is not wanting that the critics exaggerate the importance of their criticisms. Even if all they urge were true and weighty, it should lead us only to suspend our judgment. But the critics are specialists, and it is proverbial that specialists are bad judges. And here it is possible for one who cannot pose as a theologian or a scholar to meet them on more than equal terms. With them it is enough that evidence of a certain kind points in one direction. But they in whom the judicial faculty is developed will pause and ask, " What is to be said upon the other side ? " and " Will the proposed

---

* The ruins of Borsippa are practically unexplored ; and considering the character of the inscriptions found on other Chaldean sites, we may expect to obtain hereafter very full State records of the capital.

decision harmonise with all the facts?" Questions of this kind, however, have no existence for the critics. If they ever presented themselves to Professor Driver's mind, it is to be regretted that he failed to take account of them when stating the general results of his inquiry. And if ignored by an author so willing to reach the truth, they need not be looked for in the writings of the sceptics and apostates.

I have hitherto been dealing with presumptions and inferences and arguments. To deny that these have weight would be both dishonest and futile. It may be conceded that if the Book of Daniel had been brought to light within the Christian era, they would suffice to bar its admission to the Canon. But to the Christian the Book is accredited by the Lord Jesus Christ Himself; and in presence of this one fact the force of these criticisms is dispelled like mist before the sun. The very prediction which the rationalists most cavil at, He has adopted in that discourse which is the key to all unfulfilled prophecy ; * and if Daniel be proved a fraud, He whom we own as Lord is discredited thereby.

Such an argument as this the rationalists of the German school despise. And with them the mention of Daniel in the Book of Ezekiel counts for nothing, though according to their own canons it ought to

---

* Matt. xxiv.

outweigh much of the negative evidence they adduce. Daniel is not mentioned by other prophets ; therefore, they argue, Daniel is a myth. Three times the prophecies of Ezekiel speak of him ; therefore, they infer, some other Daniel is intended. Their argument is based on the silence of the sacred and other books of the Jews. A man so eminent as the Daniel of the exile would not, they urge, have been thus ignored. And yet they conjecture the career of another Daniel of equal, or even greater eminence, whose very existence has been forgotten ! It is not easy to deal with such casuists. But there is one argument, at least, which they cannot rob us of.

They have got rid of the second chapter and the seventh, and the closing vision of the Book, but the great central prophecy of the Seventy Weeks remains ; and this affords proof of the Divine authority of Daniel, which cannot be destroyed. Let them fix the date of the Book where they will, they fail to account for this. From one definitely recorded historical event—the edict to rebuild Jerusalem, to another definitely recorded historical event—the public manifestation of the Messiah, the length of the intervening period was predicted ; and with accuracy absolute and to the very day the prediction has been fulfilled.

To elucidate that prophecy this volume has been written, and as the result constitutes my personal contribution to the controversy, I may be pardoned for explaining the steps by which it has been reached. The vision refers to 70 sevens of years, but I deal here only with the 69 " weeks " of the twenty-fifth verse.   Here are the words :—

" Know therefore and discern that from the going forth of the commandment to restore and to build Jerusalem unto the Messiah, the Prince, shall be seven weeks and threescore and two weeks : it shall be built again with street and moat, even in troublous times." *

Now it is an undisputed fact that Jerusalem was rebuilt by Nehemiah, under an edict issued by Arta- xerxes (Longimanus), in the twentieth year of his reign.   Therefore, notwithstanding the doubts which controversy throws upon everything, the conclusion is obvious and irresistible that this was the epoch of the prophetic period.   But the month date was Nisan, and the sacred year of the Jews began with the phasis of the Paschal moon.   I appealed, therefore, to the Astronomer Royal, the late Sir George Airy, to cal- culate for me the moon's place for March in the year in question, and I thus ascertained the date required —March 14th, B.C. 445.

This being settled, one question only remained, Of what kind of year does the era consist ?   And

---

* I follow the marginal reading of the R.V., which was the reading adopted by the American Company.

the answer to this is definite and clear. That it is
the ancient year of 360 days* is plainly proved in
two ways. First, because, according to Daniel and
the Apocalypse, $3\frac{1}{2}$ prophetic years are equal to 1,260
days ; and, secondly, because it can be proved that
the 70 years of the " Desolations " were of this
character ; and the connection between the period of
the " Desolations " and the era of the " weeks " is one
of the few universally admitted facts in this controversy. The " Desolations " began on the 10th
Tebeth, B.C. 589 (a day which for four-and-twenty
centuries has been commemorated by the Jews as a
fast), and ended on the 24th Chisleu, B.C. 520.†

Having thus settled the *terminus a quo* of the
" weeks," and the form of year of which they are
composed, nothing remains but to calculate the duration of the era. Its *terminus ad quem* can thus with
certainty be ascertained. Now 483 years (69 × 7)
of 360 days contain 173,880 days. And a period
ot 173,880 days, beginning March 14th, B.C. 445,
ended upon that Sunday in the week of the crucifixion, when, for the first and only time in His
ministry, the Lord Jesus Christ, in fulfilment of
Zechariah's prophecy, made a public entry into
Jerusalem, and caused His Messiahship to be

---

* See p. 68 *post*.
† See pp. 55, 69-71, and 237 *post*.

openly proclaimed by "the whole multitude of the disciples." *

I need not discuss the matter further here. In the following chapters every incidental question involved is fully dealt with, and every objection answered.† Suffice it to repeat that in presence of the facts and figures thus detailed no mere negation of belief is possible. These must be accounted for in some way. "There is a point beyond which unbelief is impossible, and the mind, in refusing truth, must take refuge in a misbelief which is sheer credulity."

It was not till after the preceding pages were in print that Archdeacon Farrar's *Daniel* reached my hands. Some apology is due, perhaps, to Professor Driver for bracketing such a work with his, but *The Expositor's Bible* will be read by many to whom *The Introduction* is an unknown book. Both writers agree in impugning the authenticity of the Book of Daniel ; but their relative positions are widely different, and no less so are their arguments and methods. The Christian scholar writes for scholars, desirous only to elucidate the truth. The popular theologian retails the extravagances of German scepticism for the enlightenment of an easily deluded public. As we turn from the one book to the other,

---

* Luke xix.

† See chaps. v.-x. *post*, and specially pp. 121-8.

we are reminded of the difference between a criminal trial when in charge of a responsible law officer of the Crown, and when promoted by a vindictive private prosecutor. In the one case the lawyer's aim is solely to assist the Court in arriving at a just verdict. In the other, we may be prepared for statements which are reckless, if not unscrupulous.

And here we must distinguish between the Higher Criticism as legitimately used by Christian scholars in the interests of truth, and the rationalistic movement which bears that name. If that movement leads to unbelief, it is in obedience to the law that like begets like. It is itself the offspring of scepticism. Its reputed founder set out with the deliberate design of eliminating God from the Bible. From the sceptic's point of view Eichhorn's theories were inadequate, and De Wette and others have improved upon them. But their aim and object are the same. The Bible must be accounted for, and Christianity explained, on natural principles. The miracles therefore had to be got rid of, and prophecy is the greatest miracle of all. In the case of most of the Messianic Scriptures the scepticism which had settled like a night mist upon Germany made the task an easy one; but Daniel was a difficulty. Such passages as the fifty-third chapter of Isaiah could be jauntily disposed of, but the infidel could make nothing of these visions of Daniel. The Book stands out as a witness

for God, and by fair means or foul it must be silenced.
And one method only of accomplishing this is possible.
The conspirators set themselves to prove that it was
written after the events it purports to predict. The
evidence they have scraped together is of a kind which
would not avail to convict a known thief of petty
larceny—much of it indeed has already been dis-
carded; but any sort of evidence will suffice with a
prejudiced tribunal, and from the very first the Book
of Daniel was doomed.

Dr. Farrar's book reproduces every shred of this
evidence in its baldest and crudest form. His
original contributions to the controversy are limited
to the rhetoric which conceals the weakness of falla-
cious arguments, and the dogmatism with which
he sometimes disposes of results accredited by the
judgment of authorities of the highest eminence.
Two typical instances will suffice. The first relates
to a question of pure scholarship. Referring to the
fifth chapter of Daniel he writes :—

"Snatching at the merest straws, those who try to
vindicate the accuracy of the writer . . . think that they
improve the case by urging that Daniel was made 'the
third ruler in the kingdom'—Nabunaid being the first,
and Belshazzar being the second! Unhappily for their
very precarious hypothesis, the translátion 'third ruler'
appears to be entirely untenable. It means 'one of a
board of three.'"

"Entirely untenable!" In view of the decision of

the Old Testament Company of the Revisers on this
point, the statement denotes extraordinary careless-
ness or intolerable arrogance. And I have authority
for stating that the Revisers gave the question full
consideration, and that it was only at the last revision that the alternative rendering, "rule as one
of three," was admitted into the margin. On no
occasion was it contemplated to accept it in the
text.*

The right rendering of ch. v. 29 is admittedly
"the third ruler" in the kingdom; but the authorities differ as to verses 7 and 16. Professor Driver
tells me that, in his opinion, the absolutely literal
rendering there is "rule as a third part in the kingdom," or, slightly paraphrasing the words, "rule as
one of three" (as in R.V. *margin*). Professor Kirk-
patrick, of Cambridge, has been good enough to refer
me to Kautzsch's *Die Heilige schrift des alten Testa-
ments*, as representing the latest and best German
scholarship, and his rendering of verse 7 is "third
ruler in the kingdom," with the note, "*i.e.*, either as
one of three over the whole kingdom (compare vi. 3),
or as third by the side of the king and the king's
mother." And the Chief Rabbi (whose courtesy to
me here I wish to acknowledge) writes :—

"I cannot absolutely find fault with —— for translating

---

* As I have taken up this as a test question I have inves-
tigated it closely.

the words 'the third part of the kingdom,' as he follows herein two of our Hebrew Commentators of great repute, Rashi and Ibn Ezra. On the other hand, others of our Commentators, such as Saadia, Jachja, etc., translate the passage as 'he shall be the third ruler in the kingdom.' This rendering seems to be more strictly in accord with the literal meaning of the words, as shown by Dr. Winer in his *Grammatik des Chaldaismus.* It also receives confirmation from Sir Henry Rawlinson's remarkable discovery, according to which Belshazzar was the eldest son of King Nabonidus, and associated with him in the Government, so that the person next in honour would be the *third*."

It is perfectly clear, therefore, that Dr. Farrar's statement is utterly unjustifiable. Is it to be attributed to want of scholarship, or to want of candour?

Again, referring to the prophet's third vision, Archdeacon Farrar writes :—

"The attempt to refer the prophecy of the seventy weeks primarily or directly to the coming and death of Christ . . . can only be supported by immense manipulations, and by hypotheses so crudely impossible, that they would have made the prophecy practically meaningless both to Daniel and to any subsequent reader" (p. 287).

It is not easy to deal with such a statement with even conventional respect. No honest man will deny that, whether the ninth chapter of Daniel be a prophecy or a fraud, the blessings specified in the twenty-fourth verse are Messianic. Here all Christian expositors are agreed. And though the views of some of them are marked by startling eccentricities even the wildest of them will contrast favourably with Kuenen's exegesis, which, in all its crude absurdity, Archdeacon Farrar adopts.*

Professor Driver's opinions are entitled to the greatest weight within the sphere in which he is so high an authority.† But I have ventured to suggest that his eminence as a scholar lends undue weight to his *dicta* on the general topics involved, and that he shares in the proverbial disability of experts in dealing with a mass of apparently conflicting evidence. The tone and manner in which

---

* His chapter on *The Seventy Weeks* provokes the exclamation, Is this what English theology has come to ! I do not allude to such vulgar blunders as calling Gabriel "the Archangel" (p. 275), or confounding the era of the Servitude with that of the Desolations (p. 289), but to the style and spirit of the excursus as a whole. For "immense manipulations" and "crudely impossible hypotheses" no recent English treatise can compare with it.

† I allude to his attempt to fix the date of the Book by the character of its Hebrew and Aramaic. This, moreover, is a point on which scholars differ. I have already quoted Dr. Pusey's *dictum*. Professor Cheyne says : "From the Hebrew of the Book of Daniel no important inference as to its date can be safely drawn" (*Encyc. Brit.*, "Daniel," p. 804) ; and one of the greatest authorities in England, who has been quoted in favour of fixing a late date for Daniel, writes, in answer to an inquiry I have addressed to him : "I am now of opinion that it is a very difficult task to settle the age of any portion of that Book from its language. I do not think, therefore, that my name should be quoted any more in the contest."

his inquiry is conducted shows a readiness to re-consider his position in the light of any new discoveries hereafter. In contrast with this there are no reserves in Dr. Farrar's denunciations. For him retreat is impossible, no matter what the future may disclose. But to review his book is not my purpose. The only serious counts in the indictment of Daniel have been already noticed. His treatise, however, raises a general question of transcendent importance, and to this I desire in conclusion to refer.

With him the Book of Daniel is the merest fiction, differing from other fiction of the same kind by reason of the multiplicity of its inaccuracies and errors. Its history is but idle legend. Its miracles are but baseless fables. It is, in every part of it, a work of the imagination. "*Avowed* fiction" (p. 43), he calls it, for it is so obviously a romance that the charge of fraud is due solely to the stupidity of the Christian Church in mistaking the aim and purpose of "the holy and gifted Jew" (p. 119) who wrote it.

Such are the results of his criticisms. What action shall we take upon them? Shall we not sadly, but with deliberate purpose, tear the Book of Daniel from its place in the Sacred Canon? By no means.

"These results," Dr. Farrar exclaims, "are in no way derogatory to the preciousness of this Old Testament Apocalypse. No words of mine can exaggerate the value which I attach to this part of our Canonical Scriptures. . . . Its right to a place in the Canon is undisputed and indisputable, and there is scarcely a single book of the Old Testament which can be made more richly profitable for teaching, for reproof, for correction, for instruction in righteousness, that the man of God may be complete, completely furnished unto every good work " (p. 4).

This is not an isolated statement such as charity might attribute to thoughtlessness. Like words are used again and again in praise of the book.* Daniel is nothing more than a religious novel, and yet " there is *scarcely a single book* of the Old Testament" of greater worth!

The question here is not the authenticity of Daniel but the character and value of the Holy Scriptures. Christian scholars whose researches lead them to reject any portion of the Canon are wont to urge that, in doing so, they increase the authority, and enhance the value, of the rest. But the Archdeacon of Westminster, in impugning the Book of Daniel, takes occasion to degrade and throw contempt upon the Bible as a whole.

Bishop Westcott declares that no writing in the Old Testament had so great a share in the development of Christianity as the Book of Daniel.† Or, to quote a hostile witness, Professor Bevan writes :

---

* See *ex. gr.*, pp. 36, 37, 90, 118, 125.
† Smith's *Bible Dict.*, " Daniel."

"In the New Testament Daniel is mentioned only once, but the influence of the book is apparent almost everywhere."* "There are few books," says Hengstenberg, "whose Divine authority is so fully established by the testimony of the New Testament, and in particular by our Lord Himself, as the Book of Daniel." Just as mist and storm may hide the solid rock from sight, so this truth may be obscured by casuistry and rhetoric ; but when these have spent themselves it stands out plain and clear. In all this controversy one result of the rejection of the Book of Daniel is entirely overlooked or studiously concealed. If "the Apocalypse of the Old Testament" be banished from the Canon, the Apocalypse of the New Testament must share in its exclusion. The visions of St. John are so inseparably interwoven with the visions of the great prophet of the exile, that they stand or fall together. This result the *critic* is entitled to disregard. But the homilist may by no means ignore it. And it brings into prominence the fact so habitually forgotten, that the Higher Criticism claims a position which can by no means be accorded to it. Its true place is not on the judgment seat, but in the witness chair. The Christian theologian must take account of much which criticism cannot notice without entirely abandoning its legitimate sphere and function.

* *Com. Daniel*, p. 15.

No one falls back upon this position more freely when it suits his purpose, than Archdeacon Farrar. He evades the testimony of the twenty-fourth chapter of St. Matthew by refusing to believe that our Lord ever spoke the words attributed to Him. But this undermines Christianity ; for, I repeat, Christianity rests upon the Incarnation, and if the Gospels be not inspired, the Incarnation is a myth. What is his answer to this ? I quote his words :—

" But our belief in the Incarnation, and in the miracles of Christ, rests on evidence which, after repeated examination, is to us overwhelming. Apart from all questions of personal verification, or the Inward Witness of the Spirit, we can show that this evidence is supported, not only by the existing records, but by myriads of external and independent testimonies."

This deserves the closest attention, not merely because of its bearing on the question at issue, but as a fair specimen of the writer's reasoning in this extraordinary contribution to our theological literature. Here is the Christian argument: " The Nazarene was admittedly the son of Mary. The Jews declared that He was the son of Joseph ; the Christian worships Him as the Son of God. The founder of Rome was said to be the divinely begotten child of a vestal virgin. And in the old Babylonian mysteries a similar parentage was ascribed to the martyred son of Semiramis, gazetted Queen of Heaven. What grounds have we then for distinguishing the miraculous birth at Bethlehem from these and other kindred legends of the ancient world ? To point to the resurrection is a transparent begging of the question. To appeal to human testimony is utter folly. At this point we are face to face with that to which no consensus of mere human testimony could lend even an *a priori* probability." *

On what then do we base our belief of the great central fact of the Christian system? Here the dilemma is inexorable : to disparage the Gospels, as this writer does, is to admit that the foundation of our faith is but a Galilæan legend. By no means, Dr. Farrar tells us ; we have not only " personal verification, and the Inward Witness of the Spirit, but we have also *myriads* of external and independent witnesses." No Christian will ignore the Witness of the Spirit. But the question here, remember, is one of *fact*. The whole Christian system depends upon the truth of the last verse of the first chapter of St. Matthew—I will not quote it. How then can the Holy Spirit impart to me the knowledge of the fact there stated, save by the written Word ? I believe the fact because I accept the record as God-breathed Scripture, an authoritative revelation from heaven. But to talk of personal

---

* *A Doubter's Doubts*, p. 76.

verification, or to appeal to some transcendental instinct, or to tens of thousands of external witnesses, is to divorce words from thoughts, and to pass out of the sphere of intelligent statement and common sense.*

R. A.

---

* Professor Driver has since called my attention to a note in the "Addenda" to the third edition of his *Introduction*, qualifying his admissions respecting Belshazzar. He has also informed me that Professor Sayce is the "high Assyriological authority" there referred to. This enables us to discount his retractation. When writing on (*e*) in the above Preface, I had before me pp. 524-9 of the *Higher Criticism and the Monuments*, and I was impressed by the force of the objections there urged against the Daniel story of Belshazzar. Great was my revulsion of feeling when I discovered that Professor Sayce's argument depends upon his misreading of the Annalistic tablet of Cyrus. That tablet admittedly refers throughout to Belshazzar as "the son of the King"; but when it records his death at the taking of Babylon, Professor Sayce reads "wife of the King" instead of "son of tne King," and goes on to argue that, as Belshazzar is not mentioned in the passage, he cannot have been in Babylon at the time! That "contract tablets" would be dated with reference to the reign of the *King*, and not of the Regent, is precisely what we should expect.

I have dealt fully with the Belshazzar question in my *Daniel in the Critics' Den*, to which I would refer also for a fuller reply to Dean Farrar's book. Having regard to the testimony of the Annalistic tablet, that question may be looked upon as settled. And if, when writing that work, I had had before me what the Rev. J. Urquhart brings to light about Darius the Mede, in his *Inspiration and Accuracy of Holy Scripture*, I should have considered that this, the only remaining difficulty in the Daniel controversy, was no longer a serious one.

1

INTRODUCTORY

TO living men no time can be so solemn as " the living present," whatever its characteristics; and that solemnity is immensely deepened in an age of progress unparalleled in the history of the world. But the question arises whether these days of ours are momentous beyond comparison, by reason of their being in the strictest sense *the last?* Is the world's history about to close? The sands of its destiny, are they almost run out, and is the crash of all things near at hand?

Earnest thinkers will not allow the wild utterances of alarmists, or the vagaries of prophecy-mongers, to divert them from an inquiry at once so solemn and so reasonable. It is only the infidel who doubts that there is a destined limit to the course of " this present evil world." That God will one day put forth His power to ensure the triumph of the good, is in some sense a matter of course. The mystery of revelation is not that He *will* do this, but that He *delays* to do it. Judged by the public facts around us, He is an indifferent spectator of the unequal struggle between good and evil upon earth. " I considered all the oppressions that are done under the sun ; and, behold, the tears of the oppressed, and they had no comforter ; and on the side of their oppressors there was power, but *they* had no comforter." * And how can such things be, if indeed the God who rules above is almighty and all-good ? Vice and godlessness and violence and wrong are rampant upon every side, and yet the heavens above keep silence. The infidel appeals to the fact in proof that the Christian's God is but a myth.† The

---

* Eccles. iv. i.

† According to Mill, the course of the world gives proof that both the power and the goodness of God are limited. His *Essays on Religion* clearly show that scepticism is an attitude of mind which it is practically impossible to maintain. Even with a reasoner so clear and able as Mill, it inevitably degenerates to a degrading form of *faith*. " The rational attitude of a thinking mind towards the supernatural " (he declares) '' is that of scepticism, *as distinguished from belief* on the one hand, and from atheism on the other ; " and yet he immediately proceeds to formulate a creed. It is not that there is a God, for that is only probable, but that if there be a God He is *not* almighty, and His goodness toward man is limited. (*Essays*, etc., pp. 242, 243.) He does not prove his creed, of course. Its truth is obvious to a "thinking mind." It is equally obvious that the sun moves round the earth. A man only needs to be as ignorant of astronomy as the infidel is of Christianity, and he will find the most indisputable proof of the fact every time he surveys the heavens !

Christian finds in it a further proof that the God he worships is patient and longsuffering—" patient because He is eternal," longsuffering because He is almighty, for wrath is a last resource with power.

But the day is coming when " our God shall come and *shall not keep silence*." * This is not a matter of opinion, but of faith. He who questions it has no claim whatever to the name of Christian, for it is as essentially a truth of Christianity as is the record of the life and death of the Son of God. The old Scriptures teem with it, and of all the writers of the New Testament there is not so much as one who does not expressly speak of it. It was the burden of the first prophetic utterance which Holy Writ records ; † and the closing book of the sacred Canon, from the first chapter to the last, confirms and amplifies the testimony.

The only inquiry, therefore, which concerns us relates to the nature of the crisis and the time of its fulfilment. And the key to this inquiry is the Prophet Daniel's vision of the seventy weeks. Not that a right understanding of the prophecy will enable us to prophesy. That is not the purpose for which it was given.‡ But it will prove a sufficient safeguard against error in the study. Notably it will save us

---

* Psalm l. 3.   † Jude 14.

‡ " Prophecy is not given to enable us to prophesy, but as a witness to God when the time comes."—PUSEY, *Daniel*, p. 80.

from the follies into which false systems of prophetic chronology inevitably lead those who follow them. It is not in our time only that the end of the world has been predicted. It was looked for far more confidently at the beginning of the sixth century. All Europe rang with it in the days of Pope Gregory the Great. And at the end of the tenth century the appehension of it amounted to a general panic. " It was then frequently preached on, and by breathless crowds listened to; the subject of every one's thoughts, every one's conversation." " Under this impression, multitudes innumerable," says Mosheim, " having given their property to monasteries or churches, travelled to Palestine, where they expected Christ to descend to judgment. Others bound themselves by solemn oaths to be serfs to churches or to priests, in hopes of a milder sentence on them as being servants of Christ's servants. In many places buildings were let go to decay, as that of which there would be no need in future. And on occasions of eclipses of sun or moon, the people fled in multitudes for refuge to the caverns and the rocks." *

And so in recent years, one date after another has been confidently named for the supreme crisis ; but still the world goes on. A.D. 581 was one of the first

---

* Elliott, *Horæ Apoc.* (3rd Ed.), I., 446 : and see also ch. iii., pp. 362-376.

years fixed for the event,* 1881 is among the last. These pages are not designed to perpetuate the folly of such predictions, but to endeavour in a humble way to elucidate the meaning of a prophecy which ought to deliver us from all such errors and to rescue the study from the discredit they bring upon it.

No words ought to be necessary to enforce the importance of the subject, and yet the neglect of the prophetic Scriptures, by those even who profess to believe all Scripture to be inspired, is proverbial. Putting the matter on the lowest ground, it might be urged that if a knowledge of the past be important, a knowledge of the future must be of far higher value still, in enlarging the mind and raising it above the littlenesses produced by a narrow and unenlightened contemplation of the present. If God has vouchsafed a revelation to men, the study of it is surely fitted to excite enthusiastic interest, and to command the exercise of every talent which can be brought to bear upon it.

And this suggests another ground on which, in our own day especially, prophetic study claims peculiar prominence ; namely, the testimony it affords to the Divine character and origin of the Scriptures. Though infidelity was as open-mouthed in former times, it had its own banner and its own camp, and it shocked

---

* Elliott, I., 373. Hippolytus predicted A.D. 500.

the mass of mankind, who, though ignorant of the spiritual power of religion, clung nevertheless with dull tenacity to its dogmas. But the special feature of the present age—well fitted to cause anxiety and alarm to all thoughtful men—is the growth of what may be termed religious scepticism, a Christianity which denies revelation—a form of godliness which denies that which is the power of godliness.*

Faith is not the normal attitude of the human mind towards things Divine; the earnest doubter, therefore, is entitled to respect and sympathy. But what judgment shall be meted out to those who delight to proclaim themselves doubters, while claiming to be ministers of a religion of which FAITH is the essential characteristic?

There are not a few in our day whose belief in the Bible is all the more deep and unfaltering just because they have shared in the general revolt against priest-craft and superstition; and such men are scarcely prepared to take sides in the struggle between free thought and the thraldom of creeds and clerics. But in the conflict between faith and scepticism within the pale, their sympathies are less divided. On the one side there may be narrowness, but at least there is honesty; and in such a case surely the moral element is to be considered before a claim to mental vigour and

---

* 2 Tim. iii. 5.

independence can be listened to. Moreover any claim of the kind needs looking into. The man who asserts his freedom to receive and teach what he deems truth, howsoever reached, and wheresoever found, is not to be lightly accused of vanity or self-will. His motives may be true, and right, and praiseworthy. But if he has subscribed to a creed, he ought to be careful in taking any such ground. It is not on the side of vagueness that the creeds of our British Churches are in fault, and men who boast of being free-thinkers would deserve more respect if they showed their independence by refusing to subscribe, than by undermining the doctrines they are both pledged and subsidized to defend and teach.

But what concerns us here is the indisputable fact that rationalism in this its most subtle phase is leavening society. The universities are its chief seminaries. The pulpit is its platform. Some of the most popular religious leaders are amongst its apostles. No class is safe from its influence. And if even the present could be stereotyped, it were well; but we are entered on a downward path, and they must indeed be blind who cannot see where it is leading. If the authority of the Scriptures be unshaken, vital truths may be lost by one generation, and recovered by the next; but if that be touched, the foundation of all truth is undermined, and all power of recovery is gone. The Christianized sceptic of to-day will soon give place

to the Christianized infidel, whose disciples and successors in their turn will be infidels without any gloss
of Christianity about them. Some, doubtless, will
escape; but as for the many, Rome will be the
only refuge for those who dread the goal to which
society is hastening. Thus the forces are marshal-
ling for the great predicted struggle of the future
between the apostasy of a false religion and the
apostasy of open infidelity.*

Is the Bible a revelation from God? This is now

---

* I cannot refrain from giving the following extract from an
article by Professor Goldwin Smith, in *Macmillan's Magazine*
for February 1878 :—

"The denial of the existence of God and of the future state,
in a word, is the dethronement of conscience ; and society will
pass, to say the least, through a dangerous interval before social
science can fill the vacant throne. . . . But in the meantime mankind, or some portions of it, may be in danger of an anarchy
of self-interest, compressed, for the purpose of political order,
by a despotism of force.

"That science and criticism, acting—thanks to the liberty of
opinion won by political effort—with a freedom never known
before, have delivered us from a mass of dark and degrading
superstitions, we own with heartfelt thankfulness to the de-
liverers, and in the firm conviction that the removal of false
beliefs, and of the authorities or institutions founded on them,
cannot prove in the end anything but a blessing to mankind.
But at the same time the foundations of general morality have
inevitably been shaken, and a crisis has been brought on, the
gravity of which nobody can fail to see, and nobody but a fanatic
of materialism can see without the most serious misgiving.

" There has been nothing in the history of man like the present

become the greatest and most pressing of all questions. We may at once dismiss the quibble that the Scriptures admittedly *contain* a revelation. Is the sacred volume no better than a lottery bag from which blanks and prizes are to be drawn at random, with no power of distinguishing between them till the day when the discovery must come too late! And in the present phase of the question it is no less a quibble to urge that passages, and even books, may have been added in error to the Canon. We refuse to surrender Holy Writ to the tender mercies of those who approach it with the ignorance of pagans and the animus of apostates. But for the purpose of the present controversy we might consent to strike out everything on which enlightened criticism has cast the shadow of a doubt. This, however, would only clear the way for the real question at

---

situation. The decadence of the ancient mythologies is very far from affording a parallel. . . . The Reformation was a tremendous earthquake : it shook down the fabric of mediæval religion, and as a consequence of the disturbance in the religious sphere, filled the world with revolutions and wars. But it left the authority of the Bible unshaken, and men might feel that the destructive process had its limit, and that adamant was still beneath their feet. But a world which is intellectual and keenly alive to the significance of these questions, reading all that is written about them with almost passionate avidity, finds itself brought to a crisis the character of which any one may realize by distinctly presenting to himself the idea of existence without a God."

issue, which is not as to the authenticity of one portion or another, but as to the character and value of what is admittedly authentic. We are now far beyond discussing rival theories of inspiration ; what concerns us is to consider whether the holy writings are what they claim to be, "the oracles of God." *

In the midst of error and confusion and uncertainty, increasing on every side, can earnest and devout souls turn to an open Bible, and find there "words of eternal life"? "The rational attitude of a thinking mind towards the supernatural is that of *scepticism*."† Reason may bow before the shibboleths and tricks of priestcraft—"the voice of the Church," as it is called ; but this is sheer credulity. But if GOD speaks, then scepticism gives place to *faith*.

---

* τὰ λόγια τοῦ θεοῦ (Rom. iii. 2). The old Hebrew Scriptures were thus regarded by those who were the divinely-appointed custodians of them (*ib.*) Not only by the devout among the Jews, but, as Josephus testifies, by all, they " were justly believed to be Divine," so that men were willing to endure tortures of all kinds rather than speak against them, and even "willingly to die for them" (Josephus, *Apion*, I., 8). This fact is of immense importance in relation to the Lord's own teaching on the subject. Dealing with a people who believed in the sanctity and value of every word of Scripture, He never missed an opportunity to confirm them in that belief. The New Testament affords abundant proof how unreservedly He enforced it upon His disciples. (As regards the limits and date of closing of the Canon of Scripture, *see* Pusey, *Daniel*, p. 294, etc.)

† Mill, *Essays on Religion.*

Nor is this a mere begging of the question. The proof that the voice is really Divine must be absolute and conclusive. In such circumstances, scepticism betokens mental or moral degradation, and faith is not the abnegation of reason, but the highest act of reason. To maintain that such proof is impossible, is equivalent to asserting that the God who made us cannot so speak to us that the voice shall carry with it the conviction that it is from Him; and this is not scepticism at all, but disbelief and atheism. " It pleased God to reveal His Son in me," was St. Paul's account of his conversion. The grounds of his faith were subjective, and could not be produced. In proof to others of their reality he could only appeal to the facts of his life ; though these were entirely the result, and in no sense or degree the basis, of his conviction. Nor was his case exceptional. St. Peter was one of the favoured three who witnessed every miracle, including the transfiguration, and yet his faith was not the result of these, but sprang from a revelation to himself. In response to his confession, " Thou art the Christ, the Son of the living God," the Lord declared, " Flesh and blood hath not revealed it unto thee, but my Father who is in heaven."* Nor, again, was this a special grace accorded only to apostles. "To them that have

---

* Matt. xvi. 16, 17.

obtained like precious faith with us,"* was St. Peter's address to the faithful generally. He describes them as " born again by the Word of God." So also St. John speaks of such as " born, not of blood, nor of the will of the flesh, nor of the will of man, but of God."† " Of His own will begat He us with the word of truth " is the kindred statement of St. James.‡

Whatever be the meaning of such words, they must mean something more than arriving at a sound conclusion from sufficient premises, or accepting facts upon sufficient evidence. Nor will it avail to urge that this birth was merely the mental or moral change naturally caused by the truth thus attained by natural means. The language of the Scripture is unequivocal that the power of the testimony to produce this change depended on the presence and operation of God. Pages might be filled with quotations to prove this, but two may suffice. St. Peter declares they preached the Gospel " with the Holy Ghost sent down from heaven ; "§ and St. Paul's words are still more definite : " Our Gospel came not unto you in word only, but also in power and in the Holy Ghost."‖

---

* 2 Peter i. 1.   † John i. 13.

‡ James i. 18.   § 1 Peter i. 12.

‖ ἀλλὰ καὶ ἐν δυνάμει καὶ ἐν πνεύματι ἁγίῳ. (1 Thess. i. 5.) 'But also in power, even in the Holy Ghost." There is no

And if the new birth and the faith of Christianity were thus produced in the case of persons who received the Gospel immediately from the Apostles, nothing less will avail with us who are separated by eighteen centuries from the witnesses and their testimony. God is with His people still. And He speaks to men's hearts, now, as really as He did in early times ; not indeed through inspired Apostles, and still less by dreams or visions, but through the Holy Writings which He Himself inspired ;* and as the result believers are " born of God," and obtain the knowledge of forgiveness of sins and of eternal life. The phenomenon is not a natural one, resulting from the study of the evidences ; it is *supernatural* altogether. "Thinking minds," regarding it objectively, may, if they please, maintain towards it what they deem " a rational attitude ; " but at least let them own the fact that there are thousands of credible

---

contrast intended between God on the one hand, and power on the other, nor yet between different sorts of power. To object that this referred to miracles which accompanied the preaching is to betray ignorance of Scripture. Acts xvii. represents the preaching to which the Apostle was alluding. That miraculous power existed in Gentile Churches is clear from 1 Cor. xii.; but the question is, did the gospel which produced those Churches appeal to miracles to confirm it ? Can any one read the first four chapters of 1 Cor. and retain a doubt as to the answer ?

* God is omnipresent ; but there is a real sense in which the Father and the Son are not on earth but in heaven, and in that same sense the Holy Spirit is not in heaven but on earth.

people who can testify to the reality of the experience here spoken of, and further let them recognise that it is entirely in accordance with the teaching of the New Testament.

And such persons have transcendental proof of the truth of Christianity. Their faith rests, not on the phenomena of their own experience, but on the great objective truths of revelation. Yet their primary conviction that these *are* Divine truths does not depend on the "evidences" which scepticism delights to criticise, but on something which scepticism takes no account of.*

" No book can be written in behalf of the Bible like the Bible itself. Man's defences are man's word ; they may help to beat off attacks, they may draw out some portion of its meaning. The Bible is God's word, and through it God the Holy Ghost, who spake it, speaks to the soul which closes not itself against it." †

But more than this, the well-instructed believer will find within it inexhaustible stores of proof that it is from God. The Bible is far more than a text-book of theology and morals, or even than a guide

---

* Such faith is inseparably connected with salvation, and salvation is the gift of God (Eph. ii. 8). Hence the solemn words of Christ, " I thank Thee, O Father, Lord of heaven and earth, because Thou hast hid these things from the wise and prudent, and hast revealed them unto babes " (Matt. xi. 25).

† Pusey, *Daniel*, Pref., p. xxv.

to heaven. It is the record of the progressive revelation God has vouchsafed to man, and the Divine
history of our race in connection with that revelation.
Ignorance may fail to see in it anything more than
the religious literature of the Hebrew race, and of
the Church in Apostolic times ; but the intelligent
student who can read between the lines will find
there mapped out, sometimes in clear bold outline,
sometimes dimly, but yet always discernible by the
patient and devout inquirer, the great scheme of
God's counsels and workings in and for this world
of ours from eternity to eternity.

And the study of prophecy, rightly understood,
has a range no narrower than this. Its chief value
is not to bring us a knowledge of " things to come,"
regarded as isolated events, important though this
may be; but to enable us to link the future with
the past as part of God's great purpose and plan
revealed in Holy Writ. The facts of the life and
death of Christ were an overwhelming proof of the
inspiration of the Old Testament. When, after His
resurrection, He sought to confirm the disciples'
faith, "beginning at Moses, and all the prophets,
He expounded unto them in all the Scriptures the
things concerning Himself." * But many a promise
had been given, and many a prophecy recorded,

---

* Luke xxiv. 27.

which seemed to be lost in the darkness of Israel's national extinction and Judah's apostasy. The fulfilment of them all depended on Messiah; but now Messiah was rejected, and His people were about to be cast away, that Gentiles might be taken up for blessing. Are we to conclude then that the past is wiped out for ever, and that God's great purposes for earth have collapsed through human sin? As men now judge of revelation, Christianity dwindles down to be nothing but a "plan of salvation" for individuals, and if St. John's Gospel and a few of the Epistles be left them they are content. How different was the attitude of mind and heart displayed by St. Paul! In the Apostle's view the crisis which seemed the catastrophe of everything the old prophets had foretold of God's purposes for earth, opened up a wider and more glorious purpose still, which should include the fulfilment of them all; and rapt in the contemplation, he exclaimed, "Oh the depth of the riches both of the wisdom and knowledge of God! how unsearchable are His judgments, and His ways past finding out!"*

True prophetic study is an inquiry into these unsearchable counsels, these deep riches of Divine wisdom and knowledge. Beneath the light it gives, the Scriptures are no longer a heterogeneous com-

---

* Rom. xi. 33.

pilation of religious books, but one harmonious whole, from which no part could be omitted without destroying the completeness of the revelation. And yet the study is disparaged in the Churches as being of no practical importance. If the Churches are leavened with scepticism at this moment, their neglect of prophetic study in this its true and broader aspect has done more than all the rationalism of Germany to promote the evil. Sceptics may boast of learned Professors and Doctors of Divinity among their ranks, but we may challenge them to name a single one of the number who has given proof that he knows anything whatever of these deeper mysteries of revelation.

The attempt to put back the rising tide of scepticism is hopeless. Indeed the movement is but one of many phases of the intense mental activity which marks the age. The reign of creeds is past. The days are gone for ever when men will believe what their fathers believed, without a question. Rome, in some phase of its development, has a strange charm for minds of a certain caste, and rationalism is fascinating to not a few; but orthodoxy in the old sense is dead, and if any are to be delivered it must be by a deeper and more thorough knowledge of the Scriptures.

These pages are but a humble effort to this end; but if they avail in any measure to promote the study of Holy Writ their chief purpose will be fulfilled. The reader therefore may expect to find the accuracy of the Bible vindicated on points which may seem of trifling value. When David reached the throne of Israel and came to choose his generals, he named for the chief commands the men who had made themselves conspicuous by feats of prowess or of valour. Among the foremost three was one of whom the record states that he defended a tract of lentiles, and drove away a troop of the Philistines.* To others it may have seemed little better than a patch of weeds, and not worth fighting for, but it was precious to the Israelite as a portion of the divinely-given inheritance, and moreover the enemy might have used it as a rallying ground from which to capture strongholds. So is it with the Bible. It is all of intrinsic value if indeed it be from God; and moreover, the statement which is assailed, and which may seem of no importance, may prove to be a link in the chain of truth on which we are depending for eternal life.

---

* 2 Sam. xxiii. 11, 12.

2

DANIEL AND HIS TIMES

"DANIEL *the prophet*." None can have a higher title to the name, for it was thus Messiah spoke of him. And yet the great Prince of the Captivity would himself doubtless have disclaimed it. Isaiah, Jeremiah, Ezekiel, and the rest, "spake as they were moved by the Holy Ghost;"* but Daniel uttered no such "God-breathed " words.† Like the " beloved disciple " in Messianic times, he beheld visions, and recorded what he saw. The great prediction of the seventy weeks was a message delivered to him by an angel, who spoke to him as man speaks with man. A stranger to prophet's fare ‡ and prophet's garb, he

---

* 2 Peter i. 21.

† My belief in the Divine character of the Book of Daniel will, I trust, appear plainly in these pages. The distinction I desire to mark here is between prophecies which men were inspired to utter, and prophecies like those of Daniel and St. John, who were merely the recipients of the revelation. With these, inspiration began in the *recording* what they had received.

‡ To quote Dan. i. 12 in opposition to this involves an obvious anachronism. The word "pulse," moreover, in the Hebrew

lived in the midst of all the luxury and pomp of an Eastern court. Next to the king, he was the foremost man in the greatest empire of antiquity; and it was not till the close of a long life spent in statecraft that he received the visions recorded in the latter chapters of his book.

To understand these prophecies aright, it is essential that the leading events of the political history of the times should be kept in view.

The summer of Israel's national glory had proved as brief as it was brilliant. The people never acquiesced in heart in the Divine decree which, in distributing the tribal dignities, entrusted the sceptre to the house of Judah, while it adjudged the birthright to the favoured family of Joseph ; * and their mutual jealousies and feuds, though kept in check by the personal influence of David, and the surpassing splendour of the reign of Solomon, produced a national disruption upon the accession of Rehoboam. In revolting from Judah, the Israelites also apostatized from God ; and forsaking the worship of Jehovah, they lapsed into open and flagrant idolatry. After

---

points generally to vegetable food, and would include a dish as savoury as that for which Esau sold his birthright (comp. Gen. xxv. 34). To eat animal food from the table of Gentiles would have involved a violation of the law ; therefore Daniel and his companions became " vegetarians."

* " Judah prevailed above his brethren, and of him came the chief ruler ; but the birthright was Joseph's " (1 Chron. v. 2).

two centuries and a half unillumined by a single
bright passage in their history, they passed into
captivity to Assyria; * and on the birth of Daniel a
century had elapsed since the date of their national
extinction.

Judah still retained a nominal independence,
though, in fact, the nation had already fallen into
a state of utter vassalage. The geographical position of its territory marked it out for such a fate.
Lying half-way between the Nile and the Euphrates,
suzerainty in Judea became inevitably a test by
which their old enemy beyond their southern frontier,
and the empire which the genius of Nabopolassar
was then rearing in the north, would test their rival
claims to supremacy. The prophet's birth fell about
the very year which was reckoned the epoch of
the second Babylonian Empire.† He was still a boy
at the date of Pharaoh Necho's unsuccessful invasion
of Chaldea. In that struggle his kinsman and
sovereign, the good king Josiah, took sides with
Babylon, and not only lost his life, but compromised
still further the fortunes of his house and the freedom
of his country. ‡

The public mourning for Josiah had scarcely ended

---

* The disruption was in B.C. 975, the captivity to Assyria
about B.C. 721.

† B.C. 625.

‡ 2 Kings xxiii. 29 ; 2 Chron. xxxv. 20.

when Pharaoh, on his homeward march, appeared
before Jerusalem to assert his suzerainty by claiming
a heavy tribute from the land and settling the succession to the throne. Jehoahaz, a younger son of
Josiah, had obtained the crown on his father's death,
but was deposed by Pharaoh in favour of Eliakim,
who doubtless recommended himself to the king of
Egypt by the very qualities which perhaps had induced his father to disinherit him. Pharaoh changed
his name to Jehoiakim, and established him in the
kingdom as a vassal of Egypt.*

In the third year after these events, Nebuchadnezzar, Prince Royal of Babylon,† set out upon an
expedition of conquest, in command of his father's
armies; and entering Judea he demanded the sub-
mission of the king of Judah. After a siege of which
history gives no particulars, he captured the city and
seized the king as a prisoner of war. But Jehoiakim
regained his liberty and his throne by pledging his
allegiance to Babylon; and Nebuchadnezzar withdrew with no spoil except a part of the holy vessels
of the temple, which he carried to the house of his
god, and no captives save a few youths of the seed

---

* 2 Kings xxiii. 33-35 ; 2 Chron. xxxvi. 3, 4.

† Berosus avers that this expedition was in Nabopolassar's
lifetime (Jos., *Apion*, i. 19), and the chronology proves it. See
App. I. as to the dates of these events and the chronology of
the period.

royal of Judah, Daniel being of the number, whom he selected to adorn his court as vassal princes.*
Three years later Jehoiakim revolted ; but, although during the rest of his reign his territory was frequently overrun by "bands of the Chaldees," five years elapsed before the armies of Babylon returned to enforce the conquest of Judea.†

Jehoiachin, a youth of eighteen years, who had just succeeded to the throne, at once surrendered with his family and retinue,‡ and once more Jerusalem lay at the mercy of Nebuchadnezzar. On his first invasion he had proved magnanimous and lenient, but he had now not merely to assert supremacy but to punish rebellion. Accordingly he ransacked the city for everything of value, and "carried away all Jerusalem," leaving none behind "save the poorest sort of the people of the land." §

---

* 2 Kings xxiv. 1 ; 2 Chron. xxxvi. 6, 7 ; Dan. i. 1, 2.

† 2 Kings xxiv. 1, 2. According to Josephus (*Ant.*, x. 6, § 3) Nebuchadnezzar on his second invasion found Jehoiakim still on the throne, and he it was who put him to death and made Jehoiachin king. He goes on to say that the king of Babylon soon afterwards became suspicious of Jehoiachin's fidelity, and again returned to dethrone him, and placed Zedekiah on the throne. These statements, though not absolutely inconsistent with 2 Kings xxiv., are rendered somewhat improbable by comparison with it. They are adopted by Canon Rawlinson in the *Five Great Monarchies* (vol. iii., p. 491), but Dr. Pusey adheres to the Scripture narrative (*Daniel*, p. 403).

‡ 2 Kings xxiv. 12.   § 2 Kings xxiv. 14.

Jehoiachin's uncle Zedekiah was left as king or governor of the despoiled and depopulated city, having sworn by Jehovah to pay allegiance to his Suzerain. This was "King Jehoiachin's captivity," according to the era of the prophet Ezekiel, who was himself among the captives. *

The servitude to Babylon had been predicted as early as the days of Hezekiah; † and after the fulfilment of Isaiah's prophecy respecting it, Jeremiah was charged with a Divine message of hope to the captivity, that after seventy years were accomplished they would be restored to their land.‡ But while the exiles were thus cheered with promises of good, King Zedekiah and "the residue of Jerusalem that remained in the land" were warned that resistance to the Divine decree which subjected them to the yoke of Babylon would bring on them judgments far more terrible than any they had known. Nebuchadnezzar would return to "destroy them utterly," and make their whole land "a desolation and an astonishment." § False prophets rose up, however, to feed the national vanity by predicting the speedy restoration of their independence,‖ and in spite of the solemn and repeated warnings and entreaties of Jeremiah, the weak and wicked king was deceived

---

* Ezek. i. 2.   † 2 Kings xx. 17.   ‡ Jer. xxix. 10.
§ Jer. xxiv. 8-10; xxv. 9; xxvii. 3-8.   ‖ Jer. xxviii. 1-4.

by their testimony, and having obtained a promise of armed support from Egypt, * he openly revolted.

Thereupon the Chaldean armies once more surrounded Jerusalem. Events seemed at first to justify Zedekiah's conduct, for the Egyptian forces hastened to his assistance, and the Babylonians were compelled to raise the siege and withdraw from Judea.†　But this temporary success of the Jews served only to exasperate the King of Babylon, and to make their fate more terrible when at last it overtook them. Nebuchadnezzar determined to inflict a signal chastisement on the rebellious city and people ; and placing himself at the head of all the forces of his empire, ‡ he once more invaded Judea and laid siege to the Holy City.

The Jews resisted with the blind fanaticism which a false hope inspires; and it is a signal proof of the natural strength of ancient Jerusalem, that for eighteen months § they kept their enemy at bay, and yielded at last to famine and not to force. The place was then given up to fire and sword. Nebuchadnezzar "slew their young men with the sword in the house of their sanctuary, and had no compassion upon young man or maiden, old man, or him that stooped for age ; he gave them all into his

---

* Ezek. xvii. 15.　　　† Jer. xxxvii. 1, 5, 11.

‡ 2 Kings xxv. 1 ; *and see* Jer. xxxiv. 1.

§ 2 Kings xxv. 1-3.

hand. And all the vessels of the house of God, great and small, and the treasures of the house of the Lord, and the treasures of the king and of his princes, all these he brought to Babylon. And they burnt the house of God, and brake down the wall of Jerusalem, and burnt all the palaces thereof with fire, and destroyed all the goodly vessels thereof. And them that had escaped from the sword carried he away to Babylon, where they were servants to him and his sons, until the reign of the kingdom of Persia: to fulfil the word of the Lord by the mouth of Jeremiah."*

As He had borne with their fathers for forty years in the wilderness, so for forty years this last judgment lingered, "because He had compassion on His people and on His dwelling place."† For forty years the prophet's voice had not been silent in Jerusalem ; "but they mocked the messengers of God, and despised His words, and misused His prophets, until the wrath of the Lord arose against His people, till there was no remedy."‡

---

* 2 Chron. xxxvi. 17-21.

† *Ibid.* xxxvi. 15.

‡ *Ibid.* v. 16. This period is no doubt the forty years of Judah's sin, specified in Ezek. iv. 6. Jeremiah prophesied from the thirteenth year of Josiah (B.C. 627) until the fall of Jerusalem in the eleventh year of Zedekiah (B.C. 587). See Jer. i. 3, and xxv. 3.

The 390 years of Israel's sin, according to Ezek. iv. 5, appear

Such is the sacred chronicler's description of the first destruction of Jerusalem, rivalled in later times by the horrors of that event under the effects of which it still lies prostrate,[5] and destined to be surpassed in days still to come, when the predictions of Judah's supreme catastrophe shall be fulfilled.*

---

to have been reckoned from the date of the covenant of blessing to the ten tribes, made by the prophet Ahijah with Jeroboam, presumably in the second year before the disruption, *i.e.*, B.C. 977 (1 Kings xi. 29-39).

* The horrors of the siege and capture of Jerusalem by Titus surpass everything which history records of similar events. Josephus, who was himself a witness of them, narrates them in all their awful details. His estimate of the number of Jews who perished in Jerusalem is 1,100,000. "The blood runs cold, and the heart sickens, at these unexampled horrors ; and we take refuge in a kind of desperate hope that they have been exaggerated by the historian." "Jerusalem might almost seem to be a place under a peculiar curse ; it has probably witnessed a far greater portion of human misery than any other spot upon the

[5] See Appendix 4, p. 305 note 5.

3

THE KING'S DREAM
AND THE PROPHET'S VISIONS

THE distinction between the Hebrew and the Chaldee portions of the writings of Daniel* affords a natural division, the importance of which will appear on a careful consideration of the whole. But for the purpose of the present inquiry, the book will more conveniently divide itself between the first six chapters and the last, the former portion being primarily historical and didactic, and the latter containing the record of the four great visions granted to the prophet in his closing years. It is with the visions that here we are specially concerned. The narrative of the third, fourth, fifth, and sixth chapters is beyond the scope of these pages, as having no immediate bearing upon the prophecy. The second chapter, however, is of great importance, as giving the foundation of the later visions.†

---

* "The Chaldee portion of Daniel commences at the fourth verse of the second chapter, and continues to the end of the seventh chapter."—TREGELLES, *Daniel*, p. 8.

† The following analysis of the Book of Daniel may help the study of it :—

In a dream, King Nebuchadnezzar saw a great image, of which the head was gold, the breasts and arms silver, the body brass, the legs iron, and the feet partly iron and partly potter's ware. Then a stone, hewn without hands, struck the feet of the image and it fell and crumbled to dust, and the stone became a great mountain and filled the whole earth.*

The interpretation is in these words :—

" Thou, O king, art a king of kings ; for the God

Chap. I. The capture of Jerusalem. The captivity of Daniel and his three companions, and their fortunes in Babylon (B.C. 606).

Chap. II. Nebuchadnezzar's dream of THE GREAT IMAGE (B.C. 603-2).

Chap. III. Nebuchadnezzar's golden image set up for all his subjects to worship. Daniel's three companions cast into the fiery furnace.

Chap. IV. Nebuchadnezzar's dream about his own insanity, and Daniel's interpretation of it. Its fulfilment.

Chap. V. Belshazzar's feast. Babylon taken by Darius the Mede (B.C. 538).

Chap. VI. Daniel is promoted by Darius ; refuses to worship him, and is cast into a den of lions. His deliverance and subsequent prosperity (? B.C. 537).

Chap. VII. Daniel's vision of THE FOUR BEASTS (? B.C. 541).

Chap. VIII. Daniel's vision of THE RAM AND THE GOAT (? B.C. 539).

Chap. IX. Daniel's prayer : the prophecy of THE SEVENTY WEEKS (B.C. 538).

Chaps. X.- XII. Daniel's LAST VISION (B.C. 534).

* The difficulty connected with the date of this vision (the second year of Nebuchadnezzar) is considered in App. I. *post.*

of heaven hath given thee a kingdom, power, and strength and glory. And wheresoever the children of men dwell, the beasts of the field and the fowls of the heaven hath He given into thine hand, and hath made thee ruler over them all. Thou art this head of gold. And after thee shall arise another kingdom inferior to thee, and another third kingdom of brass, which shall bear rule over all the earth. And the fourth kingdom shall be strong as iron ; forasmuch as iron breaketh in pieces and subdueth all things : and as iron that breaketh all these, shall it break in pieces and bruise. And whereas thou sawest the feet and toes part of potter's clay and part of iron, the kingdom shall be divided ; but there shall be in it of the strength of the iron, forasmuch as thou sawest the iron mixed with miry clay. And as the toes of the feet were part of iron and part of clay, so the kingdom shall be partly strong, and partly broken. And whereas thou sawest iron mixed with miry clay, they shall mingle themselves with the seed of men : but they shall not cleave one to another, even as iron is not mixed with clay. And in the days of these kings shall the God of heaven set up a kingdom which shall never be destroyed : and the kingdom shall not be left to other people, but it shall break in pieces and consume all these kingdoms, and it shall stand for ever. Forasmuch as thou sawest that the stone was cut out of the mountain without hands, and that it brake in pieces the iron, the brass, the clay, the silver, and the gold; the great God hath made known to the king what shall come to pass hereafter: and the dream is certain, and the interpretation thereof sure." *

The predicted sovereignty of Judah passed far beyond the limits of mere supremacy among the tribes of Israel. It was an imperial sceptre which was entrusted to the Son of David. "I will make him my firstborn, higher than the kings of the earth." †
"All things shall fall down before him, all nations shall serve him." ‡ Such were the promises which Solomon inherited; and the brief glory of his reign gave proof how fully they might have been realized,§ had he not turned aside to folly, and bartered for present sensual pleasures the most splendid prospects which ever opened before mortal man. Nebuchadnezzar's dream of the great image, and Daniel's vision in interpretation of that dream, were a Divine revelation that the forfeited sceptre of the house of David had passed to Gentile hands, to remain with them until the day when "the God of heaven shall set up a kingdom which shall never be destroyed." ‖

It is unnecessary here to discuss in detail the earlier portions of this prophecy. There is, in fact,

---

* Dan. ii. 37-45.   § 2 Chron. ix. 22-28.
† Psalm lxxxix. 27.   ‖ Dan. ii. 44.
‡ Psalm lxxii. 11.

no controversy as to its general character and scope; and bearing in mind the distinction between what is doubted and what is doubtful, there need be no controversy as to the identity of the empires therein described with Babylonia, Persia, Greece, and Rome. That the first was Nebuchadnezzar's kingdom is definitely stated,* and a later vision as expressly names the Medo-Persian empire and the empire of Alexander as being distinct "kingdoms" within the range of the prophecy.† The fourth empire, there-fore, must of necessity be Rome. But it is sufficient here to emphasize the fact, revealed in the plainest terms to Daniel in his exile, and to Jeremiah in the midst of the troubles at Jerusalem, that thus the sovereignty of the earth, which had been forfeited by Judah, was solemnly committed to the Gentiles.‡

---

* Dan. ii. 37, 38. † Dan. viii. 20, 21.

‡ *Cf.* Dan. ii. 38, and Jer. xxvii. 6, 7.—The statement of Gen. xlix. 10 may seem at first sight to clash with this : " The sceptre shall not depart from Judah, nor a law-giver from be-tween his feet, until Shiloh come." But, as events prove, this cannot mean that royal power was to be exercised by the house of Judah until the advent of Christ. Hengstenberg has rightly interpreted it *(Christology,* Arnold's trans., § 78) : " Judah shall not cease to exist as a tribe, nor lose its superiority, until it shall be exalted to higher honour and glory through the great Redeemer, who shall spring from it, and whom not only the Jews, but all the nations of the earth shall obey." As he points out, "*until* not unfrequently means *up to* and *afterwards.*" (*See ex. gr.* Gen xxviii. 15.) The meaning of the prophecy,

The only questions which arise relate, first to the character of the final catastrophe symbolized by the fall and destruction of the image, and secondly to the time of its fulfilment ; and any difficulties which have been raised depend in no way upon the language of the prophecy, but solely upon the preconceived views of interpreters. No Christian doubts that the "stone cut out without hands" was typical either of Christ Himself or of His kingdom. It is equally clear that the catastrophe was to occur when the fourth empire should have become divided, and be "partly strong and partly brittle." Therefore its fulfilment could not belong to the time of the first advent. No less clear is it that its fulfilment was to be a sudden crisis, to be followed by the establishment of "a kingdom which shall never be destroyed." Therefore it relates to events still to come. We are dealing here, not with prophetic theories, but with the meaning of plain words; and what the prophecy foretells is not the rise and spread of a " *spiritual* kingdom " in the midst of earthly kingdoms, but the establishment of a kingdom which "shall break in pieces and consume all these kingdoms."*

---

therefore, was not that Judah was to exercise royal power *until* Christ, and then lose it, which is the lame and unsatisfactory gloss usually adopted ; but that the pre-eminence of Judah is to be irrevocably established in Christ—not spiritually, but in fact, in the kingdom of which Daniel prophesies.

* To believe that such a prophecy can ever be realized may

The interpretation of the royal dream raised the captive exile at a single bound to the Grand-Vizier-ship of Babylon,* a position of trust and honour which probably he held until he was either dismissed or withdrew from office under one or other of the two last kings who succeeded to Nebuchadnezzar's throne. The scene on the fatal night of Belshazzar's feast suggests that he had been then so long in retirement, that the young king-regent knew nothing of his fame.† But yet his fame was still so great with older men, that notwithstanding his failing years, he was once more called to the highest office by Darius, when the Median king became master of the broad-walled city.‡

But whether in prosperity or in retirement, he was true to the God of his fathers. The years in which his childhood in Jerusalem was spent, though poli-tically dark and troubled, were a period of the brightest spiritual revival by which his nation had

---

seem to betoken fanaticism and folly, but at least let us accept the language of Scripture, and not lapse into the blind absurdity of expecting the fulfilment of theories based on what men con-jecture the prophets ought to have foretold.

* Dan. ii. 48.

† This appears from the language of the queen-mother, Dan. v. 10-12. But chap. viii. 27 shows that Daniel, even then, held some appointment at the court.

‡ Dan. vi. 1, 2. Daniel cannot have been less than eighty years of age at this time. See chron. table, App. I. *post.*

ever been blessed, and he had carried with him to the court of Nebuchadnezzar a faith and piety that withstood all the adverse influences which abounded in such a scene.*

The Daniel of the second chapter was a young man just entering on a career of extraordinary dignity and power, such as few have ever known. The Daniel of the seventh chapter was an aged saint, who, having passed through the ordeal scathless, still possessed a heart as true to God and to His people as when, some threescore years before, he had entered the gates of the broad-walled city a captive and friendless stranger. The date of the earlier vision was about the time of Jehoiakim's revolt, when their ungovernable pride of race and creed still led the Jews to dream of independence. At the time of the later vision more than forty years had passed since Jerusalem had been laid in ruins, and the last king of the house of David had entered the brazen gates of Babylon in chains.

Here again the main outlines of the prophecy seem

---

* It is improbable that Daniel was less than twenty-one years of age when placed at the head of the empire in the second year of Nebuchadnezzar. The age to which he lived makes it equally improbable that he was more. His birth would thus fall, as before suggested, about B.C. 625, the epoch of Nabopolassar's era, and some three years later was Josiah's passover, the like of which had never been held in Israel from the days of Samuel (2 Chron. xxxv. 18, 19).

clear. As the four empires which were destined successively to wield sovereign power during "the times of the Gentiles" are represented in Nebuchadnezzar's dream by the four divisions of the great image, they are here typified by four wild beasts.* The ten toes

---

* The following is the vision as recorded in Daniel vii. 2-14 :—
" Daniel spake and said, I saw in my vision by night, and, behold, the four winds of the heaven strove upon the great sea. And four great beasts came up from the sea, diverse one from another. The first was like a lion, and had eagle's wings : I beheld till the wings thereof were plucked, and it was lifted up from the earth, and made stand upon the feet as a man, and a man's heart was given to it. And, behold, another beast, a second, like to a bear, and it raised up itself on one side, and it had three ribs in the mouth of it between the teeth of it : and they said thus unto it, Arise, devour much flesh. After this I beheld, and, lo, another, like a leopard, which had upon the back of it four wings of a fowl ; the beast had also four heads ; and dominion was given to it. After this I saw in the night visions, and, behold, a fourth beast, dreadful and terrible, and strong exceedingly ; and it had great iron teeth : it devoured and brake in pieces, and stamped the residue with the feet of it : and it was diverse from all the beasts that were before it ; and it had ten horns. I considered the horns, and, behold, there came up among them another little horn, before whom there were three of the first horns plucked up by the roots : and, behold, in this horn were eyes like the eyes of man, and a mouth speaking great things. I beheld till the thrones were cast down, and the Ancient of days did sit, whose garment was white as snow, and the hair of his head like the pure wool : his throne was like the fiery flame, and his wheels as burning fire. A fiery stream issued and came forth from before him : thousand thousands ministered unto him, and ten thousand times

of the image in the second chapter have their correlatives in the ten horns of the fourth beast in the
seventh chapter. The character and course of the
fourth empire are the prominent subject of the later
vision, but both prophecies are equally explicit that
that empire in its ultimate phase will be brought
to a signal and sudden end by a manifestation of
Divine power on earth.

The details of the vision, though interesting and
important, may here be passed unnoticed, for the
interpretation given of them is so simple and so
definite that the words can leave no room for doubt
in any unprejudiced mind. " These great beasts,
which are four, are four kings" (*i.e.*, kingdoms ;
compare verse 23), "which shall arise out of the
earth ; but the saints of the Most High shall

---

ten thousand stood before him : the judgment was set, and the
books were opened. I beheld then, because of the voice of
the great words which the horn spake : I beheld even till the
beast was slain, and his body destroyed, and given to the
burning flame. As concerning the rest of the beasts, they had
their dominion taken away : yet their lives were prolonged for
a season and time. I saw in the night visions, and, behold,
one like the Son of man came with the clouds of heaven, and
came to the Ancient of days, and they brought him near before
him. And there was given him dominion, and glory, and a
kingdom, that all people, nations, and languages, should serve
him : his dominion is an everlasting dominion, which shall
not pass away, and his kingdom that which shall not be
destroyed."

take the kingdom and possess the kingdom for ever."*

The prophet then proceeds to recapitulate the vision, and his language affords an explicit answer to the only question which can reasonably be raised upon the words just quoted, namely, whether the "kingdom of the saints" shall follow immediately upon the close of the fourth Gentile empire.† "Then," he adds, " I would know the truth of the fourth beast, which was diverse from all the others, exceeding dreadful, whose teeth were of iron, and his nails of brass ; which devoured, brake in pieces, and stamped the residue with his feet ; and of the ten horns that

---

* Verses 17, 18.

† Certain writers advocate an interpretation of these visions which allots the "four kingdoms" to Babylonia, Media, Persia, and Greece. This view, with which Professor Westcott's name is identified, claims notice merely in order to distinguish it from another with which it has been confounded, even in a work of such pretensions as *The Speaker's Commentary* (Vol. vi., p. 333, *Excursus on the Four Kingdoms*). The learned author of the *Ordo Sæclorum* (§ 616, etc.), quoting Maitland, who in turn follows Lacunza (Ben Ezra), argues that the accession of Darius the Mede to the throne of Babylon did not involve a change of empire. These writers further urge that the description of the third kingdom resembles Rome rather than Greece. According to this view, therefore, the kingdoms are 1st Babylon, including Persia, 2nd Greece, 3rd Rome, 4th a future kingdom to arise in the last days. But as already noticed (p. 32, *ante*), the book of Daniel expressly distinguishes Babylon, Medo-Persia, and Greece as "kingdoms" within the scope of the prophecy.

were in his head, and of the other which came up, and before whom three fell, even of that horn that had eyes, and a mouth that spake very great things, whose look was more stout than his fellows. I beheld, and the same horn made war with the saints, and prevailed against them; until the Ancient of days came, and judgment was given to the saints of the Most High; and the time came that the saints possessed the kingdom."

Such was the prophet's inquiry. Here is the interpretation accorded to him in reply. " The fourth beast shall be the fourth kingdom upon earth, which shall be diverse from all kingdoms, and shall devour the whole earth, and shall tread it down, and break it in pieces. And the ten horns out of this kingdom are ten kings that shall arise: and another shall arise after them; and he shall be diverse from the first, and he shall subdue three kings. And he shall speak great words against the Most High, and shall wear out the saints of the Most High, and think to change times and laws; and they shall be given into his hand, until a time and times and the dividing of time. But the judgment shall sit, and they shall take away his dominion, to consume and to destroy it unto the end. And the kingdom and dominion, and the greatness of the kingdom under the whole heaven, shall be given to the people of the saints of the Most High, whose kingdom is an everlasting kingdom, and all dominions shall serve and obey Him." *

Whether history records any event which may be within the range of this prophecy is a matter of opinion. That it has not been *fulfilled* is a plain matter of fact.† The Roman earth shall one day be parcelled out in ten separate kingdoms, and out of one of these shall arise that terrible enemy of God and His people, whose destruction is to be one of the events of the second advent of Christ.

---

* Dan. vii. 19-27. On this vision see Pusey, *Daniel*, pp. 78, 79.

† The state of Europe at or after the dismemberment of the Roman Empire has been appealed to as a fulfilment of it, ignoring the fact that the territory which Augustus ruled included a considerable district both of Asia and Africa. Nor is this all. There is no presumption against finding in past times a partial accomplishment of such a prophecy, but the fact that twenty-eight different lists, including sixty-five "kingdoms," have been put forward in the controversy, is a proof how worthless is the evidence of any such fulfilment. In truth the historical school of interpreters have here, as on many other points, brought discredit upon their entire system, containing, as it does, so much that claims attention (see App. II., Note C).

4

THE VISION OF THE RIVER OF ULAI

" THE times of the Gentiles;" thus it was that Christ Himself described the era of Gentile supremacy. Men have come to regard the earth as their own domain, and to resent the thought of Divine interference in their affairs. But though monarchs seem to owe their thrones to dynastic claims, the sword or the ballot-box,—and in their individual capacity their title may rest solely upon these,—the power they wield is divinely delegated, for " the Most High ruleth in the kingdom of men, and giveth it to whomsoever He will." * In the exercise of this high prerogative He took back the sceptre He had entrusted to the house of David, and transferred it to Gentile hands ; and the history of that sceptre during the entire period, from the epoch to the close of the times of the Gentiles, is the subject of the prophet's earlier visions.

The vision of the eighth chapter of Daniel has a narrower range. It deals only with the two king-

* Dan. iv. 25.

doms which were represented by the middle portion, or arms and body, of the image of the second chapter. The Medo-Persian Empire, and the relative superiority of the younger nation, are represented by a ram with two horns, one of which was higher than the other, though the last to grow. And the rise of the Grecian Empire under Alexander, followed by its division among his four successors, is typified by a goat with a single horn between its eyes, which horn was broken and gave place to four horns that came up instead of it. Out of one of these horns came forth a little horn, representing a king who should become infamous as a blasphemer of God and a persecutor of His people.

That the career of Antiochus Epiphanes was in a special way within the scope and meaning of this prophecy is unquestioned. That its ultimate fulfilment belongs to a future time, though not so generally admitted, is nevertheless sufficiently clear. The proof of it is twofold. First, it cannot but be recognized that its most striking details remain wholly unfulfilled.* And secondly, the events described are expressly stated to be " in the last end of the indignation," † which is " the great tribulation "

---

* I allude to the 2,300 days of verse 14, and to the statement of verse 25, " He shall also stand up against the Prince of Princes, but he shall be broken without hand."

† Dan. viii. 19.

of the last days,* "the time of trouble" which is immediately to precede the complete deliverance of Judah.†

It is unnecessary, however, further to embarrass the special subject of these pages by any such discussion. So far as the present inquiry is immediately concerned, this vision of the ram and the he-goat is important mainly as explanatory of the visions which precede it.‡

---

* Matt. xxiv. 21.

† "And there shall be a time of trouble such as never was since there was a nation even to that same time ; and at that time thy people shall be delivered,"—*i.e.*, the Jews (Dan. xii. i).

‡ The following is the vision of the eighth chapter :—

"And I saw in a vision ; and it came to pass, when I saw, that I was at Shushan, in the palace, which is in the province of Elam ; and I saw in a vision, and I was by the river of Ulai. Then I lifted up mine eyes, and saw, and, behold, there stood before the river a ram which had two horns. And the two horns were high ; but one was higher than the other, and the higher came up last. I saw the ram pushing westward, and northward, and southward ; so that no beasts might stand before him, neither was there any that could deliver out of his hand ; but he did according to his will, and became great. And as I was considering, behold, an he goat came from the west, on the face of the whole earth, and touched not the ground : and the goat had a notable horn between his eyes. And he came to the ram that had two horns, which I had seen standing before the river, and ran unto him in the fury of his power. And I saw him come close unto the ram, and he was moved with choler against

One point of contrast with the prophecy of the fourth Gentile kingdom demands a very emphatic notice. The vision of Alexander's reign, followed

---

him, and smote the ram, and brake his two horns ; and there was no power in the ram to stand before him, but he cast him down to the ground, and stamped upon him : and there was none that could deliver the ram out of his hand. Therefore the he goat waxed very great ; and when he was strong, the great horn was broken ; and for it came up four notable ones, toward the four winds of heaven. And out of one of them came forth a little horn, which waxed exceeding great, toward the south, and toward the east, and toward the pleasant land. And it waxed great, even to the host of heaven ; and it cast down some of the host and of the stars to the ground, and stamped upon them. Yea, he magnified himself even to the prince of the host, and by him the daily sacrifice was taken away, and the place of his sanctuary was cast down. And an host was given him against the daily sacrifice by reason of transgression, and it cast down the truth to the ground ; and it practised, and prospered. Then I heard one saint speaking, and another saint said unto that certain saint which spake. How long shall be the vision concerning the daily sacrifice, and the trans- gression of desolation, to give both the sanctuary and the host to be trodden under foot? And he said unto me, Unto two thousand and three hundred days ; then shall the sanctuary be cleansed. And it came to pass, when I, even I Daniel, had seen the vision, and sought for the meaning, then, behold, there stood before me as the appearance of a man. And I heard a man's voice between the banks of Ulai, which called, and said, Gabriel, make this man to understand the vision. So he came near where I stood : and' when he came, I was afraid, and fell upon my face : but he said unto me, Under- stand, O son of man ; for at the time of the end shall be

by the fourfold division of his empire, suggests a rapid sequence of events, and the history of the three-and-thirty years that intervened between the battles of Issus and of Ipsus* comprises the full realization

---

the vision. Now, as he was speaking with me I was in a deep sleep on my face toward the ground : but he touched me, and set me upright. And he said, Behold, I will make thee know what shall be in the last end of the indignation : for at the time appointed the end shall be. The ram which thou sawest having two horns are the kings of Media and Persia. And the rough goat is the king of Grecia : and the great horn that is between his eyes is the first king. Now that being broken, whereas four stood up for it, four kingdoms shall stand up out of the nation, but not in his power. And in the latter time of their kingdom, when the transgressors are come to the full, a king of fierce countenance, and understanding dark sentences, shall stand up. And his power shall be mighty, but not by his own power : and he shall destroy wonderfully, and shall prosper, and practise, and shall destroy the mighty and the holy people. And through his policy also he shall cause craft to prosper in his hand ; and he shall magnify himself in his heart, and by peace shall destroy many ; he shall also stand up against the Prince of princes ; but he shall be broken without hand. And the vision of the evening and the morning which was told is true ; wherefore shut thou up the vision ; for it shall be for many days."

* It was the battle of Issus in B.C. 333, not the victory of Granicus in the preceding year, which made Alexander master of Palestine. The decisive battle which brought the Persian empire to an end, was at Arbela in B.C. 331. Alexander died B.C. 323, and the definite distribution of his territories among his four chief generals, followed the battle of Ipsus B.C. 301. In this partition Seleucus's share included Syria ("the king of the north"), and Ptolemy held the Holy Land with Egypt

of the prophecy. But the rise of the ten horns upon
the fourth beast in the vision of the seventh chapter,
appears to lie within as brief a period as was the
rise of the four horns upon the goat in the eighth
chapter; whereas it is plain upon the pages of history that this tenfold division of the Roman empire
has never yet taken place. A definite date may be
assigned to the advent of the first three kingdoms of
prophecy; and if the date of the battle of Actium be
taken as the epoch of the hybrid monster which filled
the closing scenes of the prophet's vision—and no
later date will be assigned to it—it follows that in
interpreting the prophecy, we may eliminate the
history of the world from the time of Augustus to
the present hour, without losing the sequence of the
vision.* Or in other words, the prophet's glance into
the future entirely overlooked these nineteen centuries
of our era. As when mountain peaks stand out
together on the horizon, seeming almost to touch,
albeit a wide expanse of river and field and hill may
lie between, so there loomed upon the prophet's

("the king of the south"); but Palestine afterwards was conquered and held by the Seleucidæ. Cassander had Macedon
and Greece; and Lysimachus had Thrace, part of Bithynia,
and the territories intervening between these and the Meander.

* The same remark applies to the vision of the second chapter,
the rise of the Roman empire, its future division, and its final
doom, being presented at a single view.

vision these events of times now long gone by, and times still future.

And with the New Testament in our hands, it would betray strange and wilful ignorance if we doubted the deliberate design which has left this long interval of our Christian era a blank in Daniel's prophecies. The more explicit revelation of the ninth chapter, measures out the years before the first advent of Messiah. But if these nineteen centuries had been added to the chronology of the period to intervene before the promised kingdom could be ushered in, how could the Lord have taken up the testimony to the near fulfilment of these very prophecies, and have proclaimed that the kingdom was at hand?* He who knows all hearts, knew well the issue; but the thought is impious that the proclamation was not genuine and true in the strictest sense; and it would have been deceptive and untrue had prophecy foretold a long interval of Israel's rejection before the promise could be realized.

Therefore it is that the two advents of Christ are brought seemingly together in Old Testament Scriptures. The surface currents of human responsibility and human guilt are unaffected by the changeless and deep-lying tide of the fore-knowledge and sovereignty

---

* *i.e.*, the kingdom as Daniel had prophesied of it. On this see Pusey, *Daniel*, p. 84.

of God. Their responsibility was real, and their guilt was without excuse, who rejected their long-promised King and Saviour. They were not the victims of an inexorable fate which dragged them to their doom, but free agents who used their freedom to crucify the Lord of Glory. " His blood be on us and on our children," was their terrible, impious cry before the judgment-seat of Pilate, and for eighteen centuries their judgment has been meted out to them, to reach its appalling climax on the advent of the " time of trouble such as never was since there was a nation."*

These visions were full of mystery to Daniel, and filled the old prophet's mind with troubled thoughts.†
A long vista of events seemed thus to intervene before the realization of the promised blessings to his nation, and yet these very revelations made those

---

* Dan. xii. 1 ; Matt. xxiv. 21. To discuss what would have been the course of events had the Jews accepted Christ is mere levity. But it is legitimate to inquire how the believing Jew, intelligent in the prophecies, could have expected the kingdom, seeing that the tenfold division of the Roman empire and the rise of the " little horn " had to take place first. The difficulty will disappear if we notice how suddenly the Grecian empire was dismembered on Alexander's death. In like manner, the death of Tiberius might have led to the immediate disruption of the territories of Rome, and the rise of the predicted persecutor. In a word, all that remained unfulfilled of Daniel's prophecy might have been fulfilled in the years which had still to run of the seventy weeks.

† Dan. vii. 28 ; viii. 27.

blessings still more sure. Ere long he witnessed the crash of the Babylonian power, and saw a stranger enthroned within the broad-walled city. But the change brought no hope to Judah. Daniel was restored, indeed, to the place of power and dignity which he had held so long under Nebuchadnezzar,* but he was none the less an exile ; his people were in captivity, their city lay in ruins, and their land was a wilderness. And the mystery was only deepened when he turned to Jeremiah's prophecy, which fixed at seventy years the destined era of " the desolations of Jerusalem."† So " by prayer and supplications, with fastings, and sackcloth and ashes," he cast himself on God ; as a prince among his people, confessing their national apostasy, and pleading for their restoration and forgiveness. And who can read that prayer unmoved ? " O Lord, according to all Thy righteousness, I beseech Thee, let Thine anger and Thy fury be turned away from Thy city Jerusalem, Thy holy mountain ; because for our sins, and for the iniquities of our fathers, Jerusalem and Thy people are become a reproach to all that are about us. Now, therefore, O our God, hear the prayer of Thy servant, and his supplications, and cause Thy face to shine upon Thy Sanctuary that is desolate, for the Lord's sake. O my God, incline Thine ear,

---

* Dan. ii. 48 ; vi. 2.　　　　† Dan. ix. 2.

and hear; open Thine eyes, and behold our desolations, and the city which is called by Thy name: for we do not present our supplications before Thee for our righteousnesses, but for Thy great mercies. O Lord, hear; O Lord, forgive; O Lord, hearken and do; defer not, for Thine own sake, O my God; for Thy city and Thy people are called by Thy name"*

While Daniel was thus "speaking in prayer' Gabriel once more appeared to him,†—that same angel messenger who heralded in after times the Saviour's birth in Bethlehem,—and in answer to his supplication, delivered to the prophet the great prediction of the seventy weeks.

---

* Dan. ix. 16-19.
† Dan. ix. 21. *See* chap. viii. 16.

5

THE ANGEL'S MESSAGE

"Seventy weeks are decreed upon thy people and upon thy holy city, to finish transgression, and to make an end of sins, and to make reconciliation for iniquity, and to bring in everlasting righteousness, and to seal up vision and prophecy, and to anoint the most holy.* Know therefore and discern, that from the going forth of the commandment † to restore and to build Jerusalem, unto the Messiah the Prince, shall be seven weeks, and threescore and two weeks : it shall be built again, with street and moat, even in troublous times. And after the threescore and two weeks shall Messiah be cut off, and shall have nothing : and the people of the Prince that shall come shall destroy the city and the sanctuary ; and his end thereof shall be with a flood, and even unto the end shall be war; desolations are determined. And he shall make a firm covenant ‡ with many for one week :

* " The expression does not in a single case apply to any *person*."—TREGELLES, *Daniel*, p. 98.

" These words are applied to the Nazarene, although this expression is never applied to a person throughout the Bible, but invariably denotes part of the temple, the holy of holies."— DR. HERMAN ADLER, *Sermons*, p. 109 (Trübner, 1869).

† " From the issuing of the decree."—TREGELLES, *Daniel*, p. 96.

‡ Not *the* covenant (as in A.V.: see margin). This word is rendered *covenant* when Divine things are in question, and *league* when, as here, an ordinary treaty is intended (*Cf. ex. gr.*, Josh. ix. 6, 7, 11. 15, 16).

and for the half of the week he shall cause the sacrifice and the oblation to cease, and upon the wing of abominations shall come one that maketh desolate, even until the consummation, and that determined, shall wrath be poured out upon the desolator."— Dan. ix. 24-27. R.V. (*See marginal readings.*)

SUCH was the message entrusted to the angel in response to the prophet's prayer for mercies upon Judah and Jerusalem.

To whom shall appeal be made for an interpretation of the utterance ? Not to the Jew, surely, for though himself the subject of the prophecy, and of all men the most deeply interested in its meaning, he is bound, in rejecting Christianity, to falsify not only history, but his own Scriptures. Nor yet to the theologian who has prophetic theories to vindicate, and who on discovering, perhaps, some era of seven times seventy in Israel's history, concludes that he has solved the problem, ignoring the fact that the strange history of that wonderful people is marked through all its course by chronological cycles of seventy and multiples of seventy. But any man of unprejudiced mind who will read the words with no commentary save that afforded by Scripture itself and the history of the time, will readily admit that on certain leading points their meaning is unequivocal and clear.

I. It was thus revealed that the full meed of blessing promised to the Jews should be deferred till the close of a period of time, described as " seventy sevens," after which Daniel's city and people * are to be established in blessing of the fullest kind.

II. Another period composed of seven weeks and sixty-two weeks is specified with equal certainty.

III. This second era dates from the issuing of an edict to rebuild Jerusalem,—not the temple, but *the city ;* for, to remove all doubt, " the street and wall " † are emphatically mentioned ; and a definite event, described as the cutting off of Messiah, marks the close of it.

IV. The beginning of the week required (in addition to the sixty-nine) to complete the seventy, is to be signalized by the making of a covenant or treaty by a personage described as " the Prince that shall come," or " the coming Prince," which covenant he will violate in the middle of the week by the suppression of the Jews' religion.‡

---

* If the words of verses 24 and 25 do not themselves carry conviction that Judah and Jerusalem are the subjects of the prophecy, the reader has but to compare them with the preceding verses, especially 2, 7, 12, 16, 18, and 19.

† Literally the "trench" or "scarped rampart."—TRE-GELLES, *Daniel,* p. 90

‡ The personage referred to in verse 27 is not the Messiah, but the second prince named in verse 26.   The theory which has gained currency, that the Lord made a seven years' compact with the Jews at the beginning of His ministry, would deserve a prominent place in a cyclopædia of the vagaries of religious

V. And therefore the complete era of seventy weeks, and the lesser period of sixty-nine weeks, date from the same epoch.*

The first question, therefore, which arises is whether history records any event which unmistakably marks the beginning of the era.

Certain writers, both Christian and Jewish, have assumed that the seventy weeks began in the first year of Darius, the date of the prophecy itself; and thus falling into hopeless error at the very threshold of the inquiry, all their conclusions are necessarily erroneous. The words of the angel are unequivocal: " From the issuing of the decree to restore and build Jerusalem unto the Messiah the Prince, shall be seven weeks and sixty-two weeks." That Jerusalem was in fact rebuilt as a fortified city, is absolutely certain and undoubted; and the only question in the matter is whether history records the edict for its restoration.

---

thought. We know of the old covenant, which has been abrogated, and of the new covenant, which is everlasting ; but the extraordinary idea of a seven years' covenant between God and men has not a shadow of foundation in the letter of Scripture, and is utterly opposed to its spirit.

* " The whole period of seventy weeks is divided into three successive periods,—seven, sixty-two, one, and the last week is subdivided into two halves. It is self-evident that since these parts, seven, sixty-two, one, are equal to the whole, viz., seventy, it was intended that they should be."—PUSEY, *Daniel*, p. 170.

When we turn to the book of Ezra, three several decrees of Persian kings claim notice. The opening verses speak of that strange edict by which Cyrus authorized the building of the temple. But here "the house of the Lord God of Israel" is specified with such an exclusive definiteness that it can in no way satisfy the words of Daniel. Indeed the date of that decree affords conclusive proof that it was not the beginning of the seventy weeks. Seventy years was the appointed duration of the servitude to Babylon.* But another judgment of seventy years' "*desolations*" was decreed in Zedekiah's reign,† because of continued disobedience and rebellion. As an interval of seventeen years elapsed between the date of the servitude and the epoch of the "desolations," so by seventeen years the second period overlapped the first. The servitude ended with the decree of Cyrus. The desolations continued till the second year of Darius Hystaspes.‡ And

* Jer. xxvii. 6-17 ; xxviii. 14 ; xxix. 10.

† It was foretold in the fourth year of Jehoiakim, *i.e.*, the year after the servitude began (Jer. xxv. 1, 11).

‡ Scripture thus distinguishes three different eras, all in part concurrent, which have come to be spoken of as " the captivity." First, the servitude ; second, Jehoiachin's captivity ; and third, the desolations. " The servitude " began in the third year of Jehoiakim, *i.e.*, B.C. 606, or before 1st Nisan (April) B.C. 605, and was brought to a close by the decree of Cyrus seventy years later. " The captivity " began in the eighth year of Nebu-

it was the era of the *desolations*, and not of the servitude which Daniel had in view.*

The decree of Cyrus was the Divine fulfilment of the promise made to the captivity in the twenty-ninth chapter of Jeremiah, and in accordance with that promise the fullest liberty was granted to the exiles to return to Palestine. But till the era of the desolations had run its course, not one stone was to be set upon another on Mount Moriah. And this explains the seemingly inexplicable fact that the firman to build the temple, granted to eager agents by Cyrus in the zenith of his power, remained in abeyance till his death; for a few refractory Samaritans were allowed to thwart the execution of this the most solemn edict ever issued by an Eastern despot, an edict in respect of which a Divine sanction seemed to confirm the unalterable will of a Medo-Persian king.†

---

chadnezzar, according to the Scriptural era of his reign, *i.e.*, in B.C. 598 ; and the *desolations* began in his seventeenth year, B.C. 589, and ended in the second year of Darius Hystaspes— again a period of seventy years. *See* App. I. upon the chronological questions here involved.

  * Dan. ix. 2 is explicit on this point :—" I, Daniel, understood by books the number of the years whereof the word of the Lord came to Jeremiah the prophet, *that he would accomplish seventy years in the desolations of Jerusalem.*"

  † " The law of the Medes and Persians, which altereth not" (Dan. vi. 12). Canon Rawlinson assumes that the temple was

When the years of the desolations were expired,
a Divine command was promulgated for the building
of the sanctuary, and in obedience to that command,
without waiting for permission from the capital, the
Jews returned to the work in which they had so long
been hindered.* The wave of political excitement
which had carried Darius to the throne of Persia, was
swelled by religious fervour against the Magian
idolatry.† The moment therefore was auspicious for
the Israelites, whose worship of Jehovah commanded
the sympathy of the Zoroastrian faith ; and when the
tidings reached the palace of their seemingly seditious action at Jerusalem, Darius made search among
the Babylonian archives of Cyrus, and finding the

---

fifteen or sixteen years in building, before the work was stopped
by the decree of the Artaxerxes mentioned in Ezra iv. (*Five
Great Mon.*, vol. iv., p. 398.) But this is entirely opposed to
Scripture. The foundation of the temple was laid in the
second year of Cyrus (Ezra iii. 8-11), but no progress was made
till the second year of Darius, when the *foundation* was again
laid, for not a stone of the house had yet been placed (Hag.
ii, 10, 15, 18). The building, once begun, was completed
within five years (Ezra vi. 15). It must be borne in mind that
the *altar* was set up, and sacrifice was renewed immediately
after the return of the exiles (Ezra iii. 3, 6).

* Ezra v. 1, 2, 5.

† *Five Great Mon.*, vol. iv., p. 405. But Canon Rawlinson
is wholly wrong in inferring that the known religious zeal
of Darius was the motive which led to the action of the Jews.
See Ezra v.

decree of his predecessor, he issued on his own behalf
a firman to give effect to it.*

And this is the second event which affords a
possible beginning for the seventy weeks.† But
though plausible arguments may be urged to prove
that, either regarded as an independent edict, or as
giving practical effect to the decree of Cyrus, the act
of Darius was the epoch of the prophetic period, the
answer is clear and full, that it fails to satisfy the
angel's words. However it be accounted for, the fact
remains, that though the "desolations" were accomplished, yet neither the scope of the royal edict, nor
the action of the Jews in pursuance of that edict,
went beyond the building of the Holy Temple,
whereas the prophecy foretold a decree for the
building of the *city ;* not the street alone, but the
fortifications of Jerusalem.

Five years sufficed for the erection of the building
which served as a shrine for Judah during the five
centuries which followed.‡ But, in striking contrast
with the temple they had reared in days when the
magnificence of Solomon made gold as cheap as
brass in Jerusalem, no costly furniture adorned the

---

* Ezra vi.

† This is the epoch fixed upon by Mr. Bosanquet in *Messiah
the Prince.*

‡ The temple was begun in the second, and completed in
the sixth year of Darius (Ezra iv. 24 ; vi. 15.)

second house, until the seventh year of Artaxerxes
Longimanus, when the Jews obtained a firman "to
beautify the house of the Lord."* This letter further
authorized Ezra to return to Jerusalem with such
of the Jews as desired to accompany him, and there
to restore fully the worship of the temple and the
ordinances of their religion. But this third decree
makes no reference whatever to building, and it might
be passed unnoticed were it not that many writers
have fixed on it as the epoch of the prophecy. The
temple had been already built long years before, and
the city was still in ruins thirteen years afterwards.
The book of Ezra therefore will be searched in vain
for any mention of a " commandment to restore and
build Jerusalem." But we only need to turn to the
book which follows it in the canon of Scripture to
find the record which we seek.

The book of Nehemiah opens by relating that
while at Susa,† where he was cup-bearer to the great
king, " an honour of no small account in Persia,"‡
certain of his brethren arrived from Judea, and he
" asked them concerning the Jews that had escaped,
which were left of the captivity, and concerning

---

* Ezra vii. *See* verses 19 and 27.

† For a description of the ruins of the great palace at Susa,
see Mr. Wm. Kennett Loftus's *Travels and Researches in
Chaldea and Susiana*, chap. xxviii.

‡ *Herodotus*, iii., 34.

Jerusalem." The emigrants declared that all were "in great affliction and reproach," "the wall of Jerusalem also was broken down, and the gates thereof were burned with fire." * The first chapter closes with the record of Nehemiah's supplication to "the God of heaven." The second chapter narrates how "in the month Nisan, in the twentieth year of Artaxerxes," he was discharging the duties of his office, and as he stood before the king his countenance betrayed his grief, and Artaxerxes called on him to tell his trouble. "Let the king live for ever," Nehemiah answered, "why should not my countenance be sad, when *the city, the place of my fathers' sepulchres, lieth waste, and the gates thereof are burned with fire !*" "For what dost thou make request ?" the king demanded in reply. Thereupon Nehemiah answered thus : "If it please the king, and if thy servant have found favour in thy sight, *that thou wouldest send me unto Judah, unto THE CITY of my fathers' sepulchres, THAT I MAY BUILD IT.*"† Artaxerxes fiated the petition, and forthwith issued the necessary orders to give effect to it. Four months later, eager hands were busy upon the ruined walls of Jerusalem, and before the Feast of Tabernacles the city was once more enclosed by gates and a rampart.‡

---

* Neh. i. 2.　　　† Neh. ii. 5.　　　‡ Neh. vi. 15.

But, it has been urged, " The decree of the twentieth
year of Artaxerxes is but an enlargement and renewal
of his first decree, as the decree of Darius confirmed
that of Cyrus." * If this assertion had not the sanction
of a great name, it would not deserve even a passing
notice. If it were maintained that the decree of the
seventh year of Artaxerxes was " but an enlargement

---

* Pusey, *Daniel*, p. 171. Dr. Pusey adds, " The little colony
which Ezra took with him of 1,683 males (with women and children some 8,400 souls) was itself a considerable addition to
those who had before returned, *and involved a rebuilding of
Jerusalem.* This rebuilding of the city and reorganization of
the polity, begun by Ezra, and carried on and perfected by
Nehemiah, corresponds with the words of Daniel, ' From the
going forth of a commandment to restore and build Jerusalem'"
(p. 172). This argument is the feeblest imaginable, and indeed
this reference to the decree of the seventh year of Artaxerxes
is a great blot on Dr. Pusey's book. If an immigration of 8,400
souls involved a rebuilding of the city, and therefore marked
the beginning of the seventy weeks, what shall be said of the
immigration of 49,697 souls seventy-eight years before ? (Ezra
ii. 64, 65.) Did this not involve a rebuilding ? But, Dr. Pusey
goes on to say, " *The term also corresponds,*" *i.e.*, the 483 years,
to the time of Christ. Here is obviously the real ground for
his fixing the date B.C. 457, or more properly B.C. 458, as given
by Prideaux, whom unfortunately Dr. Pusey has followed at
this point. With more *naiveté* the author of the *Connection*
pleads that the years will not tally if any other date be assigned,
and therefore the decree of the seventh of Artaxerxes must
be right ! (Prid., *Con.*, I., 5, B.C. 458.) Such a system of interpretation has done much to discredit the study of prophecy
altogether.

and renewal" of his predecessors' edicts, the statement would be strictly accurate. That decree was
mainly an authority to the Jews "to beautify the
House of the Lord, which is in Jerusalem," * in exten-
sion of the decrees by which Cyrus and Darius permitted them to *build* it. The result was to produce
a gorgeous shrine in the midst of a ruined city. The
movement of the seventh of Artaxerxes was chiefly
a religious revival,† sanctioned and subsidized by
royal favour; but the event of his twentieth year was
nothing less than the restoration of the autonomy
of Judah. The execution of the work which Cyrus
authorized was stopped on the false charge which the
enemies of the Jews carried to the palace, that their
object was to build not merely the Temple, but the
city. "A rebellious city" it had ever proved to each
successive suzerain, "for which cause"—they declared
with truth—its destruction was decreed. "We certify
the king" (they added) "that *if this city be builded
again, and the walls thereof set up*, thou shalt have
no portion on this side the river." ‡ To allow the
building of the temple was merely to accord to a
conquered race the right to worship according to
the law of their God, for the religion of the Jew
knows no worship apart from the hill of Zion. It

---

* Ezra vii. 27.   † Ezra vii. 10.
‡ *i.e., Euphrates.*   Ezra iv. 16.

was a vastly different event when that people were permitted to set up again the far-famed fortifications of their city, and entrenched behind those walls, to restore under Nehemiah the old polity of the Judges.*
This was a revival of the national existence of Judah, and therefore it is fitly chosen as the epoch of the prophetic period of the seventy weeks.

The doubt which has been raised upon the point may serve as an illustration of the extraordinary bias

---

* "This last is the only decree which we find recorded in Scripture which relates to the restoring and building of the city. It must be borne in mind that the very existence of a place *as a city* depended upon such a decree ; for before that any who returned from the land of captivity went only in the condition of sojourners ; it was the decree that gave them a recognized and distinct political existence."—TREGELLES, *Daniel*, p. 98.

"On a sudden, however, in the twentieth year of Artaxerxes, Nehemiah, a man of Jewish descent, cup-bearer to the king, received a commission to rebuild the city with all possible expedition. The cause of this change in the Persian politics is to be sought, not so much in the personal influence of the Jewish cup-bearer, as in the foreign history of the times. The power of Persia had received a fatal blow in the victory obtained at Cnidos by Conon, the Athenian admiral. The great king was obliged to submit to a humiliating peace, among the articles of which were the abandonment of the maritime towns, and a stipulation that the Persian army should not approach within three days' journey of the sea. Jerusalem, being about this distance from the coast, and standing so near the line of communication with Egypt, became a post of the utmost importance."
—MILMAN, *Hist. Jews* (3rd Ed.), i., 435.

which seems to govern the interpretation of Scripture, in consequence of which the plain meaning of words is made to give place to the remote and the less probable. And to the same cause must be attributed the doubt which some have suggested as to the identity of the king here spoken of with Artaxerxes Longimanus.*

The question remains, whether the date of this edict can be accurately ascertained. And here a most striking fact claims notice. In the sacred narrative the date of the event which marked the beginning of the seventy weeks is fixed only by reference to the regnal era of a Persian king. Therefore we must needs turn to secular history to ascertain the epoch, and *history dates from this very period.* Herodotus, "the father of history," was the contemporary of Artaxerxes, and visited the Persian court.† Thucydides, "the prince of historians," also was his contemporary. In the great battles of Marathon and Salamis, the history of Persia had become interwoven with events in Greece, by which its chronology

---

* "Artaxerxes I. reigned forty years, from 465 to 425. He is mentioned by Herodotus once (vi. 98), by Thucydides frequently. Both writers were his contemporaries. There is every reason to believe that he was the king who sent Ezra and Nehemiah to Jerusalem, and sanctioned the restoration of the fortifications."—RAWLINSON, *Herodotus*, vol. iv., p. 217.

† The year in which he is said to have recited his writings at the Olympic games, was the very year of Nehemiah's mission.

can be ascertained and tested ; and the chief chronological eras of antiquity were current at the time.*
No element is wanting, therefore, to enable us with
accuracy and certainty to fix the date of Nehemiah's
edict.

True it is that in ordinary history the mention of
"the twentieth year of Artaxerxes" would leave in
doubt whether the era of his reign were reckoned from
his actual accession, or from his father's death ; † but
the narrative of Nehemiah removes all ambiguity upon
this score. The murder of Xerxes and the beginning
of the usurper Artabanus's seven months' reign was
in July B.C. 465 ; the accession of Artaxerxes
was in February B.C. 464.‡ One or other of these

---

* The era of the Olympiads began B.C. 776; the era of Rome
(A.U.C.) B.C. 753 ; and the era of Nabonassar, B.C. 747.

† "The seven months of Artabanus were by some added to
the last year of Xerxes, and by others were included in the reign
of Artaxerxes."—CLINTON, *Fasti Hellenici*, vol. ii., p. 42.

‡ It has been shown already that the accession of Xerxes is
determined to the beginning of 485 B.C. His twentieth year was
completed in the beginning of 465 B.C., and his death would
happen in the beginning of the Archonship of Lysitheus. The
seven months of Artabanus, completing the twenty-one years,
would bring down the accession of Artaxerxes (after the removal
of Artabanus) to the beginning of 464, in the year of Nabonassar
284, where it is placed by the canon. *Note b* : "We may place
the death of Xerxes in the first month of that Archon (*i.e.*, of
Lysitheus), July B.C. 465, and the succession of Artaxerxes in the
eighth month, February B.C. 464."—CLINTON, *Fasti Hellenici*,
vol. ii., p. 380.

dates, therefore, must be the epoch of Artaxerxes' reign. But as Nehemiah mentions the Chisleu (November) of one year, and the following Nisan (March) as being both in the same year of his master's reign, it is obvious that, as might be expected from an official of the court, he reckons from the time of the king's accession *de jure*, that is from July B.C. 465. The twentieth year of Artaxerxes therefore began in July B.C. 446, and the commandment to rebuild Jerusalem was given in the Nisan following. The epoch of the prophetic cycle is thus definitely fixed as in the Jewish month Nisan of the year B.C. 445.*

---

* See Appendix II., Note A, on the chronology of the reign of Artaxerxes Longimanus.

6

THE PROPHETIC YEAR

I N English ears it must sound pedantic to speak of
"weeks" in any other than the familiar acceptation of the term. But with the Jew it was far otherwise. The effect of his laws was fitted "to render the
word *week* capable of meaning a seven of years almost
as naturally as a seven of days. Indeed the gene-
rality of the word would have this effect at any rate.
Hence its use to denote the latter in prophecy is not
mere arbitrary symbolism, but the employment of a
not unfamiliar and easily understood language."*

Daniel's prayer referred to seventy years fulfilled :
the prophecy which came in answer to that prayer
foretold a period of seven times seventy still to come.

But here a question arises which never has received
sufficient notice in the consideration of this subject.
None will doubt that the era is a period of years ;
but of what kind of year is it composed? That the
Jewish year was lunisolar appears to be reasonably

---

* Smith's *Bib. Dict.*, III., 1726, "Week." Greek and Latin
philosophers too have known of 'weeks of years.'" — PUSEY,
Daniel, p. 167.

certain. If tradition may be trusted, Abraham pre-
served in his family the year of 360 days, which he
had known in his Chaldean home.* The month
dates of the flood (150 days being specified as the
interval between the seventeenth day of the second
month, and the same day of the seventh month)
appear to show that this form of year was the
earliest known to our race. Sir Isaac Newton states,
that "all nations, before the just length of the solar
year was known, reckoned months by the course of
the moon, and years by the return of winter and
summer, spring and autumn ; and in making calendars for their festivals, they reckoned thirty days to
a lunar month, and twelve lunar months to a year,
taking the nearest round numbers, whence came the
division of the ecliptic into 360 degrees." And in
adopting this statement, Sir G. C. Lewis avers that
"all credible testimony and all antecedent probability
lead to the result that a solar year containing twelve
lunar months, determined within certain limits of error,
has been generally recognised by the nations adjoin-
ing the Mediterranean, from a remote antiquity." †

But considerations of this kind go no further than

---

* *Encyc. Brit.* (6th ed.), title " *Chronology.*" See also Smith's
Bib. Dict., title " *Chronology,*" p. 314.

† *Astronomy of the Ancients*, chap. i., § 7. Are not the
hundred and eighty days of the great feast of Xerxes intended
to be equivalent to six months? (Esther i. 4.)

to prove how legitimate and important is the question here proposed. The inquiry remains whether any grounds exist for reversing the presumption which obtains in favour of the common civil year. Now the prophetic era is clearly seven times the seventy years of the "desolations" which were before the mind of Daniel when the prophecy was given. Is it possible then to ascertain the character of the years of this lesser era?

One of the characteristic ordinances of the Jewish law was, that every seventh year the land was to lie fallow, and it was in relation to the neglect of this ordinance that the era of the desolations was decreed. It was to last "until the land had enjoyed her Sabbaths; for so long as she lay desolate, she kept Sabbath, to fulfil threescore and ten years." * The essential element in the judgment was, not a ruined city, but a land laid desolate by the terrible scourge of a hostile invasion,† the effects of which were perpetuated by famine and pestilence, the continuing proofs of the Divine displeasure. It is obvious therefore, that the true epoch of the judgment is not, as has been generally assumed, the capture of Jerusalem, but the invasion of Judea. From the time the Babylonian armies entered the land, all agricultural

---

* 2 Chron. xxxvi. 21 ; cf. Lev. xxvi. 34, 35.
† Compare Jer. xxvii. 13 ; and Hag. ii. 17.

pursuits were suspended, and therefore the desolations may be reckoned from the day the capital was invested, namely, the tenth day of the tenth month in the ninth year of Zedekiah. This was the epoch as revealed to Ezekiel the prophet in his exile on the banks of the Euphrates,* and for twenty-four centuries the day has been observed as a fast by the Jews in every land.

The close of the era is indicated in Scripture with equal definiteness, as "the four-and-twentieth day of the ninth month in the second year of Darius.† " Consider now " (the prophetic word declared) " from this day and upward—from the four-and-twentieth day of the ninth month, even from the day that the foundation of the Lord's temple was laid—consider it : *from this day I will bless you.*" Now from the tenth day of Tebeth B.C. 589,‡ to the twenty-fourth day of Chisleu B.C. 520,§ was a period of 25,202 days ; and seventy years of 360 days contain exactly 25,200 days. We may conclude, therefore, that the era of the " desolations " was a period of seventy years of 360 days, beginning the day after the Baby-

---

* Ezek. xxiv. 1, 2.

† Hag. ii. 10, 15-19. The books of Haggai and Zechariah give in full the prophetic utterances which the narrative of Ezra (iv 24 ; v. 1-5) mentions as the sanction and incentive under which the Jews returned to the work of setting up their temple.

‡ The ninth year of Zedekiah. See App. I. *post*.

§ The second year of Darius Hystaspes.

lonian army invested Jerusalem, and ending the day before the foundation of the second temple was laid.*

But this inquiry may be pressed still further. As the era of the "desolations" was fixed at seventy years, because of the neglect of the Sabbatic years,† we might expect to find that a period of seven times seventy years measured back from the close of the seventy years of "indignation against Judah," would bring us to the time when Israel entered into their full national privileges, and thus incurred their full responsibilities. And such in fact will be found upon inquiry to be the case. From the year succeeding the dedication of Solomon's temple, to the year before the foundation of the second temple was laid, was a period of 490 years of 360 days.‡

---

* The date of the Paschal new moon, by which the Jewish year is regulated, was the evening of the 14th March in B.C. 589, and about noon on 1st April B.C. 520. According to the phasis the 1st Nisan in the former year was probably the 15th or 16th March, and in the latter the 1st or 2nd April.

† 2 Chron. xxxvi. 21 ; Lev. xxvi. 34, 35.

‡ The temple was dedicated in the eleventh year of Solomon, and the second temple was founded in B.C. 520. The intervening period reckoned exclusively was 483 years = 490 lunisolar years of 360 days. It is noteworthy that the interval between the dedication of Solomon's temple and the dedication of the second temple (B.C. 515) was 490 years. A like period had elapsed between the entrance into Canaan and the foundation of the kingdom under Saul. These cycles of 70, and multiples of 70, in Hebrew history are striking and interesting. See App. 1.

It must be admitted, however, that no argument based on calculations of this kind is final.* The only data which would warrant our deciding unreservedly that the prophetic year consists of 360 days, would be to find some portion of the era subdivided into the days of which it is composed. No other proof can be wholly satisfactory, but if this be forthcoming, it must be absolute and conclusive. And this is precisely what the book of the Revelation gives us.

As already noticed, the prophetic era is divided into two periods, the one of 7 + 62 heptades, the other of a single heptade.† Connected with these eras, two "princes" are prominently mentioned; first, the Messiah, and secondly, a prince of that people by whom Jerusalem was to be destroyed,—a personage of such pre-eminence, that on his advent his identity is to be as certain as that of Christ Himself. The first era closes with the "cutting off" of Messiah; the beginning of the second era dates from the signature of a "covenant," or treaty, by this second "prince,"

---

* Though it is signally confirmed by the undoubted fact that the Jewish Sabbatical year was conterminous, not with the solar, but with the ecclesiastical year.

† The division of the 69 weeks into 7 + 62 is accounted for by the fact that the first 49 years, during which the restoration of Jerusalem was completed, ended with a great crisis in Jewish history, the close of the prophetic testimony. Forty-nine years from B.C. 445 brings us to the date of Malachi's prophecy.

with or perhaps in favour of "the many," * that is the Jewish nation, as distinguished probably from a section of pious persons among them who will stand aloof. In the middle of the heptade the treaty is to be violated by the suppression of the Jews' religion, and a time of persecution is to follow.

Daniel's vision of the four beasts affords a striking commentary upon this. The identity of the fourth beast with the Roman empire is not doubtful, and we read that a "king" is to arise, territorially connected with that empire, but historically belonging to a later time ; he will be a persecutor of "the saints of the Most High," and his fall is to be immediately followed by the fulfilment of Divine blessings upon the favoured people—the precise event which marks the close of the "seventy weeks." The duration of that persecution, moreover, is stated to be "a time and times, and the dividing of time,"—a mystical expression, of which the meaning might be doubtful, were it not that it is used again in Scripture as synonymous with three and a half years, or half a prophetic week.† Now there can be no reasonable doubt of the identity of the king of Daniel vii. 25 with the first "beast" of the thirteenth chapter of Revelation. In the Revelation he is likened to a

---

* "The multitude."—TREGELLES, *Daniel*, p. 97.

† Rev. xii. 6, 14.

leopard, a bear, and a lion,—the figures used for
Daniel's three first beasts. In Daniel there are ten
kingdoms, represented by ten horns. So also in
Revelation. According to Daniel, "he shall speak
great words against the Most High, and wear out the
saints of the Most High : " according to Revelation,
"he opened his mouth in blasphemy against God,"
"and it was given unto him to make war with
the saints and to overcome them." According to
Daniel, "they shall be given into his hand until a
time and times and the dividing of time," or three
and a half years : according to Revelation, "power
was given unto him to continue forty and two
months."

It is not impossible, of course, that prophecy may
foretell the career of two different men, answering
the same description, who will pursue a precisely
similar course in similar circumstances for a similar
period of three and a half years ; but the more
natural and obvious supposition is that the two are
identical. Owing to the very nature of the subject,
their identity cannot be logically demonstrated, but
it rests upon precisely the same kind of proof upon
which juries convict men of crimes, and convicted
prisoners are punished.

Now this seventieth week is admittedly a period
of seven years, and half of this period is three times
described as " a time, times, and half a time," or " the

dividing of a time ; " * twice as forty-two months ; †
and twice as 1,260 days.‡   But 1,260 days are exactly
equal to forty-two months of thirty days, or three and
a half years of 360 days, whereas three and a half
Julian years contain 1,278 days.   It follows therefore
that the prophetic year is not the Julian year, but
the ancient year of 360 days.§

---

* Dan. vii. 25 ; xii. 7 ; Rev. xii. 14.

† Rev. xi. 2 ; xiii. 5.

‡ Rev. xi. 3 ; xii. 6.

§ It is noteworthy that the prophecy was given at Babylon,
and the Babylonian year consisted of twelve months of thirty
days.   That the prophetic year is not the ordinary year is no
new discovery.   It was noticed sixteen centuries ago by Julius
Africanus in his *Chronography*, wherein he explains the seventy
weeks to be weeks of *Jewish* (lunar) years, beginning with the
twentieth of Artaxerxes, the fourth year of the 83rd Olympiad,
and ending in the second year of the 202nd Olympiad ; 475
Julian years being equal to 490 lunar years.

7

THE MYSTIC ERA OF THE WEEKS

THE conclusions arrived at in the preceding chapter suggest a striking parallel between Daniel's earlier visions and the prophecy of the seventy weeks. History contains no record of events to satisfy the predicted course of the seventieth week. The Apocalypse was not even written when that period ought chronologically to have closed, and though eighteen centuries have since elapsed, the restoration of the Jews seems still but a chimera of sanguine fanatics.[6] And be it remembered that the purpose of the prophecy was not to amuse or interest the curious. Of necessity some mysticism must characterize prophetic utterances, otherwise they might be "fulfilled to order" by designing men; but once the prophecy comes side by side with the events of which it speaks, it fails of one of its chief purposes if its relation to them be doubtful. If any one will learn the connection between prophecy and its fulfilment, let him read the fifty-third chapter of Isaiah, and compare it with the story of the Passion: so

---

[6] See Appendix 4, p. 305 note 6.

vague and figurative that no one could have acted out the drama it foretold ; but yet so definite and clear that, once fulfilled, the simplest child can recognize its scope and meaning. If then the event which constitutes the epoch of the seventieth week must be as pronounced and certain as Nehemiah's commission and Messiah's death, it is of necessity still future.

And this is precisely what the study of the seventh chapter of Daniel will have led us to expect. All Christian interpreters are agreed that between the rise of the fourth beast and the growth of the ten horns there is a gap or parenthesis in the vision ; and, as already shown, that gap includes the entire period between the time of Christ and the division of the Roman earth into the ten kingdoms out of which the great persecutor of the future is to arise. This period, moreover, is admittedly unnoticed also in the other visions of the book. There is therefore a strong *à priori* probability that it would be overlooked in the vision of the ninth chapter.

More than this, there is not only the same reason for this mystic foreshortening in the vision of the seventy weeks, as in the other visions,* but that reason applies here with special force. The seventy weeks were meted out as the period during which Judah's blessings were deferred. In common with

---

* See pp. 44—47, *ante.*

all prophecy, the meaning of this prophecy will be
unmistakable when its ultimate fulfilment takes
place, but it was necessarily conveyed in a mystical
form in order to shut up the Jews to the responsibility of accepting their Messiah. St. Peter's
inspired proclamation to the nation at Jerusalem,
recorded in the third chapter of Acts, was in accordance with this. The Jews looked merely for a return
of their national supremacy, but God's first purpose
was redemption through the death of the great Sin-
bearer. Now, the sacrifice had been accomplished,
and St. Peter pointed to Calvary as the fulfilment of
that "which God before had showed by the mouth
of all His prophets;" and he added this testimony,
"Repent ye therefore, and turn again, that your sins
may be blotted out, that so there may come seasons
of refreshing from the presence of the Lord ; and that
He may send the Christ, who hath been appointed for
you, even Jesus." *   The realization of these blessings
would have been the fulfilment of Daniel's prophecy,
and the seventieth week might have run its course
without a break. But Judah proved impenitent and
obdurate, and the promised blessings were once again
postponed till the close of this strange era of the
Gentile dispensation.

But it may be asked, Was not the Cross of Christ

---

* Acts iii. 19, 20, Revised Version.

the fulfilment of these blessings? A careful study of the Angel's words* will show that not so much as one of them has been thus accomplished. The sixty-ninth week was to end with Messiah's death ; the close of the seventieth week was to bring to Judah the full enjoyment of the blessings resulting from that death. Judah's transgression has yet to be restrained, and his sins to be sealed up. The day is yet future when a fountain shall be opened for the iniquity of Daniel's people,† and righteousness shall be ushered in for them. In what sense were vision and prophet sealed up at the death of Christ, considering that the greatest of all visions was yet to be given,‡ and the days were still to come when the words of the prophets were to be fulfilled ? § And whatever meaning is to be put upon "anointing the most holy," it is clear that Calvary was not the accomplishment of it.‖

---

* Dan. ix. 24.   † Zech. xiii. 1.

‡ The Revelation.   § Luke xxi. 22.

‖ *See* p. 51, *ante.* All these words point to practical benefits to be conferred in a practical way upon the people, at the second advent of Christ. Isaiah i. 26 is a commentary on "bringing in righteousness." To take it as synonymous with declaring God's righteousness (Rom. iii. 25) is doctrinally a blunder and an anachronism. To any whose views of "reconciliation" are not based on the use of the word in Scripture, "making reconciliation for iniquity" will seem an exception. The Hebrew verb *caphar* (to make atonement or reconciliation) means literally "to

But is it consistent with fair argument or common-sense to urge that an era thus chronologically defined should be indefinitely interrupted in its course? The

---

cover over " sin (*see* its use in Gen. vi. 14), to do away with a charge against a person by means of bloodshedding, or otherwise (*ex. gr.* by intercession, Exod. xxxii. 30), so as to secure his reception into Divine favour. The following is a list of the passages where the word is used in the first three books of the Bible : Gen. vi. 14 (*pitch*) ; xxxii. 20 (*appease*) ; Exod. xxix. 33, 36, 37 ; xxx. 10, 15, 16 ; xxxii. 30 ; Lev. i. 4; iv. 20, 26, 31, 35 ; v. 6, 10, 13, 16, 18 ; vi. 7, 30; vii. 7 ; viii. 15, 34 ; ix. 7; x. 17; xii, 7, 8 ; xiv. 18, 19, 20, 21, 29, 31, 53 ; xv. 15, 30 ; xvi. 6, 10, 11, 16, 17, 18, 20, 24, 27, 32, 33, 34 ; xvii. 11 ; xix. 22 ; xxiii. 28.

It will be seen that *caphar* is never used of the expiation or bloodshedding considered objectively, but of the results accruing from it to the sinner, sometimes immediately on the victim's death, sometimes conditional upon the action of the priest who was charged with the function of applying the blood. The sacrifice was not the atonement, but the means by which atonement was made. Therefore " the preposition which marks substitution is never used in connection with the word *caphar* " (Girdlestone's *Synonyms O. T.*, p. 214).

Making reconciliation, or atonement, therefore, according to the Scriptural use of the word, implies the removal of the practical estrangement between the sinner and God, the obtaining forgiveness for the sin ; and the words in Daniel ix. 24 point to the time when this benefit will be secured to Judah. " *In that day* there shall be a fountain opened to the inhabitants of Jerusalem for sin and uncleanness" (Zech. xiii. 1) ; that is, the blessings of Calvary will be theirs ; *reconciliation* will be accomplished for the people. In keeping with this, transgression will be *restrained* (*see* use of the word in Gen. viii. 2 ; Exod. xxxvi. 6) ; *i.e.*, they will cease to transgress; sins will be sealed up,—the

ready answer might be given, that if common-sense and fairness—if human judgment, is to decide the question, the only doubt must be whether the final period of the cycle, and the blessings promised at its close, be not for ever abrogated and lost by reason of the appalling guilt of that people who "killed the Prince of life."* There exists surely no presumption against supposing that the stream of prophetic time is tided back during all this interval of the apostasy of Judah. The question remains, whether any precedent for this can be discovered in the mystical chronology of Israel's history.

According to the book of Kings, Solomon began to build the temple in the 480th year after the children of Israel were come out of the land of Egypt.† This statement, than which none could, seemingly, be more exact, has sorely puzzled chronologers. By some it has been condemned as a forgery, by others it has been dismissed as a blunder; but all have agreed in rejecting it. Moreover, Scripture itself appears to clash with it. In his sermon at Pisidian Antioch ‡ St. Paul epitomizes thus the chronology of

---

ordinary word for securing a letter (1 Kings xxi. 8), or a purse or bag of treasure (Job xiv. 17) ; *i.e.*, sins will be done with and put away in a practical sense ; and vision and prophet will likewise be sealed up, *i.e.*, their functions will be at an end, for all will have been fulfilled.

    * Acts. iii. 15.   † 1 Kings vi. 1.   ‡ Acts xiii. 18-21.

this period of the history of his nation : forty years in the wilderness ; 450 years under the Judges, and forty years of the reign of Saul ; making a total of 530 years. To which must be added the forty years of David's reign and the first three years of Solomon's ; making 573 years for the very period which is described in Kings as 480 years. Can these conclusions, apparently so inconsistent, be reconciled ? *

If we follow the history of Israel as detailed in the

---

* According to Browne (*Ordo Sæc.*, §§ 254 and 268) the Exodus was on Friday the 10th April, B.C. 1586 ; the passage of Jordan was the 14th April, B.C. 1546 ; the accession of Solomon was B.C. 1016, and the foundation of the Temple was the 20th April, B.C. 1013. He therefore accepts St. Paul's statements unreservedly. Clinton conjectures that there was an interval of about twenty-seven years before the time of the Judges, and another of twelve years before the election of Saul, thus fixing on B.C. 1625 as the date of the Exode, extending the whole period to 612 years. Josephus reckons it 621 years, and this is adopted by Hales, who calls the statement in Kings "a forgery." Other chronologers assign periods varying from the 741 years of Julius Africanus to the 480 years of Usher, whose date for the Exode—B.C. 1491—has been adopted in our Bible, though clearly wrong by ninety-three years at least. The subject is fully discussed by Clinton in *Fasti Hell.*, vol. i., pp. 312-313, and by Browne, reviewing Clinton's arguments, in *Ordo Sæc.*, § 6, etc. Browne's conclusions have much to commend them. But if others are right in inserting conjectural periods, my argument remains the same, for any such periods, if they existed, were obviously excluded from the 480 years on the same principle as were the eras of the servitudes. (This subject is discussed further in App. I.)

book of Judges, we shall find that for five several periods their national existence as Jehovah's people was in abeyance. In punishment for their idolatry, God gave them up again and again, and "sold them into the hands of their enemies." They became slaves to the king of Mesopotamia for eight years, to the king of Moab for eighteen years, to the king of Canaan for twenty years, to the Midianites for seven years, and finally to the Philistines for forty years.* But the sum of $8 + 18 + 20 + 7 + 40$ years is 93 years, and if 93 years be deducted from 573 years, the result is 480 years. It is obvious, therefore, that the 480 years of the book of Kings from the Exodus to the temple is a mystic era formed by eliminating every period during which the people were cast off by God.† If, then, this principle were intelligible to the Jew in regard to history, it was

---

* Judges iii. 8, 14 ; iv. 2, 3 ; vi. 1 ; xiii. 1. The servitude of Judges x. 7, 9 affected only the tribes beyond Jordan, and did not suspend Israel's *national* position.

† The Israelites were nationally God's people as no other nation ever can be ; therefore they were dealt with in some respects on principles similar to those which obtain in the case of individuals. A life without God is death. Righteousness must keep a strict account and sternly judge ; or grace may pardon. And if God forgives, He likewise forgets the sin (Heb. x. 17) ; which doubtless means that the record is wiped out, and the period it covers is treated as though it were a blank. The days of our servitude to evil are ignored in the Divine chronology.

both natural and legitimate to introduce it in respect of an essentially mystic era like that of the seventy weeks.

But this conclusion does not depend upon argument however sound, or inference however just. It is in-disputably proved by the testimony of Christ Himself. " What shall be the sign of Thy coming, and of the end of the world ? " the disciples inquired as they gathered round the Lord on one of the last days of His ministry on earth.* In reply he spoke of the tribulation foretold by Daniel,† and warned them that the signal of that fearful persecution was to be the precise event which marks the middle of the seventieth week, namely, the defilement of the holy place by the " abomination of desolation,"—some image of himself probably, which the false prince will set up in the temple in violation of his treaty obligations to respect and defend the religion of the Jews ‡ That this prophecy was not fulfilled

---

* Matt. xxiv. 3.

† θλῖψις, Matt. xxiv. 21; Dan. xii. 1 (LXX).

‡ καὶ ἐπὶ τὸ ἱερὸν βδέλυγμα τῶν ἐρημώσεων, Dan. ix. 27; τὸ βδέλυγμα ἐρημώσεως, Dan. xii. 11 (LXX.); ὅταν οὖν ἴδητε τὸ βδέλυγμα τῆς ἐρημώσεως τὸ ῥηθὲν διὰ Δανιὴλ τοῦ προφήτου, ἑστὼς ἐν τόπῳ ἁγίῳ, Matt. xxiv. 15. *Comp.* 1 Maccabees i. 54, ᾠκοδόμησαν βδέλυγμα ἐρημώσεως ἐπὶ τὸ θυσιαστήριον. This passage in Matthew affords an unanswerable proof that all systems of interpretation which make the seventy weeks end with the coming or death of Christ, and therefore *before the destruction of Jerusalem by Titus,* are

by Titus is as certain as history can make it ; *
but Scripture itself leaves no doubt whatever on
the point.

It appears from the passages already quoted, that
the predicted tribulation is to last three and a half
years, and to date from the violation of the treaty in
the middle of the seventieth week.   What is to follow
is thus described by the Lord Himself in words of
peculiar solemnity :—"Immediately after the tribulation of those days shall the sun be darkened, and
the moon shall not give her light, and the stars shall
fall from heaven, and the powers of the heaven shall
be shaken : and then shall appear the sign of the Son
of man in heaven, and then shall all the tribes of the
earth mourn, and they shall see the Son of man coming
in the clouds of heaven with power and great glory." †
That it is to the closing scenes of the dispensation
this prophecy relates is here assumed.‡   And as these
scenes are to follow *immediately* after a persecution,

---

wholly wrong.   And that that event was not in fact the terminus
of the era is plain from Matt. xxiv. 21-29, and Dan. ix. 24.

* Making all allowance for the contemptible time-serving of
Josephus and his admiration for Titus, his testimony on this
point is too full and explicit to admit of doubt (*Wars*, vi., 2,
§ 4).

† Matt. xxiv. 29.

‡ I am aware of systems of interpretation which fritter away
the meaning of all such scriptures, but it is idle to attempt to
refute them in detail.   (*See* chap xi. *post*, and App. Note C.)

of which the era is within the seventieth week, the inference is incontestable that the events of that week belong to a time still future.*

We may conclude, then, that when wicked hands set up the cross on Calvary, and God pronounced the dread "*Lo-ammi*" † upon His people, the course of the prophetic era ceased to run. Nor will it flow on again till the autonomy of Judah is restored ; and, with obvious propriety, that is held to date from the moment their readmission into the family of nations is recognised by treaty.‡ It will, therefore, be here assumed that the former portion of the prophetic era

---

* Such was the belief of the early Church ; but the question has been argued at length out of deference to modern writers who have advocated a different interpretation of Dan. ix. 27. Hippolytus, bishop and martyr, who wrote at the beginning of the third century, is most definite on the point. Quoting the verse, he says : " By one week he meant the last week, *which is to be at the end of the whole world ;* of which week the two prophets Enoch and Elias will take up the half ; for they will preach 1,260 days, clothed in sackcloth " (Hip. on *Christ and Antichrist*). According to Browne (*Ordo Sæc.*. p. 386, *note*), this was also the view of the father of Christian chronologers, Julius Africanus. That half of the last week has been fulfilled, but the remaining three and a half years are still future, is maintained by Canon Browne himself (§ 339), who notices, what so many modern writers have missed, that the events belonging to this period are connected with the times of Antichrist.

† Rom. ix. 25, 26 ; *cf.* Hos. i. 9, 10.

‡ *i.e.*, the covenant mentioned in Dan. ix. 27.

has run its course, but that the events of the last seven years have still to be accomplished. The last point, therefore, necessary to complete the chain of proof is to ascertain the date of " Messiah the Prince."

8

"MESSIAH THE PRINCE"

JUST as we find that in certain circles people who are reputed pious are apt to be regarded with suspicion, so it would seem that any writings which claim Divine authority or sanction inevitably awaken distrust. But if the evangelists could gain the same fair hearing which profane historians command; if their statements were tested upon the same principles on which records of the past are judged by scholars, and evidence is weighed in our courts of justice, it would be accepted as a well-established fact of history that our Saviour was born in Bethlehem, at a time when Cyrenius was Governor of Syria, and Herod was king in Jerusalem. The narrative of the first two chapters of St. Luke is not like an ordinary page of history which carries with it no pledge of accuracy save that which the general credit of the writer may afford. The evangelist is treating of facts of which he had "perfect understanding from the very first;" * in which, more-

* Luke i. 3.

over, his personal interest was intense, and in respect
of which a single glaring error would have prejudiced
not only the value of his book, but the success of
that cause to which his life was devoted, and with
which his hopes of eternal happiness were identified.

The matter has been treated as though this
reference to Cyrenius were but an incidental allusion,
in respect of which an error would be of no importance; whereas, in fact, it would be absolutely vital.
That the true Messiah must be born in Bethlehem
was asserted by the Jew and conceded by the
Christian : that the Nazarene was born in Bethlehem
the Jew persistently denied. If even to-day he could
disprove that fact, he would justify his unbelief; for
if the Christ we worship was not by right of birth
the heir to David's throne, He is not the Christ
of prophecy. Christians soon forgot this when they
had no longer to maintain their faith against the
unbroken front of Judaism, but only to commend it
to a heathen world. But it was not forgotten by
the immediate successors of the apostles. Therefore it was that in writing to the Jews, Justin Martyr
asserted with such emphasis that Christ was born
during the taxing of Cyrenius, appealing to the lists
of that census as to documents then extant and
available for reference, to prove that though Joseph
and Mary lived at Nazareth, they went up to
Bethlehem to be enrolled, and that thus it came to

pass the Child was born in the royal city, and not in the despised Galilean village.*

And these facts of the pedigree and birth of the Nazarene afforded almost the only ground upon which issue could be joined, where one side maintained, and the other side denied, that His Divine character and mission were established by transcendental proofs. None could question that His acts were more than human, but blindness and hate could ascribe them to Satanic power; and the sublime utterances which in every succeeding age have commanded the admiration of millions, even of those who have refused to them the deeper homage of their faith, had no charm for men thus prejudiced. But these statements about the taxing which brought the Virgin Mother up to Bethlehem, dealt with plain facts which required no moral fitness to appreciate them. That in such a matter a writer like St. Luke could be in error is utterly improbable, but that

---

* Bethlehem, "in which Jesus Christ was born, as you may also learn from the lists of the taxing which was made in the time of Cyrenius, the first Governor of yours in Judea."—*Apol.*, i., § 34.

"We assert Christ to have been born a hundred and fifty years ago, under Cyrenius."—*Ibid.*, § 46.

"But when there was an enrolment in Judea, which was then made first under Cyrenius, he went up from Nazareth, where he lived, to Bethlehem, of which place he was, to be enrolled," etc.—*Dial. Trypho*, § 78.

the error would remain unchallenged is absolutely incredible ; and we find Justin Martyr, writing nearly a hundred years after the evangelist, appealing to the fact as one which was unquestionable. It may, therefore, be accepted as one of the most certain of the really certain things of history, that the first taxing of Cyrenius was made before the death of Herod, and that while it was proceeding Christ was born in Bethlehem.

Not many years ago this statement would have been received either with ridicule or indignation. The evangelist's mention of Cyrenius appeared to be a hopeless anachronism ; as, according to un-doubted history, the period of his governorship and the date of his "taxing" were nine or ten years later than the nativity. Gloated over by Strauss and others of his tribe, and dismissed by writers unnum-bered either as an enigma or an error, the passage has in recent years been vindicated and explained by the labours of Dr. Zumpt of Berlin.

By a strange chance there is a break in the history of this period, for the seven or eight years beginning B.C. 4.* The list of the governors of Syria, therefore, fails us, and for the same interval P. Sulpicius Quirinus, the Cyrenius of the Greeks, disappears from history.

---

* Josephus here leaves a gap in his narrative ; and through the loss of MSS., the history of Dion Cassius, the other authority for this period, is not available to supply the omission.

But by a series of separate investigations and arguments, all of them independent of Scripture, Dr. Zumpt has established that Quirinus was *twice* governor of the province, and that his first term of office dated from the latter part of B.C. 4, when he succeeded Quinctilius Varus. The unanimity with which this conclusion has been accepted renders it unnecessary to discuss the matter here. But one remark respecting it may not be out of place. The grounds of Dr. Zumpt's conclusions may be aptly described as a chain of circumstantial evidence, and his critics are agreed that the result is reasonably certain.* To make that certainty absolute, nothing

---

* Dr. Zumpt's labours in this matter were first made public in a Latin treatise which appeared in 1854. More recently he has published them in his *Das Geburtsjahr Christi* (Leipzig, 1869). The English reader will find a summary of his arguments in Dean Alford's *Greek Test.* (Note on Luke ii. 1), and in his article on *Cyrenius* in Smith's *Bible Dict.;* he describes them as "very striking and satisfactory." Dr. Farrar remarks, "Zumpt has, with incredible industry and research, all but established in this matter the accuracy of St. Luke, by proving the extreme *probability* that Quirinus was *twice* governor of Syria" (*Life of Christ*, vol. i., p. 7, *note*). See also an article in the *Quarterly Review* for April 1871, which describes Zumpt's conclusions as "very nearly certain," "all but certain." The question is discussed also in Wieseler's *Chron. Syn.* (Venables's trans.)

In his Roman history, Mr. Merivale adopts these results unreservedly. He says (vol. iv., p. 457), "A remarkable light has been thrown upon the point by the demonstration, as it seems to be, of Augustus Zumpt in his second volume of *Commentationes*

is wanting but the positive testimony of some historian of repute. If, for example, one of the lost fragments of the history of Dion Cassius were brought to light, containing the mention of Quirinus as governing the province during the last months of Herod's reign, the fact would be deemed as certain as that Augustus was emperor of Rome. A Christian writer may be pardoned if he attaches equal weight to the testimony of St. Luke. It will, therefore, be here assumed as absolutely certain that the birth of Christ took place at some date not earlier than the autumn of B.C. 4.*

The dictum of our English chronologer, than whom none more eminent or trustworthy can be appealed to, is a sufficient guarantee that this conclusion is consistent with everything that erudition can bring to bear upon the point. Fynes Clinton sums up his

---

Epigraphicæ, that Quirinus (the Cyrenius of St. Luke ii.) was first governor of Syria from the close of A.U. 750 (B.C. 4), to A.U. 753 (B.C. 1)."

* The birth of our Lord is placed in B.C. 1, by Pearson and Hug; B.C. 2, by Scaliger; B.C. 3, by Baronius, Calvisius, Süskind, and Paulus; B.C. 4, by Lamy, Bengel, Anger, Wieseler, and Greswell; B.C. 5, by Usher and Petavius; B.C. 7, by Ideler and Sanclementi (Smith's *Bible Dict.*, " Jesus Christ," p. 1075).

It should be added that Zumpt's date for the nativity is fixed on independent grounds in B.C. 7. Following Ideler, he concludes that the conjunction of the planets Jupiter and Saturn, which occurred in that year, was the " Star " which led the Magi to Palestine.

discussion of the matter thus: " The nativity was not more than about eighteen months before the death of Herod, nor less than five or six. The death of Herod was either in the spring of B.C. 4, *or the spring of* B.C. 3. The earliest possible date then for the nativity is the autumn of B.C. 6 (U.C. 748), eighteen months before the death of Herod in B.C. 4. *The latest will be the autumn of* B.C. 4 (U.C. 750), about six months before his death, assumed to be in spring B.C. 3." * This opinion has weight, not only because of the writer's eminence as a chronologist, but also because his own view as to the actual date of the birth of Christ would have led him to narrow still more the limits within which it must have occurred, if his sense of fairness had permitted him to do so. Moreover, Clinton wrote in ignorance of what Zumpt has since brought to light respecting the census of Quirinus. The introduction of this new element into the consideration of the question, enables us with absolute confidence, adopting Clinton's dictum, to assign the death of Herod to the month Adar of B.C. 3, and the nativity to the autumn of B.C. 4.

That the least uncertainty should prevail respecting the time of an event of such transcendent interest to mankind is a fact of strange significance. But whatever doubt there may be as to the birth-date of

---

* *Fasti Romani*, A.D. 29.

the Son of God, it is due to no omission in the sacred page if equal doubt be felt as to the epoch of His ministry on earth. There is not in the whole of Scripture a more definite chronological statement than that contained in the opening verses of the third chapter of St. Luke. "In the fifteenth year of the reign of Tiberius Cæsar, Pontius Pilate being governor of Judæa, and Herod being tetrarch of Galilee, and his brother Philip tetrarch of Ituræa and of the region of Trachonitis, and Lysanias the tetrarch of Abilene, Annas and Caiaphas being the high priests, the word of God came unto John the son of Zacharias in the wilderness."

Now the date of Tiberius Cæsar's reign is known with absolute accuracy ; and his fifteenth year, reckoned from his accession, began on the 19th August, A.D. 28. And further, it is also known that during that year, so reckoned, each of the personages named in the passage, actually held the position there assigned to him. Here then, it might be supposed, no difficulty or question could arise. But the evangelist goes on to speak of the beginning of the ministry of the Lord Himself, and he mentions that "He was about thirty years of age when He began."* This statement, taken in connection with the date

---

* Luke iii. 23. Such is the right rendering of the verse. The Revised Version renders it :—" And Jesus Himself, when He began *to teach*, was about thirty years of age."

commonly assigned to the nativity, has been supposed to require that "the fifteenth year of Tiberius" shall be understood as referring, not to the epoch of his reign, but to an earlier date, when history testifies that certain powers were conferred on him during the two last years of Augustus. All such hypotheses, however, "are open to one overwhelming objection, viz., that the reign of Tiberius, as beginning from 19th August, A.D. 14, was as well known a date in the time of Luke, as the reign of Queen Victoria is in our own day; and no single case has ever been, or can be, produced, in which the years of Tiberius were reckoned in any other manner."*

---

* Lewin, *Fasti Sacri*, p. liii. Diss., chap. vi. The joint-principate theory of the reign of Tiberius, elaborately argued for by Greswell, is essential with writers like him, who assign the crucifixion to A.D 29 or 30. Sanclementi, indeed, finding "that nowhere in histories, or on monuments, or coins, is a vestige to be found of any such mode of reckoning the years of this emperor," *disposes of* the difficulty by taking the date in Luke iii. 1 to refer, not to John the Baptist's ministry, but to Christ's death. Browne adopts this in a modified form, recognizing that the hypothesis above referred to "falls under fatal objections." He remarks that "it is improbable to the last degree" that Luke, who wrote specially for a Roman officer, and generally for Gentiles, would have so expressed himself as to be certainly misunderstood by them. Therefore, though the statement of the evangelist clashes with his conclusion as to the date of the Passion, he owns his obligation to accept it. See *Ordo Sæc.*, §§ 71 and 95.

Nor is there any inconsistency whatever between these statements of St. Luke and the date of the nativity (as fixed by the evangelist himself), under Cyrenius, in the autumn of B.C. 4; for the Lord's ministry, dating from the autumn of A.D. 28, may in fact have begun before His thirty-first year expired, and cannot have been later than a few months beyond it. The expression " *about* thirty years " implies some such margin.* As therefore it is wholly unnecessary, it becomes wholly unjustifiable, to put a forced and special meaning on the evangelist's words; and by the fifteenth year of Tiberius Cæsar he must have intended what all the world would assume he meant, namely, the year beginning 19th August, A.D. 28. And thus, passing out of the region of argument and controversy, we reach at last a well-ascertained date of vital importance in this inquiry.

The first Passover of the Lord's public ministry on earth is thus definitely fixed by the Gospel narrative itself, as in Nisan A.D. 29. And we are thus enabled to fix 32 A.D. as the year of the crucifixion.†

---

* As Dean Alford puts it (*Gr. Test.*, *in loco*) : " This ὡσεὶ τριάκοντα admits of considerable latitude, but only in one direction, viz., *over thirty years*."

† " It seems to me absolutely certain that our Lord's ministry lasted for some period above three years " (Pusey, *Daniel*, p. 176, and *see* p. 177, *note*⁷). This opinion is now held so universally, that it is no longer necessary to set forth in detail the grounds on which it rests ; indeed, recent writers generally assume

This is opposed, no doubt, to the traditions embodied in the spurious *Acta Pilati* so often quoted in this controversy, and in the writings of certain of the fathers, by whom the fifteenth year of Tiberius was held to be itself the date of the death of Christ; " by some, because they confounded the date of the baptism with the date of the Passion; by others, because they supposed both to have happened in one year; by others, because they transcribed from their predecessors without examination."*

An imposing array of names can be cited in support of any year from A.D. 29 to A.D. 33 ; but such testimony is of force only so long as no better can be found. Just as a seemingly perfect chain of circum-

without proof that the ministry included four Passovers. The most satisfactory discussion of the question which I know of is in Hengstenberg's *Christology* (Arnold's trans., §§ 755-765). St. John mentions expressly three Passovers at which the Lord was present; and if the feast of John v. 1 be a Passover, the question is at an end. It is now generally admitted that that feast was either *Purim* or *Passover*, and Hengstenberg's proofs in favour of the latter are overwhelming. The feast of *Purim* had no Divine sanction. It was instituted by the decree of Esther, Queen of Persia, in the 13th year of Xerxes (B.C. 473), and it was rather a social and political than a religious feast, the service in the synagogue being quite secondary to the excessive eating and drinking which marked the day. It is doubtful whether our Lord would have observed such a feast at all ; but that, contrary to the usual practice, He would have specially gone up to Jerusalem to celebrate it, is altogether incredible.

* Clinton's *Fasti Rom.*, A.D. 29.

stantial evidence crumbles before the testimony of a single witness of undoubted veracity and worth, and the united voice of half a county will not support a prescriptive right, if it be opposed to a single sheet of parchment, so the cumulative traditions of the Church, even if they were as definite and clear as in fact they are contradictory and vague, would not outweigh the proofs to which appeal has here been made.

One point more, however, claims attention. Numerous writers, some of them eminent, have discussed this question as though nothing more were needed in fixing the date of the Passion than to find a year, within certain limits, in which the paschal moon was full upon a Friday. But this betrays strange forgetfulness of the intricacies of the problem. True it is that if the system by which to-day the Jewish year is settled had been in force eighteen centuries ago, the whole controversy might turn upon the week date of the Passover in a given year ; but on account of our ignorance of the embolismal system then in use, no weight whatever can be attached to it.* While the Jewish year was the old lunisolar

---

* "The month began at the phasis of the moon . . . and this happens, according to Newton, when the moon is eighteen hours old. Therefore the fourteenth Nisan might commence when the moon was 13d. 18h. old, and wanted 1d. oh. 22m. to the full. [The age of the moon at the full will be 14d. 18h. 22m.] But sometimes the *phasis* was delayed till the moon was 1d. 17h.

year of 360 days, it is not improbable they adjusted it, as for centuries they had probably been accustomed to do in Egypt, by adding annually the "complimentary days" of which Herodotus speaks.* But it is not to be supposed that when they adopted the present form of year, they continued to correct the calendar in so primitive a manner. Their use of the metonic cycle for this purpose is comparatively modern.† And

---

old; and then if the first Nisan were deferred till the *phasis*, the fourteenth would begin only 1 h. 22 m. before the full. This precision, however, in adjusting the month to the moon did not exist in practice. The Jews, like other nations who adopted a lunar year, and supplied the defect by an intercalary month, failed in obtaining complete accuracy. We know not what their method of calculation was at the time of the Christian era" (*Fasti Rom.*, vol. ii., p. 240); A.D. 30 is the only year between 28 and 33 in which the phasis of the full moon was on a Friday. In A.D. 29 the full moon was on Saturday, and the phasis on Monday. (*See* Wurm's Table, in Wiesler's *Chron. Syn.*, Venables's trans., p. 407).

* *Herod.* ii. 4.

† It was about A.D. 360 that the Jews adopted the metonic cycle of nineteen years for the adjustment of their calendar. Before that time they used a cycle of eighty-four years, which was evidently the calippic period of seventy-six years with a Greek octaëteris added. This is said by certain writers to have been in use at the time of our Lord, but the statement is very doubtful. It appears to rest on the testimony of the later Rabbins. Julius Africanus, on the other hand, states in his *Chronography* that "the Jews insert three intercalary months every eight years." For a description of the modern Jewish calendar see *Encyc. Brit.* (9th ed., vol. v., p. 714).

it is probable that with the lunar year they obtained also under the Seleucidæ the old eight years' cycle for its adjustment. The fact that this cycle was in use among the early Christians for their paschal calculations,* raises a presumption that it was borrowed from the Jews ; but we have no certain knowledge upon the subject.

Indeed, the only thing reasonably certain upon the matter is that the Passover did *not* fall upon the days assigned to it by writers whose calculations respecting it are made with strict astronomical accuracy,† for the *Mishna* affords the clearest proof that the beginning of the month was not determined by the *true* new moon, but by the first appearance of her disc ; and though in a climate like that of Palestine this would seldom be delayed by causes which would operate in murkier latitudes, it doubtless sometimes

---

* Browne, *Ordo Sæc.*, § 424.

† See *ex. gr.* Browne *Ordo Sæc.*, § 64. He avers that " if in a given year the paschal moon was at the full at any instant between sunset of a Thursday and sunset of a Friday, the day included between the two sunsets was the 15th Nisan ; " and on this ground he maintains that A.D. 29 is the only possible date of the crucifixion. As his own table shows, however, no possible year (*i.e.*, no year between 28 and 33) satisfies this requirement ; for the paschal full moon in A.D. 29 was on Saturday the 16th April, not on Friday the 18th March. This view is maintained also by Ferguson and others. It may be accounted for, perhaps, by the fact that till recent years the *Mishna* was not translated into English.

happened "that neither sun nor stars for many days appeared."* These considerations justify the statement that in any year whatever the 15th Nisan may have fallen on a Friday.†

For example, in A.D. 32, the date of the true new moon, by which the Passover was regulated, was the night (10ʰ 57ᵐ) of the 29th March. The ostensible date of the 1st Nisan, therefore, according to the phasis, was the 31st March.‡ It may have

---

* Acts xxvii. 20. Treatise *Rosh Hashanah* of the *Mishna* deals with the mode in which, in the days of the "second temple," the feast of the new moon was regulated. The evidence of two competent witnesses was required by the Sanhedrim to the fact that they had *seen* the moon, and the numerous rules laid down for the journey and examination of these witnesses prove that not unfrequently they came from a distance. Indeed, the case of their being "a day and a night on the road" is provided for (ch. i., § 9). The proclamation by the Sanhedrim, therefore, may have been sometimes delayed till a day or even two after the phasis, and sometimes the phasis was delayed till the moon was 1 d. 17 h. old [Clinton, *Fasti Rom.*, vol. ii., p. 240]; so that the 1st Nisan may have fallen several days later than the true new moon. Possibly, moreover, it may have been still further delayed by the operation of rules such as those of the modern Jewish calendar for preventing certain festivals from falling on incompatible days. It appears from the *Mishna* ("*Pesachim*") that the present rules for this purpose were not in force; but yet there may have been similar rules in operation.

† See *Fasti Rom.*, vol. ii., p. 240, as to the impossibility of determining in what years the Passover fell on Friday.

‡ *See* p. 99, *ante* (note.)

been delayed, however, till the 1st April; and in that case the 15th Nisan should apparently have fallen on Tuesday the 15th April. But the calendar may have been further disturbed by intercalation. According to the scheme of the eight years' cycle, the embolismal month was inserted in the third, sixth, and eighth years, and an examination of the calendars from A.D. 22 to A D. 45 will show that A.D. 32 was the third year of such a cycle. As, therefore, the difference between the solar year and the lunar is $11\frac{1}{4}$ days, it would amount in three years to $33\frac{3}{4}$ days, and the intercalation of a thirteenth month (*Ve-adar*) of thirty days would leave an epact still remaining of $3\frac{3}{4}$ days ; and the " ecclesiastical moon " being that much before the real moon, the feast day would have fallen on the Friday (11th April), exactly as the narrative of the Gospels requires.*

---

* The following is the scheme of the octaëteris :—

" The solar year has a length of $365\frac{1}{4}$ days ; 12 lunar months make 354 days. The difference, which is called the epact or epagomené, is $11\frac{1}{4}$ days. This is the epact of the first year. Hence the epact of the second year $= 22\frac{1}{2}$ days ; of the third, $33\frac{3}{4}$. These $33\frac{3}{4}$ days make one lunar month of 30 days, which is added to the third lunar year as an intercalary or thirteenth month ($\dot{\epsilon}\mu\beta o\lambda\iota\sigma\mu\acute{o}s$), and a remainder or epact of $3\frac{3}{4}$ days. Hence the epact of the fourth year $= 11\frac{1}{4} + 3\frac{3}{4} = 15$ days ; that of the fifth year $= 26\frac{1}{4}$; of the sixth, $37\frac{1}{2}$, which gives a second embolism of 30 days with an epact of $7\frac{1}{2}$. The epact, therefore, of the seventh year is $18\frac{3}{4}$, and of the eighth $= 18\frac{3}{4}$

This, moreover, would explain what, notwithstanding all the poetry indulged in about the groves and grottoes of Gethsemane, remains still a difficulty. Judas needed neither torch nor lantern to enable him to track his Master through the darkest shades and recesses of the garden, nor was it, seemingly, until he had fulfilled his base and guilty mission that the crowd pressed in to seize their victim. And no traitor need have been suborned by the Sanhedrim to betray to them at midnight the object of their hate, were it not that they dared not take Him save by stealth.* Every torch and lamp increased the risk of rousing the sleeping millions around them, for that night all Judah was gathered to the capital

---

$+ 11\frac{1}{4}$ = just 30, which is the third embolism with no epact remaining."—BROWNE, *Ordo Sæc.*, § 424.

The days of the Paschal full moon in the years A.D. 22-37 were as follows ; the embolismal years, according to the octaëteris, being marked E :—

A.D.					A.D.				
22,	.	.	.	5th April	30,	.	.	.	6th April
23,	.	.	.	25th March	31,	.	.	.	27th March
24,	.	.	.	12th April	32 E,	.	.	.	14th April
25,	.	.	.	1st April	33,	.	.	.	3rd April
26,	.	.	.	21st March	34,	.	.	.	23rd March
27 E,	.	.	.	9th April	35 E,	.	.	.	11th April
28,	.	.	.	29th March	36,	.	.	.	30th March
29 E,	.	.	.	17th April	37 E,	.	.	.	18th April

* Luke xxii. 2-6.

to keep the Paschal feast.* If, then, the full moon were high above Jerusalem, no other light were needed to speed them on their guilty errand; but if, on the other hand, the Paschal moon were only ten or eleven days old upon that Thursday night, she would certainly have been low on the horizon, if she had not actually set, before they ventured forth. These suggestions are not made to confirm the proof already offered of the year date of the death of Christ, but merely to show how easy it is to answer objections which at first sight might seem fatal.

---

* Josephus testifies that an "innumerable multitude" came together for the feast (*Ant.*, xvii., 9, § 3); and he computes that at a Passover before the siege of Jerusalem upwards of 2,700,200 persons actually partook of the Paschal Supper, besides the foreigners present in the city (*Wars*, vi., 9, § 3).

9

THE PASCHAL SUPPER

THE trustworthiness of witnesses is tested, not by the amount of truth their evidence contains, but by the absence of mistakes. A single glaring error may serve to discredit testimony which seemed of the highest worth. This principle applies with peculiar force in estimating the credibility of the Gospel narratives, and it lends an importance that can scarcely be exaggerated to the question which arises in this controversy, Was the betrayal in fact upon the night of the Paschal Supper? If, as is so commonly maintained, one or all of the Evangelists were in error in a matter of fact so definite and plain, it is idle to pretend that their writings are in any sense whatever God-breathed.*

---

* θεοπνευστος, 2 Tim. iii. 16. *See* Browne's *Ordo Sæc.*, §§ 65-70, for an exhaustive discussion of this question, in proof that "the three first Gospels are at variance on this point with the fourth." The matter is treated of in books without number. I here deal only with the salient points in the controversy. Arguments based upon the Sabbatical observance of the 15th Nisan being inconsistent with the events of the morning of the crucifixion are worthless. "To strain at a gnat and swallow a camel" was

The testimony of the first three Gospels is united, that the Last Supper was eaten at the Jewish Passover. The attempt to prove that it was an anticipatory celebration, without the paschal sacrifice, though made with the best of motives, is utterly futile. " Now on the first day of unleavened bread " (St. Matthew declares),* " the disciples came to Jesus, saying, Where wilt thou that we make ready for Thee to eat the Passover ? " It was the proposal not of the Lord, but of the disciples, who, with the knowledge of the day and of the rites pertaining to it, turned to the Master for instructions. With yet greater definiteness St. Mark narrates that this took place on the first day of unleavened bread, *when they killed the Passover.*†

---

characteristic of the men who were the actors in these scenes. If any one have doubts of it, let him read the *Mishna*. And points such as that the Jews were forbidden to leave their houses on the night of the Supper, depend upon confounding the commands given for the night of the Exodus with the law relative to its annual celebration. As well might it be urged that the Lord sanctioned and took part in a violation of the law because He reclined at supper, instead of standing girded and shod as enjoined in Exod. xii.

* Matt. xxvi. 17 (Revised Version). In the Authorized Version out translators have perverted the verse. It was not the first day of the *feast*, but τῇ πρώτῃ τῶν ἀζύμων, or, as St. Luke calls it, ἡ ἡμέρα τῶν ἀζύμων, viz., the day on which leaven was banished from their houses, the 14th Nisan, on the evening of which the Passover was eaten.

† Mark xiv. 12.

And the language of St. Luke is, if possible, more unequivocal still : " Then came the day of unleavened bread, *when the Passover must be killed*." *

But it is confidently asserted that the testimony of St. John is just as clear and unambiguous that the crucifixion took place upon the very day and, it is sometimes urged, at the very hour of the paschal sacrifice. Many an eminent writer may be cited to support this view, and the controversy waged in its defence is endless. But no plea for deference to great names can be tolerated for a moment when the point at issue is the integrity of Holy Writ ; and despite the erudition that has been exhausted to prove that the Gospels are here at hopeless variance, none who have learned to prize them as a Divine revelation will be surprised to find that the main difficulty depends entirely on prevailing ignorance respecting Jewish ordinances and the law of Moses.

These writers one and all confound the Paschal Supper with the festival which followed it, and to which it lent its name. The supper was a memorial of the redemption of the firstborn of Israel on the night before the Exodus ; the feast was the anniversary of their actual deliverance from the house of bondage. The supper was not a part of the feast ; it was morally the basis on which the feast

---

* Luke xxii. 7.

was founded, just as the Feast of Tabernacles was based on the great sin-offering of the day of expiation which preceded it. But in the same way that the Feast of Weeks came to be commonly designated Pentecost, the feast of Unleavened Bread was popularly called the Passover.* That title was common to the supper and the feast, and included both ; but the intelligent Jew would never confound the two ; and if he spoke emphatically of the *feast* of the Passover, he would thereby mark the festival to the exclusion of the supper.†

No words can possibly express more clearly this distinction than those afforded by the Pentateuch in the final promulgation of the Law :—" In the fourteenth day of the first month is the Passover of the Lord ; and in the fifteenth day of this month is the feast."‡

Opening the thirteenth chapter of St. John in the light of this simple explanation, every difficulty vanishes. The scene is laid at the Paschal Supper,

---

* See Luke xxii. 1., and compare Josephus, *Ant.*, xiv. 2, 1, and xvii. 9, 3 : " The feast of unleavened bread, *which we call the Passover.*"

† Or if the emphasis rested on the last word, the distinction would be between Passover and Pentecost or Tabernacles.

‡ Numb. xxviii. 16, 17. Compare Exod. xii. 14-17, and Lev. xxiii. 5, 6, and mark that in the enumeration of the *feasts* in the twenty-third chapter of Exodus, the Passover (*i.e.*, the Paschal Supper) is omitted altogether.

on the eve of the festival, "before *the feast* of the Passover;"* and after the narration of the washing of the disciples' feet, the evangelist goes on to tell of the hurried departure of Judas, explaining that, to some, the Lord's injunction to the traitor was understood to mean, "Buy what we have need of *against the feast*." † The feast day was a Sabbath, when trading was unlawful, and it would seem that the needed supply for the festival was still procurable far on in the preceding night; for another of the errors with which this controversy abounds is the assumption that the Jewish day was invariably reckoned a νυκθημερον, beginning in the evening.‡

---

* John xiii. 1. The reader must carefully distinguish between verses such as this and those verses where in our English version the word "feast" is in italics, denoting that it is not in the original.

† John xiii. 29.

‡ Such, for instance, was the day of atonement (Lev. xxiii. 32) and also the weekly Sabbath. But though the Passover was eaten between six o'clock and midnight, this period was designated in the law, not the beginning of the 15th Nisan, but the evening or night of the 14th (compare Exod. xii. 6-8, and Lev. xxiii. 5). The 15th, or feast day, was reckoned, doubtless, from six o'clock the following morning, for, according to the *Mishna* (Treatise *Berachoth*), the day began at six o'clock a.m. These writers would have us believe that the disciples supposed that they were there and then eating the Passover, and yet that they imagined Judas was despatched to buy what was needed for the Passover!

Such, doubtless, was the common rule, and notably in respect of the law of ceremonial cleansing. This very fact, indeed, enables us without a doubt to conclude that the Passover on account of which the Jews refused to defile themselves by entering the judgment hall, was not the Paschal *Supper*, for that supper was not eaten till after the hour at which such defilement would have lapsed. In the language of the law, " When the sun is down he shall be clean, and shall afterwards eat of the holy things." * Not so was it with the holy offerings of the feast day, which they must needs eat before the hour at which their uncleanness would have ceased.† The only question, therefore, is whether partaking of the peace offerings of the festival could properly be designated as " eating the Passover." The law of Moses itself supplies the answer : " Thou shalt sacrifice the Passover unto the Lord thy God of the flock and *the herd . . . seven days* shalt thou eat unleavened bread *therewith*." ‡

If then the words of St. John are intelligible only when thus interpreted, and if when thus interpreted

---

* Lev. xxii. 7.

† Because the day ended at six o'clock. Moreover, we know from Jewish writers that these offerings (called in the *Talmud* the *Chagigah*) were eaten between three and six o'clock, and ceremonial uncleanness continued until six o'clock.

‡ Deut. xvi. 2, 3, and compare 2 Chron. xxxv. 7, 8.

they are consistent with the testimony of the three first Evangelists, no element is lacking to give certainty that the events of the eighteenth chapter occurred upon the *feast*-day. Or if confirmation still be needed, the closing verses of this very chapter give it, for according to the custom cited, it was at the *feast* that the governor released a prisoner to the people.* Fearing because of the populace to seize the Lord upon the *feast*-day,† the Pharisees were eager to procure His betrayal on the night of the Paschal Supper. And so it came to pass that the arraignment before Pilate took place upon the *festival*, as all the Evangelists declare.

But does not St. John expressly state that it was "the *preparation* of the Passover," and must not this necessarily mean the fourteenth of Nisan? The plain answer is, that not a single passage has been cited from writings either sacred or profane in which that day is so described ; whereas among the Jews "the preparation" was the common name for the day before the Sabbath, and it is so used by all the Evangelists. And bearing this in mind, let the reader compare the fourteenth verse of the nineteenth chapter of St. John with the thirty-first and forty-second verses of the same chapter, and he

---

* John xviii. 39. Compare Matt. xxvii. 15 ; Mark xv. 6 ; and Luke xxiii. 17.

† Matt. xxvi. 5 ; Mark xiv. 1, 2.

will have no difficulty in rendering the words in question, "it was Passover Friday."*

But yet another statement of St. John is quoted in this controversy. "That Sabbath day was an high day," he declares, and *therefore*, it is urged, it must have been the 15th of Nisan. The force of this "therefore" partly depends upon overlooking the fact that all the great sacrifices to which the 15th of Nisan largely owed its distinctive solemnity, were repeated daily throughout the festival.† On this account alone that Sabbath was "an high day." But besides, it was specially distinguished as the day on which the firstfruits of the harvest were offered in the temple; for in respect of this ordinance, as in most other points of difference between the Karaite Jews, who held to the Scriptures as their

---

* ἦν δὲ παρασκευὴ τοῦ πάσχα, compare vers. 31 and 42, and also Matt. xxvii. 62 ; Mark xv. 42 ; Luke xxiii. 54. Josephus (*Ant.*, xvi., 6, 2) cites an imperial edict relieving the Jews from appearing before the tribunals either on the Sabbath or after the ninth hour of the preparation day. It is unjustifiable to assert that the absence of the article in John xix. 14 precludes our giving this meaning to the word παρασκευὴ in that passage. In three of the other five verses cited the word is anarthrous, for in fact it had come to be the common name for the day, and the expression "Passover Friday" was as natural to a Jew as is "Easter Monday" to ourselves. (*See* Alford's note on Mark xv. 42. Still more valuable is his explanation of Matt. xxvii 62.)

† Numb. xxviii. 19-24. Compare Josephus, *Ant.*, iii. 10, 5.

only guide, and the Rabbinical Jews, who followed the traditions of the elders, the latter were entirely in the wrong.

The law enjoined that the sheaf of the firstfruits should be waved before the Lord "on the morrow after the (paschal) Sabbath,"* and from that day the seven weeks were reckoned which ended with the feast of Pentecost. But as the book of Deuteronomy expressly ordains that the weeks should be counted from the first day of the harvest,† it is evident that the morrow after the Sabbath should not be itself a Sabbath, but a working day. The true day for the ordinance, therefore, was the day of the resurrection, " the first day of the week " following the Passover,‡ when, according to the in-

---

* Lev. xxiii. 10, 11.

† Deut. xvi. 9, and comp. Lev. xxiii. 15, 16.

‡ The present Jewish calendar is so adjusted that the 14th of Nisan shall never fall upon their Sabbath (see *Encyc. Brit.*, 9th ed., title, *Hebrew Calendar*) ; and this, doubtless, was so intended, for the duties of the day were inconsistent with the due observance of the fourth commandment. Therefore " the morrow after the Sabbath" following would invariably be a working day, so that the law is perfectly consistent in providing that the sheaf should be waved on the first day of the harvest. It is only, therefore, in a cycle of years that the true day for offering the firstfruits falls on the third day from the Passover ; but in the year of the crucifixion, the great antitype, the resurrection of Christ from the dead (1 Cor. xv. 20, 23), occurred upon the very day Divinely appointed for the rite. It follows

tention of the law, the barley harvest should begin, and the first sheaf gathered should be carried to the Holy Place and solemnly waved before Jehovah. But with the Jews all this was lost in the empty rite of offering in the temple a measure of meal prepared from corn which, in violation of the law, had been garnered days before. This rite was invariably celebrated on the 16th of Nisan ; and thus synchronizing with the solemnities both of the Paschal festival and of the Sabbath, that day could not fail to be indeed " an high day."*

The argument in proof that the death of Christ was on the very day the paschal lamb was killed, has gained a fictitious interest and value from the seeming fitness of the synchronism this involves. But a closer investigation of the subject, combined with a broader view of the Mosaic types, will dissipate the force of this conclusion. The distinctive

---

that the true day of Pentecost must always be on the first day of the week (*see* Lev. xxiii. 15, 16), and therefore in that same year the true Pentecost was, not the Sabbath day on which the Jews observed the feast, but the day which followed it, a fact which confirms the presumption that the designedly ambiguous word used in Acts ii. 1, means " accomplished," in the sense of *passed*, and that it was when assembled on " the first day of the week " that the Church received the gift of the Holy Ghost.

* In truth it could not but have been the greatest Sabbath of the year, and it is idle to pretend that this is not sufficient to account for the mention made of it.

teaching of Calvinism is based on giving an exclusive
place to the great sin-offering of Leviticus, in which
substitution, in its most definite and narrowest sense,
is essential. The Passover, on the other hand, has
ever been the most popular of types. But though
the other typical sacrifices are almost entirely ignored
in the systems of our leading schools of theology,
they have no little prominence in Scripture. The
offerings which are placed first in the book of Leviticus have a large share in the theology of the
Epistle to the Hebrews,—the new Testament " Leviticus," whereas the Passover is not even once referred
to.* Now these Leviticus offerings† marked the
feast-day,‡ on which, according to the Gospels, "the
Messiah was cut off."

And other synchronisms are not wanting, still
more striking and significant. During all His
ministry on earth, albeit it was spent in humiliation
and reproach, no hand was ever laid upon the Blessed
One, save in importunate supplication or in devout
and loving service. But when at times His enemies
would fain have seized Him, a mysterious hour to

---

* The *historical* mention of the Passover in Heb. xi. 28 is of
course no exception. It has no place in the *doctrine* of the
Epistle.

† The burnt-offering, with its meat-offering, the peace-offering
(the *chagigah* of the Talmud), and the sin-offering (Lev. i.-iv.).

‡ Num. xxviii. 17-24.

come was spoken of, in which their hate should be unhindered. "This is your hour, and the power of darkness," He exclaimed, as Judas and the impious companions in his guilt drew round Him in the garden.* *His* hour, He called it, when He thought of His mission upon earth : *their* hour, when in the fulfilment of that mission He found Himself within their grasp.

The agonies inflicted on Him by men have taken hold on the mind of Christendom ; but beyond and above all these the mystery of the Passion is that He was forsaken and accursed of God.† In some sense, indeed, His sufferings from men were but a consequence of this ; therefore His reply to Pilate, "Thou couldst have no power at all against Me, except it were given thee from above." If men seized and slew Him, it was because God had delivered Him up. When that destined hour had struck, the mighty Hand drew back which till then had shielded Him from outrage. His *death* was not the beginning, but the close of His sufferings ; in truth, it was the hour of His triumph.

---

* Luke xxii. 53.

† No reverent mind will seek to analyse the meaning of such words, save in so far as they testify to the great fact that His sufferings and death were in expiation of our sins. But the believer will not tolerate a doubt as to the reality and depth of their meaning.

The midnight agony in Gethsemane was thus the great antitype of that midnight scene in Egypt when the destroying angel flashed through the land. And as His death was the fulfilment of His people's deliverance, so it took place upon the anniversary of "that selfsame day that the Lord did bring the children of Israel out of the land of Egpyt by their armies." *

---

* Exod. xii. 51. The Passover of the yearly celebration was but a memorial of the Passover in Egypt, which was the true type. It was killed, moreover, not at the hour of the Lord's death, but *after* that hour, between the ninth and the eleventh hour (Josephus, *Wars*, vi., 9, 3). "The elucidation of the doctrine of types, now entirely neglected, is an important problem for future theologians." This dictum of Hengstenberg's [*Christology* (Arnold's Ed.), § 765] may still be recorded as a deserved reproach upon theology, and much that has been written in this controversy might be quoted to prove its truth.

The day of the crucifixion was the anniversary not only of the Exodus, but also of the promise to Abraham (comp. Exod. xii. 41).

The day of the resurrection was the anniversary of the crossing of the Red Sea, and again of the resting of the Ark on Ararat (Gen. viii. 4). Nisan, which had been the seventh month, became the first month at the Exodus. (*See* Exod. xii. 2 ; *cf. Ordo. Sæc.*, § 299.) On the 17th Nisan the renewed earth emerged from the waters of the flood; the redeemed people emerged from the waters of the sea ; and the Lord Jesus rose from the dead.

10

FULFILMENT OF THE PROPHECY

"THE secret things belong unto the Lord our God ; but those things which are revealed belong unto us and to our children." * And among the "things which are revealed" fulfilled prophecy has a foremost place. In presence of the events in which it has been accomplished, its meaning lies upon the surface. Let the facts of the Passion be admitted, and their relation to the twenty-second Psalm is indisputable. There are profound depths of spiritual significance in the Psalmist's words, because of the nature of the facts which have fulfilled them ; but the testimony which the prophecy affords is addressed to all, and he who runs may read it. Is it possible then, it may be asked, that the true interpretation of this prophecy of the Seventy Weeks involves so much inquiry and discussion ?

Such an objection is perfectly legitimate ; but the answer to it will be found in distinguishing between the difficulties which appear in the prophecy itself, and those which depend entirely on the controversy

* Deut. xxix. 29.

to which it has given rise. The writings of Daniel have been more the object of hostile criticism than any other portion of the Scripture, and the closing verses of the ninth chapter have always been a principal point of attack. And necessarily so, for if that single passage can be proved to be a prophecy, it establishes the character of the book as a Divine revelation. Daniel's visions admittedly describe historical events between the days of Nebuchadnezzar and of Antiochus Epiphanes ; therefore scepticism assumes that the writer lived in Maccabean times. But this assumption, put forward without even a decent pretence of proof, is utterly refuted by pointing to a portion of the prophecy fulfilled at a later date ; and accordingly it is of vital moment to the sceptic to discredit the prediction of the Seventy Weeks.

The prophecy has suffered nothing from the attacks of its assailants, but much at the hands of its friends. No elaborate argument would be necessary to elucidate its meaning, were it not for the difficulties raised by Christian expositors. If everything that Christian writers have written on the subject could be wiped out and forgotten, the fulfilment of the vision, so far as it has been in fact fulfilled, would be clear upon the open page of history. Out of deference to these writers, and also in the hope of removing prejudices which are fatal to the right understanding of the subject, these difficulties have here been discussed. It now remains only to recapitulate the conclusions which have been recorded in the preceding pages.

The sceptre of earthly power which was entrusted to the house of David, was transferred to the Gentiles in the person of Nebuchadnezzar, to remain in Gentile hands " until the times of the Gentiles be fulfilled."

The blessings promised to Judah and Jerusalem were postponed till after a period described as " seventy weeks " ; and at the close of the sixty-ninth week of this era the Messiah should be " cut off."

These seventy weeks represent seventy times seven prophetic years of 360 days, to be reckoned from the issuing of an edict for the rebuilding of the city— " the street and rampart," of Jerusalem.

The edict in question was the decree issued by Artaxerxes Longimanus in the twentieth year of his reign, authorising Nehemiah to rebuild the fortifications of Jerusalem.

The date of Artaxerxes's reign can be definitely ascertained — not from elaborate disquisitions by biblical commentators and prophetic writers, but by the united voice of secular historians and chronologers.

The statement of St. Luke is explicit and unequivocal, that our Lord's public ministry began in the fifteenth year of Tiberius Cæsar. It is equally clear that it began shortly before the Passover. The date of it can thus be fixed as between August A.D. 28 and April A.D. 29. The Passover of the crucifixion therefore was in A.D. 32, when Christ was betrayed on the night of the Paschal Supper, and put to death on the day of the Paschal Feast.

If then the foregoing conclusions be well founded. we should expect to find that the period intervening between the edict of Artaxerxes and the Passion was 483 prophetic years. And accuracy as absolute as the nature of the case permits is no more than men are here entitled to demand. There can be no loose reckoning in a Divine chronology ; and if God has deigned to mark on human calendars the fulfilment of His purposes as foretold in prophecy, the strictest scrutiny shall fail to detect miscalculation or mistake.

The Persian edict which restored the autonomy of Judah was issued in the Jewish month of Nisan. It may in fact have been dated the 1st of Nisan, but no other day being named, the prophetic period must be reckoned, according to a practice common with the Jews, from the Jewish New Year's Day.* The seventy weeks are therefore to be computed from the 1st of Nisan B.C. 445.†

---

* " On the 1st of Nisan is a new year for the computation of the reign of kings, and for festivals."—*Mishna*, treatise " *Rosh Hash.*" (*See* p. 102, *ante*, note).

† The wall was finished in the twenty and fifth day of the month Elul, in fifty and two days " (Neh. vi. 15). Now fifty-

Now the great characteristic of the Jewish sacred year has remained unchanged ever since the memorable night when the equinoctial moon beamed down upon the huts of Israel in Egypt, bloodstained by the Paschal sacrifice ; and there is neither doubt nor difficulty in fixing within narrow limits the Julian date of the 1st of Nisan in any year whatever. In B.C. 445 the new moon by which the Passover was regulated was on the 13th of March at 7h. 9m. A.M.* And accordingly the 1st Nisan may be assigned to the 14th March.

---

two days, measured back from the 25th Elul, brings us to the 3rd Ab. Therefore Nehemiah must have arrived not later than 1st Ab, and apparently some days earlier (Neh. ii. 11). Compare this with Ezra's journey thirteen years before. " For upon the first day of the first month began he to go up from Babylon, and on the first day of the fifth month (Ab) came he to Jerusalem, according to the good hand of his God upon him " (Ezra vii. 9). I infer therefore that Nehemiah also set out *early* in the first month.

The chronological parallelisms between the respective journeys of Ezra and Nehemiah have suggested the ingenious theory that both went up to Jerusalem together, Ezra vii. and Neh. ii. relating to the same event. This is based upon the supposition that the regnal years of Artaxerxes, according to Persian computation, were reckoned from his birth, a supposition, however, which is fanciful and arbitrary, though described by its author as "by no means unlikely" (*Trans. Soc. Bib. Arch.*, ii.., 110 : Rev. D. H. Haigh, 4th Feb., 1873).

* For this calculation I am indebted to the courtesy of the

But the language of the prophecy is clear : " From the going forth of the commandment to restore and to build Jerusalem *unto Messiah the Prince* shall be seven weeks and threescore and two weeks." An era therefore of sixty-nine " weeks," or 483 prophetic years reckoned from the 14th March, B.C. 445, should close with some event to satisfy the words, " unto the Messiah the Prince."

The date of the nativity could not possibly have been the termination of the period, for then the sixty-nine weeks must have ended thirty-three years before Messiah's death.

If the beginning of His public ministry be fixed

Astronomer Royal, whose reply to my inquiry on the subject is appended :

> " ROYAL OBSERVATORY, GREENWICH.
> " *June* 26*th*, 1877.

" SIR,—I have had the moon's place calculated from Largeteau's Tables in Additions to the *Connaisance des Tems* 1846, by one of my assistants, and have no doubt of its correctness. The place being calculated for —444, March 12d. 20h., French reckoning, or March 12d. 8h. P.M., it appears that the said time was short of New Moon by about 8h. 47m., and therefore the New Moon occurred at 4h. 47m. A.M., March 13th, Paris time.

> " I am, etc.,
> " (Signed,) G. B. AIRY."

The new moon, therefore, occurred at Jerusalem on the 13th March, B.C. 445 (444 Astronomical) at 7h. 9m. A.M.

upon, difficulties of another kind present themselves. When the Lord began to preach, the kingdom was not presented as a fact accomplished in His advent, but as a hope the realization of which, though at the very door, was still to be fulfilled. He took up the Baptist's testimony, "The kingdom of heaven is *at hand.*" His ministry was a preparation for the kingdom, leading up to the time when in fulfilment of the prophetic Scriptures He should publicly declare Himself as the Son of David, the King of Israel, and claim the homage of the nation. It was the nation's guilt that the cross and not the throne was the climax of His life on earth.

No student of the Gospel narrative can fail to see that the Lord's last visit to Jerusalem was not only in fact, but in the purpose of it, the crisis of His ministry, the goal towards which it had been directed. After the first tokens had been given that the nation would reject His Messianic claims, He had shunned all public recognition of them. But now the twofold testimony of His words and His works had been fully rendered, and His entry into the Holy City was to proclaim His Messiahship and to receive His doom. Again and again His apostles even had been charged that they should not make Him known. But now He accepted the acclamations of "the whole multitude of the disciples," and silenced the remonstrance of the Pharisees with the indignant rebuke, " I tell you if these should hold their peace, the stones would immediately cry out." *

The full significance of the words which follow in the Gospel of St. Luke is concealed by a slight interpolation in the text. As the shouts broke forth from His disciples, " Hosanna to the Son of David ! blessed is the king of Israel that cometh in the name of the Lord ! " He looked off toward the Holy City and exclaimed, " If *thou* also hadst known, even *on this day*, the things which belong to thy peace ; but now they are hid from thine eyes ! " † The time of Jerusalem's visitation had come, and she knew it not. Long ere then the nation had rejected Him, but this was the predestined day when their choice must be irrevocable, —the day so distinctly signalised in Scripture as the fulfilment of Zechariah's prophecy, " Rejoice greatly, O daughter of Zion ! shout, O daughter of Jerusalem ! behold *thy King cometh unto thee !* " ‡ Of all the days of the ministry of Christ on earth,

---

* Luke xix. 39, 40.

† εἰ ἔγνως καὶ σὺ καί γε ἐν τῇ ἡμέρᾳ ταύτῃ τὰ προς εἰρήνην σου· κ. τ. λ. (Luke xix. 42). The received text inserts σου after ἡμέρᾳ, but the best MSS. (*Alex. Vat. Sin.*, etc.) agree in omitting it. καὶ σύ, " *thou also*, as well as these my disciples." καὶ γε et quidem— " *even*" (Alford, *Gr. Test. in loco*). The Revised Version reads, " If thou hadst known *in this day*," etc.

‡ Zech. ix. 9.

no other will satisfy so well the angel's words, " unto Messiah the Prince."

And the date of it can be ascertained.   In accordance with the Jewish custom, the Lord went up to Jerusalem upon the 8th Nisan, " six days before the Passover." *   But as the 14th, on which the Paschal Supper was eaten, fell that year upon a Thursday, the 8th was the preceding Friday.   He must have spent the Sabbath, therefore, at Bethany ; and on the evening of the 9th, after the Sabbath had ended, the Supper took place in Martha's house.   Upon the following day, the 10th Nisan, He entered Jerusalem as recorded in the Gospels.†

The Julian date of that 10th Nisan was Sunday the 6th April, A.D. 32.   What then was the length of the period intervening between the issuing of the decree to rebuild Jerusalem and the public advent of " Messiah the Prince,"—between the 14th March, B.C. 445, and the 6th April, A.D. 32 ?   THE INTERVAL CONTAINED EXACTLY AND TO THE VERY DAY

---

* "When the people were come in great crowds to the feast of unleavened bread on the *eighth* day of the month Xanthicus,' *i.e.*, Nisan (Josephus, *Wars*, vi. 5, 3).   "And the Jews' Passover was nigh at hand, and many went out of the country up to Jerusalem, before the Passover, to purify themselves. . . . Then Jesus, six days before the Passover, came to Bethany " (John xi. 55 ; xii. 1).

† Lewin, *Fasti Sacri*, p. 230.

173,880 DAYS, OR SEVEN TIMES SIXTY-NINE PRO-
PHETIC YEARS OF 360 DAYS, the first sixty-nine
weeks of Gabriel's prophecy.*

Much there is in Holy Writ which unbelief may
value and revere, while utterly refusing to accept it

---

* The 1st Nisan in the twentieth year of Artaxerxes (the edict
to rebuild Jerusalem) was 14th March, B.C. 445. (See p. 306 #7.)

The 10th Nisan in Passion Week (Christ's entry into Jerusalem) was 6th April, A.D. 32.

The intervening period was 476 years and 24 days (the days
being reckoned inclusively, as required by the language of the
prophecy, and in accordance with the Jewish practice).

But 476 × 365 = ...	173,740 days.
Add (14 March to 6th April, *both* inclusive)	24 „
Add for leap years	116 „
	173,880

And 69 weeks of prophetic years of 360 days (or 69 × 7 × 360)
= 173,880 days.

It may be well to offer here two explanatory remarks. First :
in reckoning years from B.C. to A.D., *one* year must always be
omitted ; for it is obvious, *ex. gr.*, that from B.C. 1 to A.D. 1 was
not *two* years, but one year. B.C. 1 ought to be described as
B.C. 0, and it is so reckoned by astronomers, who would describe
the historical date B.C. 445, as 444 (see note, p. 124, *ante*). And
secondly, the Julian year is 11m. 10·46s., or about the 129th
part of a day, longer than the mean solar year. The Julian
calendar, therefore, contains three leap years too many in four
centuries, an error which had amounted to eleven days in
A.D. 1752, when our English calendar was corrected by declaring
the 3rd September to be the 14th September, and by intro-
ducing the Gregorian reform which reckons three secular years

as Divine; but prophecy admits of no half-faith. The prediction of the "seventy weeks" was either a gross and impious imposture, or else it was in the fullest and strictest sense *God-breathed.** It may be that in days to come, when Judah's great home-bringing shall restore to Jerusalem the rightful owners of its soil,[9] the Jews themselves shall yet rake up from deep beneath its ruins the records of the great king's decree and of the Nazarene's rejection, and they for whom the prophecy was given will thus be confronted with proofs of its fulfilment. Meanwhile what judgment shall be passed on it by fair and thoughtful men? To believe that the facts and figures here detailed amount to nothing more than happy coincidences involves a greater exercise of faith than that of the Christian who accepts the book of Daniel as Divine. There is a point beyond which unbelief is impossible, and the mind in refusing truth must needs take refuge in a misbelief which is sheer credulity.

---

out of four as common years; *ex. gr.*, 1700, 1800 and 1900 are common years, and 2000 is a leap year. " Old Christmas day " is still marked in our calendars, and observed in some localities, on the 6th January; and to this day the calendar remains uncorrected in Russia. (See Appendix 4, p. 306 note 8.)

* θεόπνευστος (2 Tim. iii. 16).

[9] See Appendix 4, p. 306 note 9.

11

PRINCIPLES OF INTERPRETATION

"THIS is a work which I find deficient; but it is to be done with wisdom, sobriety, and reverence, or not at all." Thus wrote Lord Bacon in treating of what he describes as "history of prophecy."

"The nature of such a work," he explains, "ought to be that every prophecy of the Scripture be sorted with the event fulfilling the same, throughout the ages of the world, both for the better confirmation of faith and for the better illumination of the Church touching those parts of prophecies which are yet unfulfilled: allowing, nevertheless, that latitude which is agreeable and familiar unto Divine prophecies; being of the nature of their Author with whom a thousand years are but as one day, and therefore are not fulfilled punctually at once, but have springing and germinant accomplishment throughout many ages, though the height or fulness of them may refer to some one age."

If the many writers who have since contributed to supply the want Lord Bacon noticed, had given due heed to these wise and weighty words, prophetic study might possibly have escaped the reproach which comes of its followers being divided into hostile camps. With the Christian the fulfilment of prophecy does not belong to the region of opinion, nor even of fact, merely; it is a matter of *faith*. We have a right, therefore, to expect that it shall be definite and clear. But though the principles and maxims of interpretation gained by the study of that part of prophecy which was accomplished within the era of Holy Writ are by no means to be thrown aside when we pass out into post-apostolic times, surely there is no presumption against our finding hidden in the history of these eighteen centuries a primary and partial fulfilment even of prophecies which will unquestionably receive a final and complete accomplishment in days to come.

Only let us not forget the "wisdom, sobriety, and reverence" which such an inquiry demands. In our day prophetic students have turned prophets, and with mingled folly and daring have sought to fix the very year of Christ's return to earth,—predictions· which possibly our children's children will recall when another century shall have been added to the history of Christendom. If such vagaries brought discredit only on their authors, it were well. But though broached in direct opposition to Scripture, they have brought reproach on Scripture itself, and have given a stimulus to the jaunty scepticism of the day. We might have hoped that whatever else might be forgotten, the last words which the Lord Jesus spoke on earth would not be thus thrust aside : " *It is not for you to know the times or the seasons which the Father hath put in His own power.*" * But what was denied to inspired apostles in days of pristine faith and power, the prophecy-mongers of these last days have dared to claim ; and the result has been that the solemn and blessed hope of the Lord's return has been degraded to the level of the predictions of astrologers, to the confusion and grief of faithful hearts, and the amusement of the world.

Any man who, avoiding extravagant or fanciful views, both of history and of Scripture, points to events in the present or the past as the correlatives of a prophecy, deserves a calm and unprejudiced hearing from thoughtful men. But let him not forget that though the Scriptures he appeals to may thus receive " germinant accomplishment," " the height or fulness of them may refer " to an age still future. What is true of all Scripture is specially true of prophecy. It is ours to assign to it a meaning ; but he who really believes it to be Divine, will

---

* Acts i. 7.

hesitate to limit its meaning to the measure of his own apprehension of it.

The prophecies of Antichrist afford a signal and most apt illustration of this. Were it not for the prejudice created by extreme statements, prophetic students would probably agree that the great apostasy of Christendom displays in outline many of the main lineaments of the Man of Sin. There is, indeed, in our day a spurious liberality that would teach us to forego the indictment which history affords against the Church of Rome ; but while no generous mind will refuse to own the moral worth of those who, in England at least, now guide the counsels of that Church, the real question at issue relates to the character, not of individuals, but of a *system*.

It is the part, therefore, not of intolerant bigotry, but of true wisdom, to search the records of the past —terrible records, truly—for the means of judging of that system. The inquiry which concerns us is not whether good men are found within the pale of Rome—as though all the moral excellence of earth could avail to cover the annals of her hideous guilt ! Our true inquiry is whether she has suffered any real change in these enlightened days. Is the Church of Rome *reformed ?* With what vehemence the answer would be shrieked from every altar within her pale ! And if not, let but dark days come again, and some of the foulest scenes and blackest crimes in the history of Christendom may be re-enacted in Europe. "The true test of a man is not what he does, but what, with the principles he holds, he would do;" and if this be true of individuals, it is still more intensely true of communities. They do good service, therefore, who keep before the public mind the real character of Rome as the present day development of the apostasy.

But when these writers go on to assert that the predictions of the Antichrist have their full and final realization in the Papacy, their position becomes a positive danger to the truth. It is maintained at the cost of rejecting some of the most definite of the prophecies, and of putting a lax or fanciful interpretation upon those very Scriptures to which they appeal.

Indeed, the chief practical evil of this system of interpretation is that it creates and fosters a habit of reading the Scriptures in a loose and superficial manner. General impressions, derived from a cursory perusal of the prophecies, are seized upon and systematized, and upon this foundation a pretentious superstructure is built up. As already noticed, the Church of Rome displays the chief moral lineaments of the Man of Sin. Therefore it is an axiom of interpretation with this school that the ten-horned beast is the Papacy. But of the beast it is written that " power was given to him over all kindreds and tongues and nations, and all that dwell upon the earth shall worship him, whose names are not written in the book of life."* Are these commentators aware that one-half of Christendom is outside the pale of Rome, and in antagonism to the claims of the Papacy ? Or do they suppose that all who belong to the Greek and Protestant Churches are enrolled in the book of life ? By no means. But they would tell us the verse does not mean exactly what it says.†

Again, the ten-horned beast is the Papacy ; the second beast, the false prophet, is the Papal clergy ; Babylon is Papal Rome. And yet when we turn to the vision of the judgment of Babylon, we find that it is *by the agency of the beast* that her doom is accomplished ! " And the ten horns which thou sawest, and the beast, *these shall hate the whore* (Babylon), and shall make her desolate, and naked, and shall eat her flesh and burn her with fire ; for God hath put in their hearts to fulfil His will, and to agree, *and give their kingdom unto the beast,* until the words of God shall be fulfilled." " These

---

* Rev. xiii. 7, 8.

† According to these interpreters, such a statement must be taken *cum grano salis,* as we term it ; and the like remark applies to their rendering of *every verse* of the thirteenth chapter of Revelation.

have one mind, *and shall give their power and strength unto the beast.*" * The governments of Christendom, therefore, are to lend their power to the Roman Pontiff and priesthood in order to the destruction of Papal Rome ! † Can absurdity be more transparent and complete ?

The question here at issue must not be prejudiced by misrepresentations, or shirked by turning away to collateral points of secondary moment. It is not whether great crises in the history of Christendom, such as the fall of Paganism, the rise of the Papacy and of the Moslem power, and the Protestant reformation of the sixteenth century, be within the scope of the visions of St. John. This may readily be conceded. Neither is it whether the fact that the chronology of some of these events is marked by cycles of years composed of the precise multiples of seventy specified in the book of Daniel and the Apocalypse, be not a further proof that all forms part of one great plan. Every fresh discovery of

---

* Rev. xvii. 16, 17, 13. In ver. 16 the best reading, as given in the Revised Version, is " *and* the beast," instead of " *upon* the beast."

† Mr. Elliott's romance on this subject is disposed of by the events of recent years, which have made Rome the peaceful capital of Italy. Of the beast and false prophet it is written, " These both were cast alive into a lake of fire " (Rev. xix. 20). It may be pleasing to Protestant zeal to suppose the Roman hierarchy and priesthood are " reserved " for such a fate.

the kind ought to be welcomed by all lovers of the truth. Instead of weakening confidence in the accuracy and definiteness of the prophecies, it ought to strengthen the faith which looks for their absolute and literal fulfilment. The question is not whether the history of Christendom was within the view of the Divine Author of the prophecies, but whether those prophecies have been *fulfilled;* not whether those Scriptures have the scope and meaning which historical interpreters assign to them, but whether their scope and meaning be exhausted and satisfied by the events to which they appeal as the fulfilment of them. It is unnecessary, therefore, to enter here upon an elaborate review of the historical system of interpretation, for if it fails when tested at some one vital point, it breaks down altogether.

Does the Apocalypse, then, belong to the sphere of prophecy accomplished ? Or, to reduce the controversy to a still narrower issue, have the visions of the seals and trumpets and vials been fulfilled ? No one will dispute the fairness of this mode of stating the question, and the fairest possible method of dealing with it will be to set forth some one of the leading visions, and then quote fully and *verbatim* what the historical interpreters put forward as the meaning of it.

The opening of the sixth seal is thus recorded by St. John: " And I beheld when he had opened the sixth seal, and, lo, there was a great earthquake ; and the sun became black as sackcloth of hair, and the moon became as blood ; and the stars of heaven fell unto the earth, even as a fig-tree casteth her untimely figs, when she is shaken of a mighty wind. And the heaven departed as a scroll when it is rolled together; and every mountain and island were moved out of their places. And the kings of the earth, and the great men, and the rich men, and the chief captains, and the mighty men, and every bondman, and every freeman, hid themselves in the dens and in the rocks of the mountains ; and said to the mountains and the rocks, Fall on us, and hide us from the face of Him that sitteth on the throne, and from the wrath of the Lamb ; for the great day of His wrath is come, and who shall be able to stand ? "*

The following is Mr. Elliott's commentary upon the vision :—

"When we consider," he declares, "the terrors of these Christ-blaspheming kings of the Roman earth, thus routed with their partisans before the Christian host, and miserably flying and perishing, there was surely that in the event which, according to the usual construction of such Scripture figures, might well be deemed to answer to the symbols

---

* Rev. vi. 12-17.

of the prefigurative vision before us : in which
vision kings and generals, freemen and slaves,
appeared flying to and seeking the caves of the
rocks to hide them : to hide them from the face
of Him that sat on the throne of power, even from
the wrath of the Lamb.

" Thus under the first shocks of this great earthquake had the Roman earth been agitated, and the
enemies of the Christians destroyed or driven into
flight and consternation. Thus, in the political
heavens, had the sun of pagan supremacy been
darkened, the moon become eclipsed and blood-
red, and of the stars not a few been shaken violently
to the ground. But the prophecy had not as yet
received its entire fulfilment. The stars of the pagan
heaven had not all fallen, nor had the heaven itself
been altogether rolled up like a scroll and vanished
away. On Constantine's first triumph, and after the
first terrors of the opposing emperors and their
hosts, though their imperial edict gave to Christianity
its full rights and freedom, yet it allowed to the
heathen worship a free toleration also. But very
soon there followed measures of marked preference
in the imperial appointments to the Christians and
their faith. And at length, as Constantine advanced
in life, in spite of the indignation and resentment of
the pagans, he issued edicts for the suppression of
their sacrifices, the destruction of their temples, and

the toleration of no other form of public worship but the Christian. His successors on the throne followed up the same object by attaching penalties of the severest character to the public profession of paganism. And the result was that, before the century had ended, its stars had all fallen to the ground, its very heaven, or political and religious system, vanished, and on the earth the old pagan institutions, laws, rites, and worship been all but annihilated." *

"A more notable instance of inadequate interpretation cannot be imagined." † What wonder if men

---

* *Horæ Apoc.*, vol. i., pp. 219, 220.

† "Another such landmark is found, I believe, in the interpretation of the *sixth seal :* if it be not indeed already laid down in what has just been said. We all know what that imagery means in the rest of Scripture. Any system which requires it to belong to another period than the close approach of the great day of the Lord, stands thereby self-condemned. I may illustrate this by reference to Mr. Elliott's continuous historical system, which requires that it should mean the downfall of paganism under Constantine. A more notable instance of inadequate interpretation cannot be imagined.

"Closely connected with this last is another fixed point in interpretation. As the seven seals, so the seven trumpets and the seven vials run on to the time close upon the end. At the termination of each series, the note is unmistakably given that such is the case. Of the seals we have already spoken. As to the trumpets, it may suffice to refer to ch. x. 7 ; xi. 18 ; as to the vials, to their very designation τὰς ἐσχάτας, and to the γέγονεν of ch. xvi. 17. Any system which does not recognise this common ending of the three, seems to me to stand thereby scoff at the awful warnings of coming wrath, when they are told that THE GREAT DAY OF HIS WRATH * is past, and that it amounted to nothing more than the rout of the pagan armies before the hosts of Constantine,—an event which has been paralleled a thousand times in the history of the world ? †

For, let the point at issue be clearly kept in view. If the reign of Constantine or some other era in the history of Christendom were appealed to as affording an intermediate fulfilment of the vision, it might pass as a feeble but harmless exposition ; but these expositors daringly assert that the prophecy has no other scope or meaning.‡   They are bound to prove that the vision of the sixth seal has been *fulfilled ;* else it is obvious that all which follows it claims fulfilment likewise. If, therefore, their system failed at this point alone, its failure

---

convicted of error."—ALFORD, *Gr. Test.*, IV., Part II., ch. viii., §§ 5, 21, 22.

* ἡ ἡμέρα ἡ μεγάλη τῆς ὀργῆς αὐτοῦ (Rev. vi. 17).

† If such statements were put forward in wantonness, and not in folly, they would suggest a reference to the solemn words, " If any man shall *take away* from the words of the book of this prophecy——" (Rev. xxii. 19).

‡ When the historical interpreters approach the Second Advent, they lose the courage of their opinions, and earnestly contend for literalness, though if their scheme be genuine, the predicted return of Christ may surely have its fulfilment in the present revival of religion and the concurrent spread of Christianity.

would be absolute and complete; but in fact the instance quoted is no more than a fair example of the manner in which they fritter away the meaning of the words they profess to explain.

We are now, they tell us, in the era of the Vials. At this very hour the wrath of God is being poured out upon the earth.* Surely men may well exclaim, —comparing the present with the past, and judging this age to be more favoured, more desirable to live in than any age which has preceded it,—Is this all the wrath of God amounts to! The vials are the seven last plagues, "for in them *is filled up the wrath of God*," and we are told that the sixth is even at this moment being fulfilled in the disruption of the Turkish Empire! Can any man be so lost in the dreamland of his own lucubrations as to imagine that the collapse of the Turkish power is a Divine judgment on an unrepentant world! † Such it may

---

* "And I saw another sign in heaven, great and marvellous, seven angels having the seven last plagues, for in them is filled up the wrath of God. . . . And the seven angels came out of the temple, having the seven plagues. . . . And one of the four beasts gave unto the seven angels seven golden vials, full of the wrath of God, who liveth for ever and ever. . . . And I heard a great voice out of the temple saying to the seven angels, Go your ways, and pour out the vials of the wrath of God upon the earth " (Rev. xv. 1, 6, 7 ; xvi. 1).

† The Austrian *Pester Lloyd* of 21st Nov., 1879, in commenting on the British line of policy with regard to Turkish affairs,

appear to be to the clique of Pachas, who, ghoul-like, fatten on the misery around them ; but untold millions would hail it as a blessing to suffering humanity, and ask with wonder, If this be a crowning token of the wrath of God, how are simple souls to distinguish between the proofs of His favour and of His direst anger !

If the event were cited as a *primary* fulfilment, within this day of grace, of a prophecy which strictly belongs to the coming day of wrath, it would merit respectful attention ; but to appeal to the dismemberment of Turkey as the full realization of the vision, is the merest trifling with the solemn language of Scripture, and an outrage on common sense.

But there are principles involved in this system of interpretation far deeper and more momentous than any which appear upon the surface. It is in direct antagonism with the great foundation truth of Christianity.

St. Luke narrates * how, after the temptation, the Lord "returned in the power of the Spirit into Galilee," and entering the synagogue of Nazareth on

---

charged Lord Beaconsfield's government with "confounding Mohammedanism with the Turks, the latter having been always regarded as the scum of Mohammedanism by all Mohammedan nations who were conscious of their own strength." Prophetic students appear to be thoroughly possessed by this error.

* Luke iv. 19, 20.

the Sabbath day, as His custom was, He stood up to read. There was handed Him the book of Isaiah's prophecy, and all eyes being fastened on Him, He opened it and read these words, "The Spirit of the Lord is upon me, because He hath anointed me to preach the gospel to the poor; He hath sent me to heal the broken-hearted, to preach deliverance to the captives, and the recovering of sight to the blind, to set at liberty them that are bruised, to preach the acceptable year of the Lord."

"And the day of vengeance of our God" are the words which followed, without a break, upon the open page before Him; but, the record adds, "He closed the book, and He gave it again to the minister, and sat down." In an age to come, when the prophecy shall have its ultimate fulfilment, the day of vengeance shall mingle with blessing to His people. * But the burden of His ministry on earth was only peace. † And it is the burden of the gospel still. God's attitude toward men is grace. "GRACE REIGNS." It is not that there is grace for the penitent or the elect, but that grace is the principle on which Christ now sits upon the throne of God. "Upon His head are many crowns, but His pierced hand now holds the only sceptre," for the Father has

---

* Compare Isa. lxiii. 4 : "For the day of vengeance is in mine heart, and the year of my redeemed is come."

† "He came and preached peace" (Eph. ii. 17).

given Him the kingdom; all power is His in heaven and on earth. "The Father judgeth no man, but hath committed all judgment to the Son;"* but His mission to earth was not to judge, but only to save. And He who is thus the only Judge is now exalted to be a Saviour, and the throne on which He sits is a throne of grace. Grace is reigning, through righteousness, unto eternal life.† "The light of this glorious gospel now shines unhindered upon earth. Blind eyes may shut it out, but they cannot quench or lessen it. Impenitent hearts may heap up wrath against the day of wrath, but they cannot darken this day of mercy or mar the glory of the reign of grace."‡

It will be in "the day of wrath" that the "seven last plagues," wherein is "filled up the wrath of God," shall run their course; and it is merely trifling with solemn and awful truths to talk of their being now

---

* John v. 22. Comp iii. 17, and xii. 47.

† Rom. v. 21.

‡ *The Gospel and its Ministry*, p. 136. True it is that the great principles of God's moral government of the world remain unchanged, and sin is thus ever working out its own punishment. But this must not be confounded with immediate Divine action in judgment. "The Lord knoweth how to reserve the unjust *to the day of judgment*, to be punished" (2 Peter ii. 9). Or, according to Rom. ii. 5, "After thy hardness and impenitent heart treasurest up unto thyself wrath against *the day of wrath.*"

fulfilled. Whatever intermediate fulfilment the vision may be now receiving, the full and final realization of it belongs to a future time.

And these pages are not designed to deal with the primary and historical fulfilment of the prophecies, or, as Lord Bacon terms it, their " springing and germinant accomplishment throughout many ages." My subject is exclusively the absolute and final fulfilment of the visions in that " one age " to which, in their " height and fulness," they belong.

The Scripture itself affords many striking instances of such intermediate or primary fulfilment ; and in these the main outlines of the prophecy are realized, but not the details.   The prediction of Elijah's advent is an instance.*   In the plainest terms the Lord declared the Baptist's ministry to be within the scope of that prophecy.   In terms as clear He announced that it would be *fulfilled* in days to come, by the reappearance upon earth of the greatest of the prophets.†   St. Peter's words at Pentecost afford another illustration.   Joel's prophecy shall yet be realized to the letter, but yet the baptism of the Holy Ghost was referred to it by the inspired Apostle.‡

To speak of the *fulfilment* of these prophecies as

---

* " Behold, I will send you Elijah the prophet, before the coming of the great and dreadful day of the Lord " (Mal. iv. 5).

† Matt. xi. 14, and xvii. 11, 12.

‡ Joel ii. 28-32 ; Acts ii. 16-21.

already past, is to use language at once unscriptural and false. Far more unwarrantable still is the assertion of finality, so confidently made, of the prophecies relating to the apostasy. There is not a single prophecy, of which the *fulfilment* is recorded in Scripture, that was not realized with absolute accuracy, and in every detail; and it is wholly unjustifiable to assume that a new system of fulfilment was inaugurated after the sacred canon closed.

Two thousand years ago who would have ventured to believe that the prophecies of Messiah would receive a literal accomplishment! " Behold, a virgin shall conceive, and bear a son."* "Behold, thy King cometh unto thee: He is just, and having salvation; lowly, and riding upon an ass, and upon a colt the foal of an ass."† " They weighed for my price thirty pieces of silver;" "And I took the thirty pieces of silver and cast them to the potter in the house of the Lord."‡ "They part my garments among them, and cast lots upon my vesture."§ " They pierced my hands and my feet." ‖ " They gave me vinegar to drink."¶ " He was cut off out of the land of the living; for the transgression of my people was He stricken."**

---

* Isa. vii. 14.   † Zech. ix. 9.

‡ Zech. xi. 12, 13.   Comp. Matt. xxvii. 5, 7.

§ Psalm xxii. 18.   Comp. John xix. 23, 24.

‖ Psalm xxii. 16.   ¶ Psalm lxix. 21.   ** Isa. liii. 8.

To the prophets themselves, even, the meaning of such words was a mystery.* For the most part, doubtless, men regarded them as no more than poetry or legend. And yet these prophecies of the advent and death of Christ received their fulfilment in every jot and tittle of them. Literalness of fulfilment may therefore be accepted as an axiom to guide us in the study of prophecy.

---

* 1 Peter i. 10-12.

12

FULNESS OF THE GENTILES

THE main stream of prophecy runs in the channel of Hebrew history. This indeed is true of all revelation. Eleven chapters of the Bible suffice to cover the two thousand years before the call of Abraham, and the rest of the old Testament relates to the Abrahamic race. If for a while the light of revelation rested on Babylon or Susa, it was because Jerusalem was desolate, and Judah was in exile. For a time the Gentile has now gained the foremost place in blessing upon earth; but this is entirely anomalous, and the normal order of God's dealings with men is again to be restored. " Blindness in part is happened to Israel *until* the fulness of the Gentiles be come in. And so all Israel shall be saved, as it is written."*

The Scriptures teem with promises and prophecies

---

* Rom. xi. 25, 26. The coming in of the fulness of the Gentiles must not be confounded with the fulfilment of the times of the Gentiles (Luke xxi. 24). The one refers to spiritual blessing, the other to earthly power. Jerusalem is not to be the capital of a free nation, independent of Gentile power, until the true Son of David comes to claim the sceptre.

in favour of that nation, not a tithe of which have yet been realized. And while the impassioned poetry in which so many of the old prophecies are couched is made a pretext for treating them as hyperbolical descriptions of the blessings of the Gospel, no such plea can be urged respecting the Epistle to the Romans. Writing to Gentiles, the Apostle of the Gentiles there reasons the matter out in presence of the facts of the Gentile dispensation. The natural branches of the race of Israel have been broken off from the olive tree of earthly privilege and blessing, and, "contrary to nature," the wild olive branches of Gentile blood have been substituted for them. But in spite of the warning of the Apostle, we Gentiles have become " wise in our own conceits," forgetting that the olive tree whose " root and fatness " we partake of, is essentially Hebrew, for " the gifts and calling of God are without repentance."

The minds of most men are in bondage to the commonplace facts of their experience. The prophecies of a restored Israel seem to many as incredible as predictions of the present triumphs of electricity and steam would have appeared to our ancestors a century ago.[10] While affecting independence in judging thus, the mind is only giving proof of its own impotence or ignorance. Moreover, the position which the Jews have held for eighteen centuries is a phenomenon which itself disposes

[10] See Appendix 4, p. 306 note 10.

of every seeming presumption against the fulfilment of these prophecies.

It is not a question of how a false religion like that of Mahomet can maintain an unbroken front in presence of a true faith; the problem is very different. Not only in a former age, but in the early days of the present dispensation, the Jews enjoyed a preference in blessing, which practically amounted almost to a monopoly of Divine favour. In its infancy the Christian Church was essentially Jewish. The Jews within its pale were reckoned by thousands, the Gentiles by tens. And yet that same people afterwards became, and for eighteen centuries have continued to be, more dead to the influence of the Gospel than any other class of people upon earth. How can "this mystery," as the Apostle terms it, be accounted for, save as Scripture explains it, namely, that the era of special grace to Israel closed with the period historically within the Acts of the Apostles, and that since that crisis of their history "blindness in part is happened" to them?

But this very word, the truth of which is so clearly proved by public facts, goes on to declare that this judicial hardening is to continue only "*until* the fulness of the Gentiles be come in;" and the inspired Apostle adds, "And so all Israel shall be saved; as it is written, There shall come out of Sion the Deliverer, and shall turn away ungodliness from Jacob; for this is My covenant unto them."*

But, it may with reason be demanded, does not this imply merely that Israel shall be brought within the blessings of the Gospel, not that the Jews shall be blessed on a principle which is entirely inconsistent with the Gospel? Christianity, as a system, assumes the fact that in a former age the Jews enjoyed a peculiar place in blessing: "Christ was *a minister of the circumcision* for the truth of God, to confirm the promises made unto the fathers, and that the Gentiles might glorify God for His mercy."† But the Jews have lost their vantage-ground through sin, and they now stand upon the common level of ruined humanity. The Cross has broken down " the middle wall" which separated them from Gentiles. It has levelled all distinctions. As to guilt "there is no difference, for *all* have sinned ; " as to mercy "there is no difference, for the same Lord over all is rich unto *all* that call on Him." How then, if there be no difference, can God give blessing on a principle which implies that there *is* a difference? In a word, the fulfilment of the promises to Judah is absolutely inconsistent with the distinctive truths of the present dispensation.

---

* Rom. xi. 25, 26. Not every Israelite, but Israel as a nation (Alford, *Gr. Test., in loco*).

† Rom. xv. 8, 9.

This question is one of immense importance, and claims the most earnest consideration. Nor is it enough to urge that the eleventh chapter of Romans itself supposes that in this age the Gentile has an advantage, though not a priority, and, therefore, Israel may enjoy the like privilege hereafter. It is part of the same revelation, that although grace stoops to the Gentile just where he is, it does not confirm him in his position *as a Gentile*, but lifts him out of it and *denationalizes* him ; for in the Church of this dispensation "there is neither Jew nor Gentile."* Judah's promises, on the contrary, imply that blessing will reach the Jew as a Jew, not only recognizing his national position, but confirming him therein.

The conclusion, therefore, is inevitable, that before God can act thus, the special proclamation of grace in the present dispensation must have ceased, and a new principle of dealing with mankind must have been inaugurated.

But here the difficulties only seem to multiply and grow. For, it may be asked, does not the dispensation run its course until the return of Christ to earth ? How then can Jews be found at His coming in a place of blessing *nationally*, akin to that

---

* Gal. iii. 28. Contrast these with the Lord's words in John iv. 22, " Salvation is of the Jews."

which they held in a bygone age? All will admit that Scripture seems to teach that such will be the case.* The question still remains whether this be really intended. Does Scripture speak of any crisis in relation to the earth, to intervene before "the day when the Son of man shall be revealed"?

No one who diligently seeks the answer to this inquiry can fail to be impressed by the fact that at first sight some confusion seems to mark the statements of Scripture with respect to it. Certain passages testify that Christ will return to earth, and stand once more on that same Olivet on which His feet last rested ere He ascended to His Father;† and others tell us as plainly that He will come, not to earth, but to the air above us, and call His people up to meet Him and be with Him.‡ These Scriptures again most clearly prove that it is His believing people who shall be " caught up,"§ leaving the world to run its course to its destined doom ; while other Scriptures as unequivocally teach that it is not His people but the wicked who are to be weeded out, leaving the righteous " to shine forth in the kingdom

---

* In proof of this, appeal may be made to these very prophecies of Daniel ; and later prophecies testify to it still more plainly, notably the book of Zechariah.

† Zech. xiv. 4 ; Acts i. 11, 12.

‡ 1 Thess. iv. 16, 17.

§ *Ibid.;* 1 Cor. xv. 51, 52.

of their Father."* And the confusion apparently increases when we notice that Holy Writ seems sometimes to represent the righteous who are to be thus blessed as Jews, sometimes as Christians of a dispensation in which the Jew is cast off by God.

These difficulties admit of only one solution, a solution as satisfactory as it is simple ; namely, that what we term the second advent of Christ is not a single event, but includes several distinct manifestations. At the first of these He will call up to Himself the righteous dead, together with His own people then living upon earth. With this event this special "day of grace" will cease, and God will again revert to "the covenants" and "the promises," and that people to whom the covenants and promises belong † will once more become the centre of Divine action toward mankind.

Everything that God has promised is within the range of the believer's hope ; ‡ but this is its near horizon. All things wait on its accomplishment. Before the return of Christ to earth, many a page of prophecy has yet to be fulfilled, but not a line of Scripture bars the realization of this the Church's

---

* Matt. xiii. 40-43.   † Rom. ix. 4.

‡ "We, according to His promise, look for new heavens and a new earth" (2 Peter iii. 13). Long ages of time and events innumerable must intervene before the realization of this hope, and yet the believer is looking for it.

special hope of His coming to take His people to Himself. Here, then, is the great crisis which will put a term to the reign of grace, and usher in the destined woes of earth's fiercest trial—"the days of vengeance, that all things which are written may be fulfilled." *

To object that a truth of this magnitude would have been stated with more dogmatic clearness is to forget the distinction between doctrinal teaching and prophetic utterance. The truth of the second advent belongs to prophecy, and the statements of Scripture respecting it are marked by precisely the same characteristics as marked the Old Testament prophecies of Messiah.†

"The sufferings of Christ and the glories which should follow" were foretold in such a way that a superficial reader of the old Scriptures would have failed to discover that there were to be two advents of Messiah. And even the careful student, if unversed in the general scheme of prophecy, might have supposed that the two advents, though morally distinct, should be intimately connected in time. So is it with the future. Some regard the second advent as a single event; by others its true character is recognised, but they fail to mark the

---

* Luke xxi. 22.

† For an admirable treatise on these characteristics of prophecy, *see* Hengstenberg's *Christology*, Kregel Publications.

interval which must separate its first from its final stage. An intelligent apprehension of the truth respecting it is essential to the right understanding of unfulfilled prophecy.

But having thus clearly fixed these principal landmarks to guide us in the study, we cannot too strongly deprecate the attempt to fill up the interval with greater precision than Scripture warrants. There are definite events to be fulfilled, but no one may dogmatize respecting the time or manner of their fulfilment. No Christian who estimates aright the appalling weight of suffering and sin which each day that passes adds to the awful sum of this world's sorrow and guilt, can fail to long that the end may indeed be near ; but let him not forget the great principle that "the longsuffering of our Lord is salvation," * nor yet the language of the Psalm, " A thousand years in Thy sight are but as yesterday when it is past, and as a watch in the night." † There is much in Scripture which seems to justify the hope that the consummation will not be long delayed ; but, on the other hand, there is not a little to suggest the thought that before these final scenes shall be enacted, civilization will have returned to its old home in the east, and, perchance, a restored Babylon shall have become

---

* 2 Peter iii. 15.   † Psalm xc. 4.

the centre of human progress and of apostate religion.*

To maintain that long ages have yet to run their course would be as unwarrantable as are the predictions so confidently made that all things shall be fulfilled within the current century. It is only in so far as prophecy is within the seventy weeks of Daniel that it comes within the range of chronology at all, and Daniel's vision primarily relates to Judah and Jerusalem.†

---

* Isa. xiii. appears to connect the final fall of Babylon with the great day that is coming (*comp.* vers. 1, 9, 10, 19); and in Jer. l. the same event is connected with the future restoration and union of the two houses of Israel (ver. 20). I make the suggestion, however, merely as a *caveat* against the idea that we have certainly reached the last days of the dispensation. If the history of Christendom should run on for another thousand years, the delay would not discredit the truth of a single statement in Holy Writ.

† No one of Daniel's visions, indeed, has a wider scope. Isaiah, Jeremiah, and Ezekiel treat of Israel (or the ten tribes); but Daniel deals only with Judah.

13

SECOND SERMON ON THE MOUNT

THE connecting link between the past and the future, between the fulfilled and the unfulfilled in prophecy, will be found in the Gospel of St. Matthew.

The chief Messianic promises are grouped in two great classes, connected respectively with the names of David and of Abraham, and the New Testament opens with the record of the birth and ministry of Messiah as " the Son of David, the son of Abraham ; " * for in one aspect of His work He was "a minister of the circumcision for the truth of God, to confirm the promises made unto the fathers." † The question of the Magi, "Where is He that is born king of the Jews?" aroused a hope which was part of the national politics of Judah ; and even the base Idumean who then usurped the throne was sensible of its significance : "Herod was troubled, and all Jerusalem with him.‡

---

* Matt. i. 1.   † Rom. xv. 8.

‡ Matt. ii. 3. It must not be imagined that it was any *religious* emotion which disturbed the king. The announce-

And when the proclamation afterwards was made, first by John the Baptist, and finally by the Lord and His apostles, "The kingdom of heaven is at hand," the Jews knew well its import. It was not "the Gospel," as we understand it now, but the announcement of the near fulfilment of Daniel's prophecy.* And the testimony had a twofold accompaniment. "The Sermon on the Mount" is recorded as embodying the great truths and principles which were associated with the Kingdom Gospel; and the attendant miracles gave proof that all was Divine. And in the earlier stages of the ministry of Christ, His miracles were not reserved for those whose faith responded to His words; the only qualification for the benefit was that the recipient should belong to the favoured race. "Go not into the way of the Gentiles, and into any city of the Samaritans enter ye not: but go rather to the lost sheep of the house of Israel. And as ye go, preach, saying, The kingdom of heaven is at

---

ment of the Magi was to him what the news of the birth of an heir is to an heir-presumptive. The Magi asked, "Where is He that is born *King of the Jews?*" Herod's inquiry, therefore, to the Sanhedrim was, "Where should *Messiah* be born?" and on being referred to the prophecy which so plainly designated Bethlehem, he determined to destroy every infant child in that city and district. Herod and the Sanhedrim had not learned to spiritualize the prophecies.

* *Cf.* Pusey, *Daniel*, p. 84.

hand. Heal the sick, cleanse the lepers, raise the dead, cast out devils: freely ye have received, freely give." * Such was the commission under which the twelve went forth through that little land, to every corner of which their Master's fame had gone before them.†

But the verdict of the nation, through its accredited and responsible leaders, was a rejection of His Messianic claims.‡ The acts and words of Christ recorded in the twelfth chapter of Matthew were an open and deliberate condemnation and defiance of the Pharisees, and their answer was to meet in solemn council and decree His death.§

---

* Matt. x. 5-8. The chapter is prophetic, in keeping with the character of the book, and reaches on to the testimony of the latter days (*see ex. gr.*, ver. 23).

† Matt. iv. 24, 25.

‡ In our own time the Jews have had the temerity to publish a translation of the *Mishna*, and the reader who will peruse its treatises can judge with what contempt and loathing the Lord must have regarded the religion of those miserable men. The treatise *Sabbath* will afford an invaluable commentary on the twelfth of Matthew. The *Mishna* is a compilation of the oral traditions of the Rabbins, made in the second century, A.D., to prevent their being lost by the dispersion—the very traditions, many of them, which prevailed when the Lord was on earth, and which He so unsparingly condemned as undermining the Scriptures, for then as now the Jews regarded them as possessing a Divine sanction. (*Cf.* Lindo's *Jewish Cal.*, Introd. ; Milman's *Hist. Jews*, Book XVIII.)

§ Matt. xii. 1-14.

From that hour His ministry entered upon a new phase. The miracles continued, for He could not meet with suffering and refuse to relieve it; but those whom thus He blessed were charged "that they should not make Him known."* The Gospel of the Kingdom ceased; His teaching became veiled in parables,† and the disciples were forbidden any longer to testify to His Messiahship.‡

The thirteenth chapter is prophetic of the state of things which was to intervene between the time of His rejection and His return in glory to claim the place which in His humiliation was denied Him. Instead of the proclamation of the Kingdom, He taught them "the *mysteries* of the Kingdom."§ His mission changed its character, and instead of a King come to reign, He described Himself as a

---

* Matt. xii. 16.

† *Ibid.* xiii. 3, 13. "From the expression ἤρξατο in Mark, compared with the question of the disciples in ver. 10,—and with ver. 34,—it appears that this was the *first beginning of our Lord's teaching by parables*, expressly so delivered, and properly so called. And the natural sequence of things here agrees with and confirms Matthew's arrangement against those who would place (as Ebrard) all this chapter before the Sermon on the Mount. He there spoke *without parables*, or mainly so; and continued to do so till the rejection and misunderstanding of His teaching led to His judicially adopting the course here indicated, χωρὶς παρ. οὐδὲν ἐλάλει αὐτοῖς."— ALFORD, *Gr. Test.*, Matt. xiii. 3.

‡ *Ibid.* xvi. 20.   § *Ibid.* xiii. 11.

Sower sowing seed. Of the parables which follow, the first three, spoken to the multitude, described the outward results of the testimony in the world ; the last three, addressed to the disciples,* speak of the hidden realities revealed to spiritual minds.

But these very parables, while they taught the disciples in the plainest terms that everything was postponed which the prophets had led them to look for in connection with the Kingdom, taught them no less clearly that the day would surely come when all should be fulfilled ; when evil should be rooted out, and the Kingdom established in righteousness and peace.† They thus learned that there was to be an " age " of which prophecy took no account, and another " Advent " at its close ; and "the second Sermon on the Mount " was the Lord's reply to the inquiry, " What shall be the sign of Thy coming, and of the end of the age ? "‡

------

* As were also the interpretations of the Parables of the Sower and of the Tares.

† Matt. xiii. 41-43.

‡ Matt. xxiv. 3. "As He sat upon the Mount of Olives, the disciples came unto Him." Compare Matt. v. 1 : "He went up into a mountain, and when He was set, His disciples came unto Him." The Sermon on the Mount unfolded the principles on which the Kingdom would be set up. The King having been rejected by the nation, the second Sermon on the Mount unfolded the events which must precede His return

The twenty-fourth chapter of Matthew has been well described as "the anchor of apocalyptic interpretation," and "the touchstone of apocalyptic systems."* The fifteenth verse specifies an event and fixes an epoch, by which we are enabled to connect the words of the Lord with the visions of St. John, and both with the prophecies of Daniel. The entire passage is obviously prophetic, and its fulfilment clearly pertains to the time of the end. The fullest and most definite application of the words must therefore be to those who are to witness their accomplishment. To them it is that the warning is specially addressed, against being deceived through a false hope of the *immediate* return of Christ. †

A series of terrible events are yet to come ; but "these are the *beginning* of sorrows ;" "the end is not yet." How long these "sorrows" shall continue is not revealed. The first sure sign that the end is near will be the advent of the fiercest trial that the redeemed on earth have ever known.

---

* Alford, *Gr. Test.*, vol. iv., Pt. II. *Proleg. Rev.*

† Matt. xxiv. 4, 6. That is, the *final* stage of the advent ; not His coming as foretold in 1 Thess. iv. and elsewhere, which has no signs preceding. See p. 154, *ante*.

To refer verse 5 to the times of Barcochab involves a glaring anachronism. The *primary* reference in vers. 15-20, and, therefore, of the earlier portion of the prophecy, was to the period ending with the destruction of Jerusalem.

The fulfilment of Daniel's vision of the defilement of the Holy Place is to be the signal for immediate flight; "for then shall be *the great* tribulation," * unparalleled even in Judah's history. But, as already noticed, this last great persecution belongs to the latter half of Daniel's seventieth week,† and therefore it affords a landmark by which we can determine the character and fix the order of the chief events which mark the closing scenes foretold in prophecy.

With the clew thus obtained from the Gospel of St. Matthew, we can turn with confidence to study the Apocalyptic visions of St. John. But first it must be clearly recognised that in the twenty-fourth of Matthew, as in the book of Daniel, Jerusalem is the centre of the scene to which the prophecy relates ; and this of necessity implies that the Jews shall have been restored to Palestine before the time of its fulfilment. ‡

Objections based on the supposed improbability of such an event are sufficiently answered by marking the connection between prophecy and miracle. The history of the Abrahamic race, to which prophecy is so closely related, is little else than a record of

---

* Vers. 15-21. Comp. Dan. xii. 1. *See* p. 84, *ante.*

† *See* p. 84, *ante.*

‡ The question of their restoration to a place of blessing spiritually has already been discussed. See pp. 149-152, *ante.*

miraculous interpositions. " Their passage out of
Egypt was miraculous. Their entrance into the
promised land was miraculous. Their prosperous
and their adverse fortunes in that land, their servitudes and their deliverances, their conquests and
their captivities, were all miraculous. The entire
history from the call of Abraham to the building
of the sacred temple was a series of miracles. It
is so much the object of the sacred historians to
describe these that little else is recorded. . . .
There are no historians in the sacred volume of
the period in which miraculous intervention was
withdrawn. After the declaration by the mouth
of Malachi that a messenger should be sent to
prepare the way, the next event recorded by any
inspired writer is the birth of that messenger. But
of the interval of 400 years between the promise
and the completion no account is given." *

The seventy years from Messiah's birth to the
dispersion of the nation were fruitful in miracle and
prophetic fulfilment. But the national existence of
Israel is as it were the stage on which alone the
drama of prophecy can, in its fulness, be displayed ;
and from the Apostolic age to the present hour,
not a single public event can be appealed to as
affording indisputable proof of *immediate* Divine

---

* Clinton, *Fasti H.*, vol. i., p. 243.

intervention upon earth.* A silent heaven is a
leading characteristic of the dispensation in which
our lot is cast. But Israel's history has yet to be
completed ; and when that nation comes again upon
the scene, the element of miraculous interpositions
will mark once more the course of events on earth.

On the other hand, the analogy of the past would
lead us to expect a merging of the one dispensation
in the other, rather than an abrupt transition ; and
the question is one of peculiar interest on general
grounds, whether passing events are not tending
towards this very consummation, the restoration of
the Jews to Palestine.

The decline of the Moslem power is one of the
most patent of public facts ; and if the dismemberment of the Turkish Empire be still delayed, it is due
entirely to the jealousies of European nations, whose
rival interests seem to render an amicable distribution
of its territories impossible. But the crisis cannot be
deferred indefinitely ; and when it arrives, the question
of greatest moment, next to the fate of Constantinople, will be, What is to become of Palestine ? Its
annexation by any one European state is in the
highest degree improbable. The interests of several

---

* There is, doubtless, what may be called the private miracle
of individual conversion, and the believer has transcendental
proof not only of the existence of God, but of His presence
and power with men (*see* pp. 10-14, *ante*).

of the first-rate Powers forbid it. The way will thus
be kept open to the Jews, whenever their inclinations
or their destinies lead them back to the land of their
fathers.

Not only would no hostile influence hinder their
return, but the probabilities of the case (and it is
with *probabilities*[11] that we are here concerned) are in
favour of the colonization of Palestine by that people
to whom historically it belongs. There is some
reason to believe that a movement of this kind has
already begun ; and if, whether by the Levant becoming a highway to India, or from some other
cause, any measure of prosperity should return to
those shores that were once the commercial centre
of the world, the Jews would migrate thither in
thousands from every land.

True it is that to colonize a country is one thing,
while to create a nation is another. But the testimony of Scripture is explicit that Judah's national
independence [12] is not to be regained by diplomacy or
the sword. Jerusalem is to remain under Gentile
supremacy until the day when Daniel's visions shall
be realized. In the language of Scripture, " Jerusalem shall be trodden down of the Gentiles until
the times of the Gentiles be fulfilled." * But long ere

---

* Luke xxi. 24. That is, till the end of the period during
which earthly sovereignty, entrusted to Nebuchadnezzar twenty-
five centuries ago, is to remain with the Gentiles (see p. 32, *ante*)

[11] See Appendix 4, p. 306 #11. [12] See Appendix 4, p. 307 #12.

then the Cross must supplant the Crescent in Judea, else it is incredible that the Mosque of Omar should give place to the Jewish Temple on the Hill of Zion.

If the operation of causes such as those above indicated, conjointly with the decay of the Moslem power, should lead to the formation of a protected Jewish state in Palestine, possibly with a military occupation of Jerusalem by or on behalf of some European Power or Powers, nothing more need be supposed than a religious revival among the Jews, to prepare the way for the fulfilment of the prophecies. †

"God has not cast away His people;" and when the present dispensation closes, and the great purpose has been satisfied for which it was ordained, the dropped threads of prophecy and promise will again be taken up, and the dispensation historically broken off in the Acts of the Apostles, when Jerusalem was the appointed centre for God's people on earth, ‡ will

---

† The following extract from the *Jewish Chronicle* of 9th Nov., 1849, is quoted in Mr. Newton's *Ten Kingdoms* (2nd Ed., p. 401) :—" The European Powers will not need to put themselves to the trouble of restoring the Jews individually or collectively. Let them but confer upon Palestine a constitution like that of the United States . . . and the Jews will restore *themselves*. They would then go cheerfully and willingly, and would there piously bide their time for a heaven-inspired Messiah, who is to restore Mosaism to its original splendour."

‡ Gentiles were then admitted within the pale, not on an equality, but in some sense as proselytes had been received

be resumed. Judah shall again become a nation, Jerusalem shall be restored, and that temple shall be built in which the "abomination of desolation" is to stand. †

---

within the nation. The Church was essentially Jewish. The temple was their place of resort (Acts ii. 46 ; iii. 1, v. 42). Their testimony was in the line of the old prophecies to the nation (*ibid.* iii. 19-26, see p. 78, *ante*), and even when scattered by persecution, the apostles remained in the metropolis, and those who were driven abroad evangelized only among the Jews (*ibid.* viii. 1, 4, and xi. 19). Peter refused to go among Gentiles save after a special revelation to him (*ibid.* x.), and he was put on his defence before the Church for going at all (*ibid.* xi. 2-18. Comp. chap. xv.)

† Scattered among the people will be a "remnant," who will "keep the commandments of God, and have the testimony of Jesus Christ" (Rev. xii. 17) ; Jews, and yet Christians ; Jews, but believers in the Messiah, whom the *nation* will continue to reject until the time of His appearing. It must be obvious to the thoughtful mind that such prophecies as the twenty-fourth of Matthew imply that there will be a believing people to be comforted and guided by them at the time and in the scene of their fulfilment.

14

THE PATMOS VISIONS

NARROWNESS of interpretation is the bane of apocalyptic study. "The words of this prophecy," "Things which must shortly come to pass:" such is the Divine description of the Book of the Revelation and of its contents. No one, therefore, is justified in denying to any portion of it a future application. The Book in its entirety is prophetic. Even the seven epistles, though they were undoubtedly addressed to Churches then existing, and though their intermediate reference to the history of Christendom is also clear, may well have a special voice in days to come for those who are to enter the fierce trials that shall precede the end.*

---

* The Bible is not intended for the present dispensation only, but for the people of God in every age ; and it is incredible that they who are to be so severely tried shall fail to find in it words specially fitted and intended to counsel and comfort them in view of what they are to endure. "This prophecy" is the Divine description of the Apocalypse as a whole (Rev. i. 3). Compare the "must shortly come to pass" of Rev. i. 1 with the "must shortly be done" of xxii. 6. The salutation (i. 4, 5) seems to fix the *dispensational* place of the Book as future. It is not the Father, but Jehovah ; not the Lord Jesus Christ,

In the fourth chapter the throne is set in heaven. Judgment now waits on grace ; but when the day of grace is past, judgment must intervene ere the promises and covenants, with all their rich store of blessings, can be fulfilled. But who can unfold that scroll that lies on the open hand of Him who sits upon the throne ? * No creature in the universe †

---

but " Jesus Christ the faithful witness, the Prince of the kings of the earth ; " and the Book speaks from a time when the Holy Spirit, *as a person*, will again be in heaven, to join in the salutation, which He never does in the Epistles of the New Testament.

Rev. i. 19 is frequently quoted to prove that the Book is divided, and that the latter part only is prophetic. In refutation of this, I appeal to the most candid of apocalyptic commentators, Dean Alford, who thus translates the verse : " Write therefore the things which thou sawest, and what things they signify, and the things which are about to happen after these." He explains " the things which thou sawest " to be " the vision which was but now vouchsafed thee," and the closing words as " the things which shall succeed these, *i.e.*, a future vision " (*Greek Test., in loco*).

In ch. iv. 1, Alford inclines to give to the second μετὰ ταῦτα the general meaning of "hereafter." But the presumption is that the words are used at the end of the verse in the same sense as at the beginning, *i.e.*, " after these things." The words imply that the fulfilment of the subsequent visions should be future, relatively to the fulfilment of the preceding vision, and not relatively merely to the time when the vision was given, which was a matter of course.

* Rev. v. 2.

† *Ibid.* 3. It is not, as in English Version, "no *man*," but οὐδείς. The Revised Version properly reads " no one."

may dare to look on it, and God Himself will not break a single seal of it, for the Father has ceded the prerogative of judgment. The ministry of grace may be shared by all whom grace has blessed, but the Son of man is the only Being in the universe who can take the initiative in judgment ; * and amid the anthems of the heavenly beings round the throne, and the swelling chorus of myriads of myriads of angels, echoed back by the whole creation of God, the Crucified of Calvary, " a Lamb, as it had been slain," takes up the book and prepares to break the seals.†

It is at the fifth seal that the vision crosses the lines of the *chronology* of prophecy.‡ Of the earlier seals, therefore, it is unnecessary to speak in detail. They are evidently descriptive of the events to which the Lord referred in the twenty-fourth chapter of Matthew, as preceding the great final persecution ; —wars and unceasing threats of war, kingdoms in arms rushing on one another to destruction ; and then famine, to be followed again by pestilence, hunger and the sword still claiming their victims,

---

* John v. 22-27. † Rev. v. 5-14.

‡ Because the fifth seal relates to the great persecution of the future, which, as already noticed, is within the seventieth week. The first four seals relate to the events preceding in time the fulfilment of the fifteenth verse of the twenty-fourth of Matthew. Compare the sixth and seventh verses of that chapter with Rev. vi. 1-8.

and others being seized by strange and nameless deaths in the ever-gathering horrors of these cumulative woes.*

According to the twenty-fourth chapter of Matthew, the tribulation is to be followed immediately by the signs and portents which the old prophets have declared will herald " the great and terrible day of the Lord." So in the Apocalypse the martyrs of the tribulation are seen in the fifth seal,† and in the sixth, the advent of the great day of wrath is proclaimed, the precise events being named which the Lord had spoken of on the Mount of Olives, and Joel and Isaiah had foretold long centuries before.‡

---

* Rev. vi. 2-8.   † *Ibid.* 9.

‡ "The day of the Lord cometh. . . . The sun shall be turned into darkness, and the moon into blood, before the great and the terrible day of the Lord come " (Joel ii. 1-31). "The day of the Lord cometh. . . .The sun shall be darkened in his going forth, and the moon shall not cause her light to shine" (Isa. xiii. 9, 10). "Immediately after the tribulation of those days shall the sun be darkened, and the moon shall not give her light, and the stars shall fall from heaven" (Matt. xxiv. 29). "There shall be signs in the sun, and in the moon, and in the stars" (Luke xxi. 25). "The sun became black as sackcloth of hair, and the moon became as blood " (compare Joel ii. 31), " and the stars of heaven fell unto the earth" (Rev. vi. 12, 13).

I entirely agree with the following note of Dean Alford's (*Greek Test.*, Matt. xxiv. 29) :—"Such prophecies are to be understood *literally*, and indeed, without such understanding would lose their truth and significance. The physical signs shall happen as accompaniments and intensifications of the

Like the dull, oppressive calm which precedes the fiercest storms, there is silence in heaven when the last seal is broken,* for the day of vengeance has dawned. The events of the earlier seals were Divine judgments, doubtless, but of a providential character, and such as men can account for by secondary causes. But God has at length declared Himself, and as it has been in the past, so now, the occasion is an outrage committed on His people. The cry of martyrs is come up in remembrance before God,† and it is the signal for the trumpet blasts which herald the outpouring of the long-pent-up wrath.‡

To write a commentary on the Apocalypse within the limits of a chapter would be impossible, and the attempt would involve a departure from the special purpose and subject of these pages. But it is essential to notice and keep in view the character and method of the Apocalyptic visions. The seer, be it remembered, was not privileged to read a single line of what was written " within and on the back side " of the sealed scroll of the fifth chapter ; but as each seal was broken, some prominent characteristic of a portion of its contents was communicated to him in

---

awful state of things which the description typifies." Not of course that the moon will really become blood, any more than that the stars will fall. The words describe *phenomena* which men will witness, and which will strike terror into their hearts.

* Rev. viii. 1. † *Ibid.* 3 ‡ *Ibid.* 6.

a vision. The main series of the visions, therefore, represent events in their chronological sequence. But their course is occasionally interrupted by parenthetical or episodical visions ; sometimes, as between the sixth and seventh seals, reaching on to the time of the end, and more frequently, as between the sixth and seventh trumpets, representing details chronologically within the earlier visions. The first and most important step, therefore, towards a right understanding of the Apocalypse is to distinguish between the serial and the episodical visions of the Book, and the following analysis is offered to promote and assist inquiry upon the subject.*—

Chap. vi.—The visions of the first six seals ; representing events in their chronological order.

[Chap. vii.—Parenthetical ; the first vision relating either to the faithful remnant of the fifth seal, or to an election in view of the judgments of the seventh seal ; the second, reaching on to the final deliverance.]

Chaps. viii., ix.—The opening of the seventh seal. The visions of the first six *trumpets ;* consecutive judgments, in their chronological order.

[Chaps. x.-xi. 13.—*Parenthetical*, containing the hidden mystery of the seven thunders (x. 3, 4) and

---

* The passages containing the parenthetical visions are marked in square brackets.

the testimony of the witnesses (the latter being probably within the era of the fifth seal.)]

Chap. xi. 15-19.—The seventh trumpet ; the third and last woe (comp. viii. 13 ; ix. 12 ; xi. 14), preceding the establishment of the kingdom (comp. x. 7 ; xi. 15).

[Chaps. xii.-xviii.—*Parenthetical*.]

Chap. xiii.—The rise and career of the two great blasphemers and persecutors of the last days.

Chap. xiv.—The remnant of chap. vii. seen in blessedness.

The everlasting Gospel (vers. 6, 7).

The fall of Babylon (ver. 8).

The doom of the worshippers of the Beast (vers. 9-11).

The revelation of Christ, and final judgments, (vers. 14-20).

Chap. xv.—A vision of events chronologically within chapter viii., the opening the seventh seal. (This appears from the fact that the faithful of the fifth seal are here represented as praising God in view of the judgments impending,—see vers. 2-4 ; which judgments are within the seventh seal.)

Chap. xvi.—The seven vials ; a second series of visions of the events of the seven trumpets. This appears—

First, because the seventh trumpet and the seventh vial both relate to the final catastrophe. Under the seventh trumpet, the mystery of God is finished (x. 7), and the temple of God is opened, and there are lightnings, voices, thunders, and an earthquake (xi. 19). Under the seventh vial, " It is done ! " is heard from the temple, and there are voices, thunders, lightnings, and an earthquake (xvi. 17, 18).

Second, because the sphere of the judgments is the same in the correlative visions of both series :— 1, The earth. 2, The sea. 3, The rivers. 4, The sun. 5, The pit, the seat of the beast. 6, Euphrates. 7, Heaven, the air.

[Chaps. xvii., xviii.—Detailed visions of the development and doom of Babylon, "the harlot," whose fall has been within the seventh trumpet and seventh vial ; the last series of judgments of the seventh seal (xi. 18 ; xvi. 19).]

Chap. xix.—The doom of the harlot being accomplished (ver. 2), the glory of the bride follows (ver. 7) ; the glorious revelation of Christ, and the destruction consequent thereon of the beast and false prophet (ver. 20).

Chap. xx.—Satan is bound. The millennial reign of the saints (vers. 1-4).

After the millennial reign, Satan is loosed, and once more deceives the nations. Satan is cast into the lake of fire. The judgment of the Great White Throne.

Chaps. xxi., xxii. 1-5.—The new heaven and new earth.

Chap. xxii. 6-21.—Conclusion.*

As the last trumpet and the last vial embrace the final judgments of the day of vengeance, which

---

* I purposely pass over chap. xii., because of the exceptional difficulties which attend the interpretation of it. "Anything within reasonable regard for the analogies and symbolism of the text seems better than the now too commonly received historical interpretation, with its wild fancies and arbitrary assignments of words and figures" (Alford, *Greek Test.*, Rev. xii. 15, 16). The only reasonable interpretation I have seen is that which regards the "man-child, who was to rule all nations with a rod of iron," and who "was caught up to God and His throne," as being the Lord Jesus Christ, and the woman as representing that people "of whom, as concerning the flesh, Christ came" (Rom. ix. 5). But the objections to this are considerable. First, past historical facts are thus introduced into a vision relating to the future. I am not aware of any other instance of this in Scripture Secondly, the main features of the vision after ver. 5 are not accounted for by the facts.

The following remarks are offered merely to assist inquiry and not at all as expressing a formed opinion on the matter. The 1,260 days during which the woman is persecuted is precisely the period of "the great tribulation." Ver. 7 declares that during the woman's flight, Michael the Archangel fought on her behalf. Dan. xii. 1, referring to the time of Antichrist's power, states that "at that time shall Michael stand up, the great prince which standeth for the children of the people ; and there shall be a time of trouble," etc., describing "the great tribulation" which is to continue 1,260 days.

Again, the Old Scriptures clearly point to the career of a future David, a deliverer of the Jews, who will become their earthly leader at that time, and reign over them in Jerusalem afterwards. See, *e.g.*, Ezek. xxxvii. 22-25, about David the

precede the advent of the glorious kingdom, they necessarily include the doom of the two great antichristian powers of the last days,—the imperial represented by the ten-horned beast, and the ecclesiastical typified by the scarlet woman. The visions of the thirteenth and seventeenth chapters, therefore, are interposed, descriptive of the rise and development of these powers. These accordingly give us details which relate to events within the earlier seals, for the martyrs of the fifth seal are the victims of the great persecutor of the thirteenth chapter.

If the foregoing scheme be correct in the main, the eras included in the Revelation may be divided thus :—

1. The seven Churches; the transitional period following the close of the Christian dispensation."*

2. The seven seals; the period during which all that prophecy has foretold shall precede the kingdom will be fulfilled.

Prince, who is certainly not Christ, seeing he is to have a palace in Jerusalem and a definite inheritance in the land, and who, moreover, is to offer burnt-offerings, etc. (Ezek. xlv. 17). I suppose this is the great military conqueror of Isa. lxiii. 1-3.

May not then Rev xii. refer to this personage, who is to be Christ's vicegerent on earth, and who will, in fact, rule over all nations?

* That is, assuming that this portion of the Book has a prophetical aspect.

3. The kingdom; to be followed, after a final interval of apostasy, by—

4. The eternal state; the new heaven and new earth.

It is manifestly within the period of the seals that the prophecies of Daniel have their fulfilment, and the next inquiry should be directed to ascertain the points of contact between the visions of St. John and the earlier prophecies.

As already noticed, it is only in so far as prophecy falls within the seventy weeks that it comes within the range of human chronology. And further, the seventieth week will be a definite period, of which the epoch of the middle and the end are definitely marked. The epoch of the first week, that is, of the prophetic period as a whole, was not the return of the Jews from Babylon, nor yet the rebuilding of their temple, but the signing of the Persian decree which restored their national position. So also the beginning of the last week will date, not from their restoration to Judea, nor yet from the future rebuilding of their shrine, but from the signing of the treaty by "the coming Prince," which probably will once more recognize them as a nation.*

But it is obvious that this personage must have attained to power before the date of that event;

---

* See p. 86. *ante.*

and it is expressly stated * that his rise is to be *after* that of the ten kingdoms which are hereafter to divide the Roman earth. It follows, therefore, that the development of these kingdoms, and the rise of the great Kaiser who is to wield the imperial sceptre in the last days, must be prior to the beginning of the seventieth week.†

And within certain limits, we can also fix the order of the subsequent events. The violation of the treaty by the defilement of the Holy Place is to occur " in the midst of the week."‡ That event, again, is to be the epoch of the great persecution by Antichrist,§ which is to last precisely three and a half years ; for his power to persecute the Jews is to be limited to that definite period.‖ " Immediately after the tribulation of those days shall the sun be darkened, and the moon shall not give her light."¶ Such is the statement of the twenty-fourth of Mat-

---

* Dan. vii. 24.

† I do not assert that he will have reached the zenith of his power before that date. On the contrary, it seems extremely probable that the treaty with the Jews will be one of the steps by which he will raise himself to the place he is destined to hold, and that as soon as he has attained his end, he will throw off the mask and declare himself a persecutor. So Irenæus teaches, and he possibly gives what was the tradition of the apostolic age.

‡ Dan. ix. 27.   § Matt. xxiv. 15-21.
‖ Dan. vii. 25 ; Rev. xiii. 5.   ¶ Matt. xxiv. 29.

thew ; and the sixth of Revelation exactly coincides with it, for the vision of the fifth seal embraced the period of " the tribulation " ; and when the sixth seal was opened, " the sun became black as sackcloth of hair, and the moon became as blood," and the cry went forth, " The great day of His wrath is come."*
In keeping with this, again, is the prophecy of Joel :
' The sun shall be turned into darkness, and the moon into blood, before the great and the terrible day of the Lord come."† The events of this day of vengeance are the burden of the vision of the seventh seal, including the judgment of Babylon, the scarlet woman—or the religious apostasy—by the agency of the imperial power ‡—the beast, whose fearful end is to bring the awful drama to a close.§

We have definite grounds, therefore, for assigning the following order to the events of the last days :—

1. The development of the ten kingdoms.

2. The appearance within the territorial limits of these kingdoms of an eleventh " king," who will subdue three of the ten, and will ultimately be accepted as Suzerain by all.

3. The making of a treaty by this king with, or in favour of, the Jews. *The epoch of the seventieth week.*

---

* Rev. vi. 12, 17. † Joel ii. 31.
‡ Rev. xvii. 16, 17. § Rev. xix. 20.

4. The violation of the treaty by this king after three and a half years.

5. " The great tribulation " of Scripture, the awful persecution of the last days, which shall continue three and a half years.

6. The deliverance of the Jews from their great enemy, to be followed by their final establishment in blessing. *The close of the seventieth week.*

7. " The great and terrible day of the Lord," the period of the seventh seal, beginning with a revelation of Christ to His people in Jerusalem, accompanied by appalling manifestations of Divine power and ending with His last glorious advent.

That the seventieth week will be the last seven years of the dispensation, and the term of the reign of Antichrist, is a belief as old as the writings of the Ante-Nicene Fathers. But a careful examination of the statements of Scripture will lead to some modification of this view. The fulfilment to Judah of the blessings specified in Dan. ix. 24 is all that Scripture expressly states will mark the close of the seventieth week. Antichrist will then be driven out of Judea ; but there is no reason whatever to suppose he will otherwise lose his power. As already shown, the seventieth week ends with the period of the fifth seal, whereas the fall of Babylon is within the era of the seventh seal. No one may assert that that era will be of long duration, and it will probably be

brief ; but the only certain indication of its length
is that it will be within a single lifetime, for at its
close the Antichrist is to be seized alive, and hurled
to his awful doom.*

The analogy of the past might lead us to expect
that the events foretold to occur at the end of the
seventieth week would follow immediately at its
close. But the Book of Daniel expressly teaches
that there will be an interval. Whatever view be
taken of the earlier portion of the eleventh of Daniel,
it is clear that " the king " of the thirty-sixth and
following verses is the great enemy of the last days.
His wars and conquests are predicted,† and the
twelfth chapter opens with the mention of the predicted time of trouble, " the great tribulation " of
Matthew and Revelation. The seventh verse specifies the duration of the " time of trouble" as " a
time, times, and a half," which, as already shown,‡
is the half week, or 1,260 days. But the eleventh
verse expressly declares that from the date of the
event which is to divide the week, and which, according to Matthew xxiv., is to be the signal of persecution, there shall be 1,290 days ; and the twelfth

---

* Rev. xix. 20.

† He is neither king of the north nor of the south, for both
these kings shall invade his territory (ver. 40), *i.e.*, the powers
which shall then respectively possess Syria and Egypt.

‡ See p. 73, *ante.*

verse postpones the blessing to 1,335 days, or seventy-five days beyond the close of the prophetic weeks.

If therefore "the day of the Lord" follows immediately upon the close of the seventieth week, it seems that Judah's complete deliverance is not to take place until after that final period has begun. And this is expressly confirmed by the fourteenth chapter of Zechariah. It is a prophecy than which none is more definite, and the difficulties which beset the interpretation of it are in no degree overcome by refusing to read it literally. It seems to teach that at that time Jerusalem is to be taken by the allied armies of the nations, and that at the moment when a host of prisoners are being led away, God will intervene in some miraculous way, as when He destroyed the army of Pharaoh at the Exodus.*

---

* "The day of battle" (Zech. xiv. 3). The prophet adds: "And His feet shall stand on that day upon the Mount of Olives." I cannot conceive how any one can suppose this to be the great and final advent in glory as described in Matt. xxiv. 30 and other Scriptures.

"The prophecy (Zech. xiv.) seems literal. If Antichrist be the leader of the nations, it seems inconsistent with the statement that he will at this time be sitting in the temple as God at Jerusalem; thus Antichrist outside would be made to besiege Antichrist within the city. But difficulties do not set aside revelations; the event will clear up seeming difficulties" (Fausset's *Commentary, in loco*). It is idle to speculate on such a matter, but I presume the city will have revolted against the

Comparison with the prophecy of the twenty-fourth chapter of St. Matthew is the surest and strictest test which can be applied to these conclusions. After fixing the epoch and describing the character of the great persecution of the last days, the Lord thus enumerates the events which are to follow at its close:*—First the great natural phenomena predicted; then the appearance of the sign of the Son of man in heaven; then the mourning of the tribes of the land;† and finally the glorious advent.

---

great enemy during his absence at the head of the armies of the empire, and that thereupon he will turn back to reconquer it. History repeats itself. Moreover, there is no reason to believe that he will reside in Jerusalem, though presumably he will have a palace there, and as part of a blasphemous pageant, will sit enthroned in the temple. That Jerusalem should be captured by a hostile army at such a time will seem less strange if it be remembered first that the true people of God therein shall have warning to leave the city at the beginning of these troubles (Matt. xxiv. 15, 16), and secondly, that the deliverance of the capital is to be the last act in the deliverance of Judah (See Zech. xii. 7).

* Immediately after the tribulation of those days shall "the sun be darkened, and the moon shall not give her light, and the stars shall fall from heaven, and the powers of the heavens shall be shaken : and then shall appear the sign of the Son of man in heaven ; and then shall all the tribes of the earth mourn, and they shall see the Son of man coming in the clouds of heaven, with power and great glory " (Matt. xxiv. 29, 30).

† κόψονται πᾶσαι αἱ φυλαὶ τῆς γῆς.   Comp. Zech. xii. 12 (LXX), κόψεται ἡ γῆ κατὰ φυλὰς φυλὰς.

That there will be *no* interval between the persecution and the "great signs from heaven"* which are to follow it, is expressly stated ; they are to occur "*immediately* after the tribulation." That an interval shall separate the other events of the series is equally clear. From the defilement of the Holy Place, to the day when the tribulation shall end, and the "fearful sights" and "great signs" from heaven shall strike terror into men's hearts, shall be a definite period of 1,260 days ;† and yet when He goes on to speak of the Advent, the Lord declares that that day is known to the Father only: it should be His people's part to watch and wait. He had already warned them against being deceived by expecting His Advent before the fulfilment of all that must come to pass.‡ Now He warns them against apostasy after the accomplishment of all things, because of the delay which even then shall still mark His coming.§

---

* Luke xxi. 11.

† Therefore if the Advent synchronized with these events, any one then living would be able to fix the date of it, once the epoch of the tribulation were known ; whereas the chapter clearly shows that an interval will follow after all has been fulfilled, long enough to weed out mere professors, who, tired of waiting, will apostatize (Matt. xxiv. 48), and to lull even true disciples to a sleep from which their Lord's return will rouse them (*Ibid.* xxv. 5).

‡ Matt. xxiv. 4-28.

§ Matt. xxiv. 42-51, and xxv. 1-13 : "THEN shall the kingdom of heaven be likened unto ten virgins." ⌈τότε, "*at the*

The words of Christ are unequivocally true, and He never enjoins upon His people to live in expectation of His coming, save at a time when nothing intervenes to bar the fulfilment of the hope. Fatalism is as popular among Christians as with the worshippers of Mahomet; and it is forgotten that though the dispensation has run its course these eighteen centuries, it might have been brought to a close at any moment. Hence the Christian is taught to live, "looking for that blessed hope."* It will be otherwise in days to come, when the present dispensation shall have closed with the first stage of the Advent. Then the word will be, not "Watch, for ye know not what hour your Lord doth come,"†—that belongs to the time when all shall have been fulfilled,—but "Take heed that no man deceive you, all these things must come to pass, but the end is not yet."‡

---

period spoken of at the end of the last chapter, viz., the coming of the Lord to His personal reign " (Alford, *Gr. Test., in loco.*)] Though applicable to every age in which there is a waiting people on earth, the parable will have its full and special application in the last days to those who shall be looking back on the complete page of prophecy fulfilled. The entire passage from chap. xxiv. 31, to chap. xxv. 30, is parenthetical, relating especially to that time.

Titus ii. 12, 13.   † Matt. xxiv. 42.   ‡ *Ibid.* 4, 6.

15

THE COMING PRINCE

" WHAT is it that all Europe is looking for ? "—
the words are quoted from a leading article
in the *Times* newspaper, on the recent finding of
Agamemnon's tomb.* "What is it that all Europe
is looking for ? It is the KING OF MEN, the great
head of the Hellenic race, the man whom a thousand
galleys and a hundred thousand men submitted to
on a simple recognition of his personal qualities,
and obeyed for ten long years. . . . The man who
can challenge for his own the shield of Agamemnon,
now waiting for the challenge, is the true Emperor
of the East, and the easiest escape from our present
difficulties."

The realization of this dream will be the fulfilment
of prophecy.

True it is that popular movements characterize
the age, rather than the power of individual minds.
It is an age of mobs. Democracy, not despotism,
is the goal towards which civilization is tending.
But democracy in its full development is one of the

---

* The *Times*, Monday, 18th December, 1876.

surest roads to despotism. First, the revolution ;
then, the *plebiscite ;* then, the despot. The Cæsar
often owes his sceptre to the mob. A man of
transcendent greatness, moreover, never fails to leave
his mark upon his times. And the true King of
Men must have an extraordinary combination of
great qualities. He must be "a scholar, a statesman, a man of unflinching courage and irrepressible
enterprise, full of resources, and ready to look in
the face a rival or a foe." * The opportunity too
must synchronize with his advent. But the voice
of prophecy is clear, that the HOUR is coming, and
the MAN.

In connection with this dream or legend of the
reappearance of Agamemnon, it is remarkable that
the language of Daniel's second vision has led some
to fix on Greece as the very place in which the Man
of prophecy shall have his rise ; † and it leaves no

---

* The *Times*, 18th December, 1876.

† That Antichrist is to arise from the eastern part of the
Roman empire, and from that part of the east which fell under
the rule of Alexander's successors, is rendered unquestionable
by this chapter. But, seeing that in the eleventh chapter he
is mentioned as conflicting with the king of the north (*i.e.*, the
king of Syria), and also with the king of the south (*i.e.*, the
king of Egypt), it is plain that he does not arise either from
Egypt or Syria. He must, therefore, arise either from Greece
or from the districts immediately contiguous to Constantinople.
It is true that if he arose from the latter, or indeed from either

doubt whatever that he will appear within the territorial limits of the old Grecian empire.

Having predicted the formation of the four kingdoms into which Alexander's conquests became divided at his death, the angel Gabriel—the divinely-appointed interpreter of the vision—proceeded thus to speak of events which must take place in days to come. "In the latter time of their kingdom, when the transgressors are come to the full, a king of fierce countenance, and understanding dark sentences, shall stand up. And his power shall be mighty, but not by his own power; and he shall destroy wonderfully, and shall prosper, and practise, and shall destroy the mighty and the holy people. And through his policy also, he shall cause craft to prosper in his hand; and he shall magnify himself

---

of the four, he would be esteemed Greek in origin, because all the four were divisions of the Greek empire ; but it seems far more probable that Greece proper will be the place of his rise. He is described as 'waxing great towards the south and towards the east, and towards the pleasant land ;' that is, toward Egypt, Syria, and Palestine—a description that would geographically suit the position of one who was supposed to be in Greece.

"Moreover, a 'little horn' (an emblem not of that which he is as an individual, but of that which he is as a monarch) is a symbol that well suits one who should arise from one of those petty principalities which once abounded in Greece, and have even still their memorial in the throne of the sovereigns of Montenegro."—NEWTON *Ten Kingdoms*, p. 193.

in his heart, and by peace shall destroy many. He shall also stand up against the Prince of princes ; but he shall be broken without hand." *

In the vision of the seventh chapter, the last great monarch of the Gentiles was represented only as a blasphemer and a persecutor : " He shall speak great words against the Most High, and shall wear out the saints of the Most High ; " but here he is described as being also a general and a diplomatist. Having thus obtained a recognised place in prophecy, he is alluded to in the vision which follows as "the Prince who is coming," †—a well-known personage, whose advent had already been foretold ; and the mention of him in Daniel's fourth and final vision is so explicit, that having regard to the vital importance of establishing the personality of this " King," the passage is here set forth at length.

" And the king shall do according to his will ; and he shall exalt himself, and magnify himself above every god, and shall speak marvellous things against the God of gods, and shall prosper till the indignation be accomplished : for that that is determined shall be done. Neither shall he regard the God of his fathers, nor the desire of women, nor regard any god : for he shall magnify himself above all. But in

---

* Dan viii. 23-25. The entire passage is quoted at pp. 43-46, *ante* (note).

† Dan. ix. 26,

his estate he shall honour the God of forces; and a
god whom his fathers knew not shall he honour with
gold, and silver, and with precious stones, and pleasant things. Thus shall he do in the most strong
holds with a strange god, whom he shall acknowledge
and increase with glory: and he shall cause them to
rule over many, and shall divide the land for gain.
And at the time of the end shall the king of
the south push at him: and the king of the north
shall come against him like a whirlwind, with
chariots, and with horsemen, and with many ships;
and he shall enter into the countries, and shall over-
flow and pass over. He shall enter also into the
glorious land, and many countries shall be over-
thrown; but these shall escape out of his hand, even
Edom, and Moab, and the chief of the children of
Ammon. He shall stretch forth his hand also upon
the countries: and the land of Egypt shall not
escape. But he shall have power over the treasures
of gold and of silver, and over all the precious things
of Egypt; and the Libyans and the Ethiopians shall
be at his steps. But tidings out of the east and out
of the north shall trouble him : therefore he shall go
forth with great fury to destroy, and utterly to make
away many. And he shall plant the tabernacles of
his palace between the seas in the glorious holy
mountain ; yet he shall come to his end, and none
shall help him. And at that time shall Michael

stand up, the great prince which standeth for the children of thy people; and there shall be a time of trouble, such as never was since there was a nation even to that same time : and at that time thy people shall be delivered, every one that shall be found written in the book."*

---

* Dan. xi. 36-45 ; xii. 1. I am inclined to believe that the entire passage from ver. 5 of Dan. xi. will receive a future fulfilment, and I have no doubt of this as regards the passage beginning with ver. 21. See especially ver. 31. But the future application of the portion quoted in the text is unquestionable. Although the chapter in part refers to Antiochus Epiphanes, "there are traits which have nothing to correspond to them in Antiochus, which are even the exact contradictory of the character of Antiochus, but which do reappear in St. Paul's account of the Antichrist to come." I quote from Dr. Pusey. He adds (*Daniel*, p. 93): "The image of the Antichrist of the Old Testament melts into the lineaments of the Antichrist himself. . . . One trait only of the anti-religious character of Antichrist was true of Antiochus also ; 'he shall speak marvellous things against the God of gods.' Blasphemy against God is an essential feature of any God-opposed power or individual. It belongs to Voltaire as much as to Antiochus. All besides has no place in him. . . . The characteristics of this infidel king are (1) self-exaltation above every god ; 'he shall magnify himself above every god ;' (2) contempt of all religion ; (3) blasphemy against the true God ; (4) apostasy from the God of his fathers ; (5) disregarding the desire of women ; (6) the honouring of a god whom his fathers knew not. Of all these six marks, one only, in the least, agrees with Antiochus." The entire passage is valuable, and the arguments conclusive. A remark at p. 96 suggests that Dr.

The burden of Daniel's prophecies is Judah and Jerusalem, but the Apocalyptic visions of the beloved disciple have a wider scope. The same scenes are sometimes presented, but they are displayed upon a grander scale. The same actors appear, but in relation to larger interests and events of greater magnitude. In Daniel, the Messiah is mentioned only in relation to the earthly people, and it is in the same connection also that the false Messiah comes upon the stage. In the Apocalypse the Lamb appears as the Saviour of an innumerable multitude " out of all nations, and kindreds, and peoples, and tongues," * and the Beast is seen as the persecutor of all who name the name of Christ on earth. The visions of St. John, moreover, include an opened heaven, while the glimpses Daniel was vouchsafed of "things to come" are limited to earth.

The attempt to fix the meaning of every detail of these visions is to ignore the lessons to be derived from the Messianic prophecies fulfilled at the first

---

Pusey identifies this king with the second " Beast " of Rev. xiii., and this view is maintained by others on the ground that a " Beast " in prophecy typifies kingly power. This is true generally, but the second beast of Rev. xiii. is expressly called " the false Prophet" (Rev. xix. 20) ; and the passage proves that he is immediately connected with the first beast, and claims no position independently of him. The difficulties in the way of supposing him to be a king in his own right are insuperable.   * Rev. vii. 9.

advent.* The old Scriptures taught the pious Jew to look for a personal Christ—not a system or a dynasty, but a *person*. They enabled him, moreover, to anticipate the leading facts of His appearing. Herod's question, for example, " Where should Christ be born ? " admitted of a definite and unhesitating answer, " In Bethlehem of Judea."† But to assign its place and meaning to every part of the mingled vision of suffering and glory was beyond the power even of the inspired prophets themselves."‡ So also is it with the prophecies of Antichrist. The case indeed is stronger still, for while they " who waited for re-demption in Israel " had to glean the Messianic prophecies from Scriptures which seemed to the careless reader to refer to the sufferings of the old Hebrew prophets or the glories of their kings, the predictions of Antichrist are as distinct and definite as though the statements were historical and not prophetic.§

---

* A similar remark applies to the refusal to recognise the main outlines of the character and history of Antichrist. Ful-filled prophecy is our only safe guide in studying the unfulfilled.

† Matt. ii. 4. *Cf.* Micah v. 2.

‡ I Peter i. 10-12.

§ The religious sceptic may refuse to accept their literal meaning, and the profane sceptic, in rejecting the fanciful interpretations of the pious, may dismiss the prophecies them-selves as incredible ; but this is only a further proof that their definiteness is too pronounced to admit of the half-faith accorded to other Scriptures.

And yet the task of the expositor is beset with real difficulties. If the book of Daniel might be read by itself no question whatever could arise. "The Coming Prince" is there presented as the head of the revived Roman empire of the future, and a persecutor of the saints. There is not a single statement respecting him that presents the smallest difficulty. But some of the statements of St. John seem inconsistent with the earlier prophecies. According to Daniel's visions the sovereignty of Antichrist appears confined to the ten kingdoms, and his career seems limited to the duration of the seventieth week. How then can this be reconciled with the statement of St. John that "power was given him over all kindreds and tongues and nations, and all that dwell upon the earth shall worship him"?* Is it credible, moreover, that a man endowed with such vast supernatural powers, and filling so marvellous a place in prophecy, will be restrained within the narrow limits of the Roman earth?

If these points be urged as objections to the truth of Scripture it is enough to mark that the prophecies of Christ were beset with kindred difficulties. Such prophecies are like the disjointed

---

* Rev. xiii. 7, 8. In the best reading of ver. 7, the same four words occur as in vii. 9—" nations, kindreds, people, and tongues.'

pieces of an elaborate and intricate mosaic. To
fit each into its place would baffle our utmost
ingenuity. To discover the main design is all we
can expect ; or if more be demanded of us, it is
enough to show that no part is inconsistent with
the rest. And these results will reward the student
of the Apocalyptic visions of Daniel and St. John,
if only he approach them untrammeled by the crude
views which prevail respecting the career of Antichrist.

These visions are not a history, but a drama. In
the twelfth chapter of Revelation we see the woman
in her travail. In the twenty-first chapter she is
manifested in her final glory. The intervening
chapters afford brief glimpses of events which fill
up the interval. It is with the thirteenth and seventeenth chapters that we have specially to do in
connection with the present subject, and it is clear
that the later vision unfolds events which come first
in the order of time.

The false church and the true are typified under
kindred emblems. Jerusalem, the Bride, has its
counterpart in Babylon, the Harlot. In the same
sense in which the New Jerusalem is the Jewish
church, so likewise Babylon is the apostasy of Rome.
The heavenly city is mother of the redeemed for
ages past : * the earthly city is mother of the harlots

---

* Gal. iv. 26.

and abominations of the earth. * The victims who
have perished in the persecutions of Antichristian
Papal Rome are estimated at *fifty millions* of human
beings ; but even this appalling record will not be
the measure of her doom. The blood of "holy
apostles and prophets,"—the martyred dead of ages
before the Papacy arose, and even of pre-Messianic
times, will be required of her when the day of
vengeance comes. †

As it is only in its Jewish aspect that the Church
is expressly symbolized as the Bride,‡ so also it
is at a time when this, their normal relationship,
has been regained by the covenant people, that
the apostate church of Christendom, in the full
development of its iniquity, appears as the Harlot.§

* Rev. xvii. 5.

† Rev. xviii. 20. So also in xvii. 6, the *saints* (the
slaughtered dead of Old Testament times) are distinguished
from the martyrs of Jesus. Luke xi. 50, 51 sets forth the
principle of God's judgments.

‡ In Scripture the church of this dispensation is symbolized
as the Body of Christ, never as the Bride. From the close
of John Baptist's ministry the Bride is never mentioned until
she appears in the Apocalypse (John iii. 29 ; Rev. xxi. 2, 9).
The force of the "nevertheless" in Eph. v. 33 depends on the
fact that the Church is the *Body*, not the Bride. The earthly
relationship is readjusted by a heavenly standard. Man and
wife are *not* one body, but Christ and His church are one body,
therefore a man is to love his wife " *even as himself.*"

§ This, I believe, is the element of truth in the view of
Auberlen and others, that the woman of chap. xvii. is the

The vision clearly indicates moreover a marked revival of her influence. She is seen enthroned upon the ten-horned Beast, herself arrayed in royal hues and decked with gold and costliest gems. The infamous greatness of Papal Rome in times gone by shall yet be surpassed by the splendour of her glories in dark days to come, when, having drawn within her pale it may be all that usurps the name of Christ on earth,* she will claim as her willing vassal the last great monarch of the Gentile world.

As regards the duration of this period of Rome's final triumphs, Scripture is silent; but the crisis which brings it to a close is definitely marked : " The ten horns and the Beast shall hate the whore, and shall make her desolate and naked, and shall eat her flesh and burn her with fire."†

One point in the angel's description of the Beast in relation to the harlot claims special notice. The seven heads have a twofold symbolism. When

---

woman of chap. xii., "the faithful city become an harlot" (Isa. i. 21).

* " I incline to think that the judgment (chap. xviii. 2) and the spiritual fornication (chap. xviii. 3), though finding their culmination in Rome, are not restricted to it, but comprise the whole apostate church, Roman, Greek, and even Protestant, in so far as it has been seduced from its first love to Christ, and (has) given its affections to worldly pomps and idols."–- REV. A. R. FAUSSET'S *Commentary.*

† Rev. xvii. 16. *See* p. 136, *ante* (note).

viewed in connection with the harlot, they are "seven mountains on which the woman sits;" but in their special relation to the Beast they have a different significance. The angel adds, "*and they are seven kings;*" that is "kingdoms," the word being used "according to its strict prophetic import, and to the analogy of that portion of the prophecy which is here especially in view." *

In the seventh chapter of Daniel the Beast is identified with the Roman Empire. In the thirteenth of Revelation he is identified also with the lion, the bear, and the panther, the three first "kingdoms" of Daniel's vision. But here he is seen as the heir and representative, not of these alone, but of all the great world-powers which have set themselves in opposition to God and to His people. The seven heads typify these powers. "Five are fallen, and one is." Egypt, Nineveh, Babylon, Persia, Greece, had fallen; and Rome then held the sceptre of earthly sovereignty, the sixth in succession to the empires already named.† "And the other is not

---

* ALFORD, *Greek Test. in loco.* Comp. Dan. vii. 17-23.

† Just as the mention of the ten horns upon the beast has set men trying to discover in the past a tenfold division of the Roman earth, so also these seven heads have suggested the idea of seven successive forms of government in the Roman empire. Neither of these conceptions would ever have been heard of, but for the prophecy of which they are supposed to be the fulfilment. The second, though not so visionary as

yet come, and when he cometh he must continue a short space." Here the prophecy is marked by the same strange "foreshortening" already noticed in each of Daniel's visions. While Rome was the sixth kingdom, the seventh is the confederacy of the latter days, heading up in "the Coming Prince." The Coming Prince himself, in the full and final development of his power, is called the eighth, though belonging to the seven.* The importance of these conclusions will appear in the sequel.

The subject of the twelfth chapter is the dragon, the woman in her travail, the birth of the man-child and his rapture to heaven ; the conflict in heaven between the archangel and the dragon; † the dragon's banishment to earth ; his persecution of the woman, and her flight to the wilderness, where she is sustained

---

the first, is open to the special objection that the word πίπτω betokens a violent fall, such as the catastrophe of ancient Babylon, or of the Babylon of the Apocalypse (comp. Rev. xviii. 2). It is wholly unsuitable to express such changes as marked the government of ancient Rome.

* Rev. xvii. 10 expressly states that the duration of the seventh will be brief. Dean Alford's comment on this is not marked by his usual candour. The words in ver. 11 are ἐκ τῶν ἑπτά, but this cannot mean merely that the Beast is "the successor and result of the seven" (Alford), for ver. 10 limits the entire succession to seven. Though because of his awful pre-eminence he is described as the eighth, yet he is really the supreme head of the seventh.

† Verse 7 ; comp. Dan. xii. 1.

for "a time, and times, and half a time," or 1,260 days * (the second half of Daniel's seventieth week). The chapter ends by the statement that, baffled in attempting to destroy the woman, the dragon "went to make war with the remnant of her seed, which keep the commandments of God, and have the testimony of Jesus Christ." The thirteenth chapter, crossing the lines of Daniel's visions, represents the fulfilment of the dragon's purpose through the agency of the man of prophecy, whom he energizes to this end. Whatever meaning be attached to the birth and rapture of the woman's child, there can be no reasonable doubt that the obedient, faithful "remnant of her seed" is the Jewish Church of the latter days, the persecuted "saints of the Most High" of Daniel's prophecy.

The serpent, the woman, and the man, appear together on the earliest page of Scripture, and they reappear upon the latest. But how significant and terrible the change! No longer the subtle tempter, Satan is now displayed in all his awfulness as the great fiery dragon,† who seeks to destroy the woman's

---

* Verses 6, 14. *See* p. 179, *ante* (note).

† δράκων πυῤῥὸς μέγας, Rev. xii. 3. "He is πυῤῥός perhaps, for the combined reasons of the wasting properties of fire, and the redness of blood" (Alford, *Greek Test., in loco*). Compare ver. 9, "The great dragon was cast out, that old serpent, called the Devil and Satan." The dragon both of Scripture and of heathen mythology is a serpent, and both refer to Satan. It is

promised seed. And instead of the humbled penitent of Eden, the man appears as a wild beast,* a monster, both in power and wickedness. The serpent's victim has become his willing slave and ally.

God has found a man to fulfil all His will, and to Him He has given up His throne, with all power in heaven and " on earth." This will hereafter be travestied by Satan, and the coming man shall have the dragon's "power, and his throne, and great authority."† Both the Dragon and the Beast are seen crowned with royal diadems.‡ Once, and only once, again in Scripture the diadem is mentioned, and then it is as worn by Him whose name is " King of kings and Lord of lords."§ It must be as pretenders to His power that the Beast and the Dragon claim it.

The personality of Satan and his interest in and close connection with our race throughout its history, are among the most certain though most mysterious facts of revelation. The popular classification of angels, men, and devils, as including intelligent

---

described by Homer as of huge size, coiled like a snake, of blood-red or dark colour, and many-headed. " He seems to use the words δράκων and ὄφις indifferently for a serpent " (Liddell and Scott).

* The θηρίον or wild-beast of Rev. xiii., etc., must not be confounded with the ζῶον or living-being of chap. iv., most unfortunately rendered *beast* in E.V.

† Rev. xiii. 2.   ‡ Rev. xii. 3 ; xiii. 1.   § Rev. xix. 12-16.

creation, is misleading. The *angels** that fell are "reserved in everlasting chains, under darkness, unto the judgment of the Great Day."† *Demons* are frequently mentioned in the narrative of the Gospels, and they have also a place in the doctrine of the Epistles. But THE DEVIL is a being who, like the Archangel, seems, in his own domain, to have no peer. ‡

---

* That is, the beings who before their fall were angels ot God The word *angel* in its secondary sense means no more than a messenger or attendant, and Satan has his angels (Rev. xii. 7). The word is used of John Baptist's disciples in Luke vii. 24.

† Jude 6.

‡ Our translators have used the word *devil* as a generic term for fallen beings other than men, but the word from which it is derived has not this scope in Greek. A διάβολος is a slanderer, and the word is so used in 1 Tim. iii. 11 ; 2 Tim. iii. 3 ; Titus ii. 3. But *the* διάβολος is Satan, of whom alone the term is used elsewhere in the New Testament, save only in John vi. 70, where it is applied to Judas Iscariot. The word δαιμόνιον, which occurs fifty-two times in the Gospels, and seven times in the rest of the New Testament, is invariably rendered *devil*, save in Acts xvii. 18 (*gods*). In classical Greek it means generally the Deity, especially an inferior god ; and in the New Testament, an evil spirit, a *demon*.

The ultimate reference of Ezek. xxviii. appears to be to Satan, and in the passage beginning, " Thou hast been in Eden in the garden of God," he is apostrophised as " the anointed cherub" (ver. 14). The cherubim appear to have some special relation to our race and world, hence their connection with the tabernacle. Can it be that our earth was at one time their domain, that Satan was of their number, and that he recognised in Adam a creature appointed to succeed him in the very scene of his glory and his fall ?

Another fact which claims notice here is the hold which serpent worship has had upon mankind. Among the nations of the ancient world there was scarcely one in whose religious system it had not a place. In heathen mythology there is scarcely a hero or a god whose history is not connected in some way with the sacred serpent. " Wherever the devil reigned the serpent was held in some peculiar veneration." *

The true significance of this depends on a just appreciation of the nature of idol worship. It may be questioned whether idolatry as popularly understood has ever prevailed except among the most debased and ignorant of races. It is not the emblem that is worshipped, but a power or being which the emblem represents. When the Apostle warned the Corinthian Church against participating in anything devoted to an idol, he was careful to explain that the idol in itself was nothing. " But " (he declared) " the things which the Gentiles sacrifice, they sacrifice to *demons*, not to God, and I would not that ye should have fellowship with demons." †

---

* Bp. Stillingfleet ; quoted in *Encyc. Metro.*, article on " Serpent Worship," *q.v.* In Bryant's *Ancient Mythology* will be found a chapter on Ophiolatry (vol. ii., p. 197, 3rd ed., and see also p. 458) which fully warrants the general statements of the text.

† 1 Cor. x. 20. *See* p. 206, *ante* (note).

This will afford an insight into the character of the predicted serpent worship of the last days.* Satan's master lie will be a travesty of the incarnation: he will energize a man who will claim universal worship as being the manifestation of the Deity in human form. And not only will there be a false Messiah, but another being, his equal in miraculous power, yet having for his only mission to obtain for him the homage of mankind. The mystery of the Godhead will thus be parodied by the mystery of iniquity, and the Father, the Son, and the Spirit will have their counterpart in the Dragon, the Beast, and the False Prophet.†

A silent heaven marks this age of grace. Whirlwind and earthquake and fire may awe, yet, as in the days of the old Hebrew prophet,‡ God is not in these, but in the "still small voice" which tells of

---

* "All the world wondered after the Beast; and they worshipped the Dragon (serpent) which gave power unto the Beast; and they worshipped the Beast" (Rev. xiii. 3, 4).

† The lamb-like Beast of Rev. xiii. 11, called the False Prophet in Rev. xix. 20. The language of xiii. 3, 12, suggests that there will be some impious travesty of the resurrection of our Lord.

‡ "The Lord passed by, and a great and strong wind rent the mountains, but the Lord was not in the wind; and after the wind an earthquake, but the Lord was not in the earthquake; and after the earthquake a fire, but the Lord was not in the fire; and after the fire, *a still small voice*" (1 Kings xix. 11, 12).

mercy and seeks to win lost men from the power of darkness to Himself. But the very silence which betokens that the throne of God is now a throne of grace is appealed to as the crowning proof that God is but a myth; and the coarse blasphemer's favourite trick is to challenge the Almighty to declare Himself by some signal act of judgment. In days to come, the impious challenge will be taken up by Satan, and death shall seize on men who refuse to bow before the image of the Beast.*

The Antichrist will be more than a profane and brutal persecutor like Antiochus Epiphanes and some of the Emperors of Pagan Rome; more than a vulgar impostor like Barcochab.† Miracles alone can silence the scepticism of apostates, and in the

---

* In the persecutions under Pagan Rome, death was often the penalty for refusing to worship Cæsar's image; but Rev. xiii. 15 clearly points to some mysterious death which shall result in the very presence of the image of the future Cæsar. The same power which will enable the False Prophet to give life to the image, will destroy the life of him who refuses to worship it.

† In one of the darkest hours of their history, when the continued persecution of the Jews threatened the race with utter extinction, Barcochab proclaimed himself the Messiah, and led them in a revolt against the Romans, which ended in a carnage of the ill-fated people more horrible than any which had preceded it (A.D. 130-132). The man seems to have been a contemptible impostor who duped the people by juggler's tricks, such as blowing fire from his mouth; and yet

exercise of all the Dragon's delegated power, the Beast will command the homage of a world that has rejected grace. "All that dwell upon the earth shall worship him, whose names are not written in the book of life."* If it were possible, the very elect would be deceived by his mighty " signs and wonders " ;† but faith, divinely given, is a sure, as it is the only, safeguard against credulity and superstition.

But this is what he will become in the zenith of his career. In his origin he is described as a " little horn,"‡—like Alexander of Macedon, the king of a petty kingdom. Possibly he will be the head of some new Principality to arise in the final dismemberment of Turkey; it may be on the banks of the Euphrates, or perhaps upon the Asian shore of the Ægean Sea. The name of Babylon is strangely connected with events to come, and Pergamus, so long the home of serpent worship in its vilest forms, is the only place on earth which Scripture has identified with Satan's throne.§

Of the great political changes which must precede his advent, the most conspicuous are the restoration

---

he attained to such an eminence, and brought about disasters so terrible, that some have sought to find in his career the fulfilment of the prophecies of Antichrist.

   * Rev. xiii. 8.   † Matt. xxiv. 24.

   ‡ Dan. vii. 8.   § Rev. ii. 13.

of the Jews to Palestine, and the predicted division of the Roman earth. The former of these events has already been considered in a previous chapter, and as regards the latter there is but little to be said. The attempt to enumerate the ten kingdoms of the future would involve a profitless inquiry.* History repeats itself; and if there be any element of periodicity in the political diseases by which nations are afflicted, Europe will inevitably pass through another crisis such as that which darkened the last decade of the eighteenth century. And should another revolution produce another Napoleon, it is impossible to foretell how far kingdoms may become consolidated, and boundaries may be changed. Moreover in forecasting the fulfilment of these prophecies, we are dealing with events which, while they may occur within the lifetime of living men, may yet be delayed for centuries. Our part is not to prophecy, but only to interpret; and we may well rest content with the certainty that when the Apocalyptic visions are in fact fulfilled, their fulfilment will be clear, not merely to minds educated in mysticism, but to all who are capable of observing public facts.

Through the gradual unfolding, it may be, of influences even now in operation; or far more pro-

---

* *See* App. 2., Note D.

bably as the outcome of some great European crisis in the future, this confederation of nations * shall be developed, and thus the stage will be prepared on which shall appear that awful Being, the great leader of men in the eventful days which are to close the era of Gentile supremacy.

If we are to understand aright the predicted course of the Antichrist's career, certain points connected with it must be clearly kept in view. The first is that up to a certain epoch he will be, notwithstanding his pre-eminence, no more than human. And here we must judge of the future by the past. At two-and-twenty years of age, Alexander crossed the Hellespont, the prince of a petty Grecian state. Four years later he had founded an Empire and given a new direction to the history of the world.

In the career of Napoleon Bonaparte, modern history affords a parallel still more striking and complete. When, now just a hundred years ago, he entered the French military school at Brienne, he was an unknown lad, without even the advantages

---

* I say *nations*, not kingdoms, advisedly, for though they will ultimately be kingdoms, *i.e.*, under monarchical government, yet *before* the advent of the Kaiser such *may* not be the case. That this division of the Roman earth will take place before his appearance is expressly stated ; but whether a year, a decade, or a century before, we are not informed.

which rank and wealth afford. So utterly obscure was his position that, not only did he owe his admission to the school to the influence of the Governor of Corsica, but calumny has found it possible to use that trifling act of friendly patronage to the disparagement of his mother's name. If then such a man, by the gigantic force of his personal qualities, combined with the accident of favouring circumstances, could attain the place which history has assigned to him, the fact affords the fullest answer to every objection which can be urged against the credibility of the predicted career of the man of prophecy.

Nor will it avail to urge that the last fifty years have so developed the mental activity of civilized races, and have produced such a spirit of independence, that the suggestion of a career like Napoleon's being repeated in days to come involves an anachronism. " In proportion as the general standard of mental cultivation is raised, and man made equal with man, the ordinary power of genius is diminished, but its extraordinary power is increased, its reach deepened, its hold rendered more firm. As men become familiar with the achievements and the exercise of talent, they learn to despise and disregard its daily examples, and to be more independent of mere men of ability ; but they only become more completely in the power of gigantic intellect, and the slaves of pre-eminent and unapproachable talent." *

By the sheer force of transcendent genius the man of prophecy will gain a place of undisputed pre-eminence in the world; but if the facts of his after career are to be understood, considerations of a wholly different kind must be taken into account. A strange crisis marks his course. At first the patron of religion, a true "eldest son of the church," he becomes a relentless and profane persecutor. At first no more than a king of men, commanding the allegiance of the Roman earth, he afterwards claims to be divine, and demands the worship of Christendom.

And we have seen how this extraordinary change in his career takes place at that epoch of tremendous import in the history of the future, the beginning of the 1,260 days of the latter half of Daniel's seventieth week. Then it is that that mysterious event takes place, described as "war in heaven" between the Archangel and the Dragon. As the result of that amazing struggle, Satan and his angels are "cast out into the earth," and the Seer bewails mankind because the devil is come down into their midst, "having great wrath because he knoweth that he hath but a short time."†

---

* Alford, *Gr. Test.* Proleg. 2 Thess., § 36.
† Rev. xii. 7, 12.

The next feature in the vision is the rise of the ten-horned Beast.* This is not the event described in the seventh of Daniel. The Beast, doubtless, is the same both in Daniel and the Apocalypse, representing the last great empire upon earth ; but in the Apocalypse it appears at a later stage of its development. Three periods of its history are marked in Daniel. In the first it has *ten* horns. In the second it has *eleven,* for the little horn comes up *among* the ten. In the third, it has but *eight,* for the eleventh has grown in power, and three of the ten have been torn away by it. Up to this point Daniel's vision represents the Beast merely as " the fourth kingdom upon earth," the Roman empire as revived in future times, and here the vision turns away from the history of the *Beast* to describe the action of the little horn as a blasphemer and persecutor.†

It is at this epoch that the thirteenth chapter of Revelation opens. The three first stages of the history of the empire are past, and a fourth has been developed. It is no longer a confederacy of nations bound together by treaty, with a Napoleon

---

† Rev. xiii. 1.

† The passage (Dan. vii. 2-14) is quoted in full at pp. 36, 37, *ante.* The distinctions above noticed clear up the seeming inconsistency between Daniel's visions and the Revelation, alluded to at p. 199, *ante.*

rising up in the midst of them and struggling for supremacy; but a confederacy of kings who are the lieutenants of one great Kaiser, a man whose transcendent greatness has secured to him an undisputed pre-eminence. And this is the man whom the Dragon will single out to administer his awful power on earth in days to come. And from the hour in which he sells himself to Satan he will be so energized by Satan, that "ALL power and signs and lying wonders" shall characterize his after course.*

There is a danger lest in dwelling on these visions as though they were enigmas to be solved, we should forget how appalling are the events of which they speak, and how tremendous the forces which will be in exercise at the time of their accomplishment. During this age of grace Satan's power on earth is so restrained that men forget his very existence. This, indeed, will be the secret of his future triumphs. And yet how unspeakably terrible must be the dragon's power, witness the temptation of our Lord! It is written, "The devil, taking Him up into an high mountain, showed unto Him all the kingdoms of the world in a moment of time; and the devil said unto Him, All this power will I give Thee,

---

* ὁ ἄνομος . . . οὗ ἐστιν ἡ παρουσία κατ᾽ ἐνέργειαν τοῦ Σατανᾶ ἐν πάσῃ δυνάμει, καὶ σημείοις, καί τέρασι ψεύδους (2 Thess. ii. 8, 9).

and the glory of them, for that is delivered unto me, and to whomsoever I will I give it. If Thou, therefore, wilt worship me, all shall be Thine." *

It is this same awful being who shall give to the Beast his throne, his power, and great authority,†— all that Christ refused in the days of His humiliation. The mind that has realized this stupendous fact will not be slow to accept what follows: "And power was given him over all kindreds, and tongues, and nations; and all that dwell upon the earth shall worship him, whose names are not written in the book of life of the Lamb."‡

Of the events which afterwards must follow upon earth, it behoves us to speak with deep solemnity and studied reserve. The phenomenon of sudden and absolute darkness is inconceivably terrible, even when eagerly looked for with full intelligence of the causes which produce it.§ How unspeakable then would be its awfulness, if unexpected, unaccounted for, and prolonged, it may be for days together. And such shall be the sign which Holy Writ declares

---

* Luke iv. 5-7.   † Rev. xiii. 2.   ‡ Rev. xiii. 7, 8.

§ The Astronomer Royal (Sir G. B. Airy) used these words in a lecture delivered at the Royal Institution, 4th July, 1853, upon the total solar eclipses of 1842 and 1851 :—" The phenomenon, in fact, is one of the most terrible that man can witness, and no degree of partial eclipses gives any idea of its horror."

shall mark the advent of earth's last great woe.[*]
The signs and wonders of Satanic power shall still
command the homage of mankind, while the thunders
of a heaven no longer silent will break forth upon
the apostate race.   Then will be the time of "the
seven last plagues," wherein " is *filled up* the wrath
of God,"—the time when "the vials of the wrath
of God" shall be poured out upon the earth.[†]   And
if in this day of grace the heights and depths of
God's longsuffering mercy transcend all human
thoughts, His WRATH will be no less Divine.   "The
day of vengeance of our God," "the great and the terrible day of the Lord,"—such are the names divinely
given to describe that time of unexampled horror.

And yet when in the midnight darkness of the
last apostasy, Divine longsuffering will only serve to
blind and harden, mercy itself shall welcome the
awful breaking of the day of vengeance, for blessing lies beyond it.   Another day is still to follow.
Earth's history, as unfolded in the Scriptures, reaches
on to a Sabbatic age of blessedness and peace ; an
age when heaven shall rule upon the earth, when
" the Lord shall rejoice in all His works,"[‡] and prove

---

[*] " The sun shall be turned into darkness . . . before the
great and the terrible day of the Lord come " (Joel ii. 31).   *See*
p. 174, *ante.*

[†] Rev. xv. 1 ; xvi. 1.   *See* pp. 142-146, *ante.*

[‡] Psalm civ. 31.

Himself to be the God of every creature He has made.*

Further still, the veil is raised, and a brief glimpse afforded us of a glorious eternity beyond, when every trace of sin shall have been wiped out for ever, when heaven will join with earth, and "the tabernale of God"—the dwelling place of the Almighty—shall be *with men*, "and He will dwell with them, and they shall be His people, and God *Himself* shall be with them, and be their God."†

It was a calamity for the Church of God when the light of prophecy became dimmed in fruitless controversy, and the study of these visions, vouchsafed by God to warn, and guide, and cheer His saints in evil days, was dismissed as utterly unprofitable. They abound in promises which God designed to feed His people's faith and fire their zeal, and a special blessing rests on those who read, and hear, and cherish them.‡ One of the most hopeful features of the present hour is the increasing interest they everywhere excite ; and if these pages should avail to deepen or direct the enthusiasm even of a few in the study of a theme which is inexhaustible, the labour they have cost will be abundantly rewarded.

---

* Psalm cxlv. 9-16.

† Rev. xxi. 3. The order of these events is noticed at pp. 177-181, *ante*.   ‡ Rev. i. 3.

APPENDIX 1

CHRONOLOGICAL TREATISE AND TABLES

THE point of contact between sacred and profane chronology, and therefore the first certain date in biblical history, is the accession of Nebuchadnezzar to the throne of Babylon (*cf.* Dan. i. 1 and Jer. xxv. 1). From this date we reckon on to Christ and back to Adam. The agreement of leading chronologers is a sufficient guarantee that David began to reign in B.C. 1056-5, and therefore that all dates subsequent to that event can be definitely fixed. But beyond this epoch, *certainty* vanishes. The marginal dates of our English Bible represent in the main Archbishop Ussher's chronology,* and notwithstanding his eminence as a chronologer some of these dates are doubtful, and others entirely wrong.

Of the doubtful dates in Ussher's scheme the

---

* Bishop Lloyd, to whom was entrusted the task of editing the A.V., in this respect made a few alterations, as *ex. gr.*, in the book of Nehemiah he rejected Ussher's chronology, and inserted the true historical date of the reign of Artaxerxes Longimanus.

reigns of Belshazzar and "Ahasuerus" may serve as examples. Belshazzar's case is specially interesting. Scripture plainly states that he was King of Babylon at its conquest by the Medo-Persians, and that he was slain the night Darius entered the city. On the other hand, not only does no ancient historian mention Belshazzar, but all agree that the last king of Babylon was Nabonidus, who was absent from the city when the Persians captured it, and who afterwards submitted to the conquerors at Borsippa. Thus the contradiction between history and Scripture appeared to be absolute. Sceptics appealed to history to discredit the book of Daniel; and commentators solved or shirked the difficulty by rejecting history. The cuneiform inscriptions, however, have now settled the controversy in a manner as satisfactory as it was unexpected. On clay cylinders discovered by Sir H. Rawlinson at Mughier and other Chaldean sites, Belshazzar (Belsaruzur) is named by Nabonidus as his eldest son. The inference is obvious, that during the latter years of his father's reign, Belshazzar was King-Regent in Babylon. According to Ptolemy's canon Nabonidus reigned seventeen years (from B.C. 555 to B.C. 538), and Ussher gives these years to Belshazzar.

In common with many other writers, Ussher has assumed that the King of the book of Esther was Darius Hystaspes, but it is now generally agreed that it is the son and successor of Darius who is there mentioned as Ahasuerus—"a name which orthographically corresponds with the Greek *Xerxes*." *

The great *durbar* of the first chapter of Esther, held in his third year (ver. 3), was presumably with a view to his expedition against Greece (B.C. 483) ; and the marriage of Esther was in his seventh year (ii. 16), having been delayed till then on account of his absence during the campaign. The marginal dates of the book of Esther should therefore begin with B.C. 486, instead of B.C. 521, as given in our English Bibles.

But these are comparatively trivial points, whereas the principal error of Ussher's chronology is of real importance. According to 1 Kings vi. 1, Solomon began to build the Temple "in the 480th year after the children of Israel were come out of the land of Egypt." The mystic character of this era of 480 years has been noticed in an earlier chapter.† Ussher assumed that it represented a strictly chronological period, and reckoning back from the third year of Solomon, he fixed the date of the Exodus as B.C. 1491,—an error which vitiates his entire system.

In Acts xiii. 18-21, St. Paul, in treating of the

---

* Rawlinson's *Herodotus*, iv., p. 212. "Xerxes (old Persian Khshayarshá) is derived by Sir H. Rawlinson from Khshaya, 'a King'" (*Ibid.* III., 446, App. Book VI. note A).

† Pages 81-85, *ante*.

interval between the Exodus and the end of Saul's reign, specifies three several periods ; viz., 40 years, *about* 450 years, and 40 years = 530 years. From the accession of David to the third year of Solomon, when the temple was founded, was forty-three years. According to this enumeration therefore, the period between the Exodus and the temple was 530 + 43 years = 573 years. Clinton, however, whose chronology has been very generally adopted, conjectures that there was an interval of twenty-seven years between the death of Moses and the first servitude, and an interval of twelve years between "Samuel the prophet" (1 Sam. vii.) and the election of Saul. Accordingly he estimates the period between the Exodus and the temple as 573 + 27 + 12 years = 612 years.*

Clinton's leading dates, therefore, are as follows :—

B.C. 4138.—Adam.

„ 2482.—The Deluge.

„ 2055.—The Call of Abraham.

„ 1625.—The Exodus.

„ 1096.—The Election of Saul.

„ 1056.—David.

" 1016.—Solomon.

---

* Josephus appears to confirm this in *Ant.* xx. 10 § 1, where he specifies 612 years between the Exodus and the temple, but in *Ant.* viii. 3 § 1, he fixes the same period at 592 years. It is supposed that in the longer era he included the twenty years during which both the temple and the palace were building.

B.C.   976.—Rehoboam.

„   606.—The Captivity (*i.e.*, the Servitude to Babylon).

In this chronology Browne proposes three corrections (*Ordo Sæc.*, §§ 10, 13) ; viz., he rejects the two conjectural terms of twenty-seven years and twelve years above noticed ; and he adds two years to the period between the Deluge and the Exodus. If this last correction be adopted (and it is perfectly legitimate, considering that *approximate* accuracy is all that the ablest chronologer can claim to have attained for this era), let *three* years be added to the period between the Deluge and the Covenant with Abraham, and the latter event becomes exactly, as it is in any case approximately, the central epoch between the Creation and the Crucifixion. The date of the Deluge will thus be put back to B.C. 2485, and therefore the Creation will be B.C. 4141.

The following most striking features appear in the chronology as thus settled :—

From Adam to the covenant with
    Abraham (B.C. 4141 to B.C 2055) is   2086 years.

From Abraham to the crucifixion of
    Christ (B.C. 2055 to A.D. 32) is   .   2086 „

From Adam to the Deluge (B.C. 4141
    to B.C. 2485) is   .   .   .   .   1656 „

From the Deluge to the Covenant
    (B.C. 2485 to B.C. 2055) is   .   .   430 „

From the Covenant to the Exodus

   (B.C. 2055 to B.C. 1625) is   .   .   430 years.

From the Exodus to the Crucifixion

   (B.C. 1625 to A.D. 32) is   .   .   1656 * „

The Covenant here mentioned is that recorded in Gen. xii. in connection with the call of Abraham. The statements of Scripture relating to this part of the chronology may seem to need explanation in two respects.

Stephen declares in Acts vii. 4 that Abraham's removal from Haran (or Charran) took place *after* the death of his father. But Abraham was only seventy-five years of age when he entered Canaan ; whereas if we assume from Gen. xi. 26 that Abraham was born when Terah was but seventy, he must have been one hundred and thirty at the call, for Terah died at two hundred and five.† The fact however is obvious from these statements, that though named first among the sons of Terah, Abraham was not the firstborn, but the youngest: Terah was seventy when his eldest son was born, and he had three sons, Haran, Nahor, and Abraham. To ascertain his age at

---

* *Cf.* Browne *Ordo Sæc.* § 13. His system, however, compels him to specify the destruction of Jerusalem (A.D. 70) as the close of the Mosaic economy, which is certainly wrong. The crucifixion was the great crisis in the history of Judah and of the world.

† Comp. Gen. xi. 26, 31, 32 ; xii. 4.

Abraham's birth we must needs turn to the history, and there we learn it was one hundred and thirty years. * And this will account for the deference Abraham paid to Lot, who, though his nephew, was nevertheless his equal in years, possibly his senior ; and moreover, as the son of Abraham's eldest brother, the nominal head of the family.†

Again.   According to Exod. xii. 40 "the sojourning of the children of Israel, who dwelt in Egypt, was 430 years."   If this be taken to mean (as the statement in Gen. xv. 13, quoted by Stephen in Acts vii. 6, might also seem to imply) that the Israelites were four centuries in Egypt, the entire chronology must be changed.   But, as St. Paul explains in Gal. iii. 17, these 430 years are to be computed from the call of Abraham, and not from the going down of Israel into Egypt.   The statement in Gen. xv. 13 is explained and qualified by the words which follow in ver. 16.   The entire period of Israel's wanderings was to be four centuries, but when the passage speaks definitely of their sojourn in Egypt it says : " In the fourth generation they shall come hither again "—a

---

* Clinton, *F. H.*, vol i., p. 299. Alford's supercilious comments on this (*Gr. Test.*, Acts vii. 4) could be easily disposed of were the occasion opportune for the discussion this would involve. Indeed a passing reference to Gen xxv. 1, 2, would have modified his statements.

† Gen. xiii. 8, 9.

word which was accurately fulfilled, for Moses was the fourth in descent from Jacob.*

It was not till 470 years after the covenant with Abraham that his descendants took their place as one of the nations of the earth. They were slaves in Egypt, and in the wilderness they were wanderers ; but under Joshua they entered the land of promise and became a nation. And with this last event begins a series of cycles of " seventy weeks " of years.

From the entrance into Canaan (B.C. 1586-5) to the establishment of the kingdom under Saul (B.C. 1096) was 490 years.

From the kingdom (B.C. 1096) to the servitude to Babylon (B.C. 606) was 490 years.

From the epoch of the servitude (B.C. 606) until the royal edict of the twentieth year of Artaxerxes Longimanus, the national independence of Judah was in abeyance, and with that date began the mystic era of 490 years, which form the "seventy weeks" of the prophecy of Daniel.

Again the period between the dedication of the first temple in the eleventh year of Solomon (B.C. 1006-5) and the dedication of the second temple in the sixth year of Darius Hystaspes of Persia (B.C. 515), was 490 years.†

---

* His mother was a daughter of Levi (Exod. ii. 1).

+ It is a remarkable coincidence that the era of the second

Are we to conclude that these results are purely accidental? No thoughtful person will hesitate to accept the more reasonable alternative that the chronology of the world is part of a Divine plan or " economy of times and seasons."

The chronological inquiry suggested by the data afforded by the books of 2 Kings, 2 Chronicles, Jeremiah, Ezekiel, and Daniel, is of principal importance, not only as establishing the absolute accuracy of Scripture, but also because it throws light upon the main question of the several eras of the captivity, which again are closely allied with the era of the seventy weeks.

The student of the book of Daniel finds every step beset with difficulties, raised either by avowed enemies, or *quasi* expositors of Holy Writ. Even the opening statement of the book has been assailed on all sides. That Daniel was made captive in the third year of Jehoiakim " is simply an invention of late Christian days," declares the author of *Messiah the Prince* (p. 42), in keeping with the style in which this writer disposes of history sacred and profane, in order to support his own theories.

In Dean Milman's History of the Jews, the page which treats of this epoch is full of inaccuracies.

---

temple was so nearly this same period of 490 years, B.C. 515 to about B.C. 18, when Herod rebuilt it.

First he confounds the seventy years of the desolations, predicted in Jer. xxv., with the seventy years of the servitude, which had already begun. Then as the prophecy of Jer. xxv. was given in the fourth year of Jehoiakim, he fixes the first capture of Jerusalem in that year, whereas Scripture expressly states it took place in Jehoiakim's third year (Dan. i. 1). He proceeds to specify B.C. 601 as the year of Nebuchadnezzar's invasion; and here the confusion is hopeless, as he mentions two periods of three years each between that date and the king's death, which nevertheless he rightly assigns to the year B.C. 598.

Again, Dr. F. W. Newman's article on the *Captivities*, in Kitto's *Cyclopædia*, well deserves notice as a specimen of the kind of criticism to be found in standard books ostensibly designed to aid the study of Scripture.

" The statement with which the book of Daniel opens is" (he maintains) "in direct collision with the books of Kings and Chronicles, which assign to Jehoiakim an eleven years' reign, as also with Jer. xxv. 1. It partially rests on 2 Chron. xxxvi. 6, which is itself not in perfect accordance with 2 Kings xxiv. In the earlier history the war broke out during the reign of Jehoiakim, who died before its close ; and when his son and successor Jehoiachin had reigned three months, the city and its king were captured. But in the Chronicles the same event is made to happen twice over at an interval of three months and ten days (2 Chron. xxxvi. 6 and 9); and even so we do not obtain accordance with the received interpretation of Dan. i. 1-3."

This writer's conclusions are adopted by Dean Stanley in his *Jewish Church* (vol. ii., p. 459), wherein he enumerates among the captives taken with Jehoiachin in the eighth year of Nebuchadnezzar, the prophet Daniel, who had gained a position at the court of Babylon six years before Jehoiachin came to the throne! *

A reference to the *Five Great Monarchies* (vol. iii., pp. 488-494), and the *Fasti Hellenici*, will show how thoroughly consistent the sacred history of this period appears to the mind of a historian or a chronologer; and moreover how completely it harmonizes with the extant fragments of the history of Berosus.

Jehoiakim did in fact reign eleven years. In his third year he became the vassal of the King of Babylon. For three years he paid tribute, and in his sixth year he revolted. There is not a shadow of reason for believing that the first verse of Daniel is spurious; and apart from all claim to Divine sanction for the book, the idea that such a writer—

---

* Compare 2 Kings xxiv. 12 with Dan. ii. 1.

a man of princely rank and of the highest culture,* and raised to the foremost place among the wise and noble of Babylonia—was ignorant of the date and circumstances of his own exile, is simply preposterous. But according to Dr. Newman, he needed to refer to the book of Chronicles for the information, and was deceived thereby! A comparison of the statements in Kings, Chronicles, and Daniel clearly establishes that the narratives are independent, each giving details omitted in the other books. The second verse of Daniel appears inconsistent with the rest only to a mind capable of supposing that the living king of Judah was placed as an ornament in the temple of Belus along with the holy vessels ; for so Dr. Newman has read it. And the apparent inconsistency in 2 Chron. xxxvi. 6 disappears when read with the context, for the eighth verse shows the writer's knowledge that Jehoiakim completed his reign in Jerusalem. Moreover the correctness of the entire history is signally established by fixing the chronology of the events, a crucial test of accuracy.

Jerusalem was first taken by the Chaldeans in the third year of Jehoiakim (Dan. i. 1). His fourth year was current with the first of Nebuchadnezzar (Jer. xxv. 1). This accords with the definite

---

* Dan. i. 3, 4.

statement of Berosus that Nebuchadnezzar's first expedition took place before his actual accession (Jos., *Apion*, i. 19). According to the canon of Ptolemy, the accuracy of which has been fully established, the reign of Nebuchadnezzar dates from B.C. 604, *i.e.*, his accession was in the year beginning the first Thoth (which fell in January) B.C. 604, and the history leaves no doubt it was early in that year. But the captivity, according to the era of Ezekiel, began in Nebuchadnezzar's eighth year (comp. Ezek. i. 2 and 2 Kings xxiv. 12) ; and in the thirty-seventh year of the captivity, Nebuchadnezzar's successor was on the throne (2 Kings xxv. 27). This would give Nebuchadnezzar a reign of at least forty-four years, whereas according to the Canon (and Berosus confirms it) he reigned only forty-three years, and was succeeded by Evil-Merodach (the Iluoradam of the Canon), in B.C. 561.

It follows therefore that Scripture antedates the years of Nebuchadnezzar, computing his reign from B.C. 605.* This would be sufficiently accounted for by the fact that, from the conquest of Jerusalem in the third year of Jehoiakim, the Jews acknowledged Nebuchadnezzar as their suzerain. It has been overlooked, however, that it is in accordance with the ordinary principle on which they reckoned

---

* Clinton, *F. H.*, vol. i., p. 367.

regnal years, computing them from Nisan to Nisan.* In B.C. 604 the 1st Nisan fell on or about the 1st April,† and according to Jewish reckoning, the King's second year would begin on that day, no matter how recently he had ascended the throne. Therefore " the fourth year of Jehoiakim that was the first year of Nebuchadnezzar " (Jer. xxv. 1), was the year beginning Nisan B.C. 605 ; and the third of Jehoiakim, in which Jerusalem was taken and the servitude began, was the year beginning Nisan B.C. 606.

This result is most remarkably confirmed by Clinton, who fixes the summer of B.C. 606 as the date of Nebuchadnezzar's first expedition.‡

It is further confirmed by, and affords the explanation of a statement of Daniel, which has been triumphantly appealed to in depreciation of the value of his book. If, it is urged, the King of Babylon kept Daniel three years in training before admitting him to his presence, how could the prophet have interpreted the King's dream in his second year ? (Dan. i. 5, 18 ; ii. 1). Daniel, a citizen of Babylon, and a courtier withal, naturally and of course computed his sovereign's reign according to

---

* See p. 240, *post*.

† The Paschal new moon, in B.C. 604, was on the 31st of March.

‡ *F. H.*, vol. i., p. 328.

the common era in use around him (as Nehemiah afterwards did in like circumstances.)* But as the prophet was exiled in B.C. 606, his three years' probation terminated at the close of B.C. 603, whereas the second year of Nebuchadnezzar, computed from his actual accession, extended to some date in the early months of B.C. 602.

Again. The epoch of Jehoiachin's captivity was in the eighth year of Nebuchadnezzar (2 Kings xxiv. 12), *i.e.*, his eighth year as reckoned from Nisan.

But the ninth year of the captivity was still current on the tenth Tebeth in the ninth year of Zedekiah and seventeenth of Nebuchadnezzar (comp. Ezek. xxiv. 1, 2, with 2 Kings xxv. 1-8).

And the nineteenth year of Nebuchadnezzar and eleventh of Zedekiah, in which Jerusalem was destroyed, was in part concurrent with the twelfth year of the captivity (comp. 2 Kings xxv. 2-8 with Ezek. xxxiii. 21).

It follows therefore that Jehoiachin (*Jeconiah*) must have been taken at *the close* of the Jewish year ("when the year was expired," 2 Chron. xxxvi. 10), that is the year preceding 1st Nisan, B.C. 597; and Zedekiah was made king (after a brief interregnum) early in the year beginning on that day.† And

---

* *See* p. 253, *post.*

† This is confirmed by Ezek. xl. 1, compared with 2 Kings xxv. 8, for the twenty-fifth year of the captivity was the fourteenth

it also follows that whether computed according to the era of Nebuchadnezzar, of Zedekiah, or of the captivity, B.C. 587 was the year in which "the city was smitten."*

The first link in this chain of dates is the third year of Jehoiakim, and every new link confirms the proof of the correctness and importance of that date. It has been justly termed the point of contact between sacred and profane history; and its importance in the sacred chronology is immense on account of its being the epoch of the servitude of Judah to the King of Babylon.

The servitude must not be confounded with the captivity, as it generally is. It was rebellion against the Divine decree which entrusted the imperial sceptre to Nebuchadnezzar, that brought on the Jews the further judgment of a national deportation, and the still more terrible chastisement of the "desolations." The language of Jeremiah is most definite in this respect. "I have given all these lands into the hand of Nebuchadnezzar, the king of Babylon, my servant." "The nation which will not serve the same Nebuchadnezzar, the king of Babylon,

___

year after the destruction of Jerusalem (viz., the nineteenth of Nebuchadnezzar), reckoned *inclusively* according to the ordinary pratice of the Jews.

* These results will appear at a glance by reference to the table appended.

that nation will I punish, saith the Lord, with the
sword, and with the famine, and with the pestilence,
until I have consumed them by his hand." But
the nations that bring their neck under the yoke
of the king of Babylon, and serve him, *those will
I let remain still in their own land*, saith the Lord,
and they shall till it and dwell therein " (Jer. xxvii.
6, 8 11 ; and comp. chap. xxxviii. 17-21).

The appointed era of this servitude was seventy
years, and the twenty-ninth chapter of Jeremiah
was a message of hope to the captivity, that at
the expiration of that period they should return to
Jerusalem (ver. 10). The twenty-fifth chapter, on
the other hand, was a prediction for the rebellious
Jews who remained in Jerusalem after the servitude
had commenced, warning them that their stubborn
disobedience would bring on them utter destruction,
and that for seventy years the whole land should
be " a desolation."

To recapitulate. The thirty-seventh year of the
captivity was current on the accession of Evil-
Merodach (2 Kings xxv. 27), and the epoch of that
king's reign was B.C. 561. Therefore the captivity
dated from the year beginning Nisan 598 and
ending Adar 597. But this was the eighth year
of Nebuchadnezzar according to Scripture reckoning.
Therefore his first year was Nisan 605 to Nisan 604.
The first capture of Jerusalem and the beginning

of the servitude was during the preceding year, 606-605. The final destruction of the city was in Nebuchadnezzar's nineteenth year, *i.e.*, 587, and the siege began 10th Tebeth (or about 25th December), 589, which was the epoch of the desolations. The burning of Jerusalem cannot have been B.C. 588, as given by Ussher, Prideaux, etc., for in that case* the captivity would have begun B.C. 599, and the thirty-seventh year would have ended before the accession of Evil-Merodach. Nor can it have been B.C. 586, as given by Jackson, Hales, etc., for then the thirty-seventh year would not have begun during Evil-Merodach's first year.†

This scheme is practically the same as Clinton's,‡ and the sanction of his name may be claimed for it, for it differs from his only in that he dates Jehoiakim's reign from *August* B.C. 609, and Zedekiah's from *June* B.C. 598, his attention not having been called to the Jewish practice of computing reigns from *Nisan ;* whereas I have fixed Nisan B.C. 608 as the epoch of Jehoiakim's reign, and ·Nisan B.C. 597 for Zedekiah's. Not of course that Nisan was in fact the month-date of the accession,

---

* As this event was in the nineteenth year of Nebuchadnezzar (2 Kings xxv. 8), and the captivity began in his eighth year (2 Kings xxiv. 12).

† Clinton, *F. H.*, vol. i., p. 319.

‡ *Ibid.*, pp. 328-329.

but that, according to the rule of the *Mishna* and the practice of the nation, the reign was so *reckoned*. Jehoiakim's date could not be Nisan B.C. 609, because his fourth year was also the first of Nebuchadnezzar, and the thirty-seventh year, reckoned from the eighth of Nebuchadnezzar, was the first of Evil-Merodach, *i.e.*, B.C. 561, which date fixes the whole chronology as Clinton himself conclusively argues.* It follows from this also that Zedekiah's date must be B.C. 597, and not 598.

The chronology adopted by Dr. Pusey † is essentially the same as Clinton's. The scheme here proposed differs from it only to the extent and on the grounds above indicated. His suggestion that the fast proclaimed in the fifth year of Jehoiakim‡ referred to the capture of Jerusalem in his third year, is not improbable, and points to Chisleu (Nov.) B.C. 606 as the date of that event. For the reasons above stated, it could not have been B.C. 607, as Dr. Pusey supposes, and the same argument proves that Canon Rawlinson's date for Nebuchadnezzar's expedition (B.C. 605) is a year too late.§

The correctness of this scheme will, I presume, be admitted, as regards the cardinal point of difference between it and Clinton's chronology, namely,

---

* *Fasti H.*, vol. i., p. 319. † *Daniel*, p. 401.
‡ Jer. xxxvi. 9. § *Five Great Mon.*, iv. 488.

that the reigns of the Jewish kings are reckoned from Nisan. It remains to notice the points of difference between the results here offered and Browne's hypotheses (*Ordo Sæc.*, §§ 162-169). He arbitrarily assumes that Jehoiachin's captivity and Zedekiah's reign began *on the same day*. This leads him to assume further (1) that they were *reckoned* from the same day, viz., the 1st Nisan, and (2) that Nebuchadnezzar's royal years dated from some date between 1st Nisan and 10 Ab 606 (§ 166). Both these positions are untenable. (1) The Jews certainly reckoned the reigns of their kings from 1st Nisan, but there is no proof that they so reckoned the years of ordinary periods or eras such as the captivity. (2) The presumption is strong, confirmed by all the synchronisms of the chronology, that they computed Nebuchadnezzar's royal era either according to the Chaldean reckoning, as in Daniel, or according to their own system, as in the other books.

The following table will show at a glance the several eras of the servitude to Babylon, king Jehoiachin's captivity, and the desolations of Jerusalem.

In using the table it is essential to bear in mind two points already stated. 1. The year given in the first column is the Jewish year beginning the 1st Nisan (March—April). For example, B.C. 604 is the year beginning the 1st April, 604 ; and B.C. 589 is the year beginning the 15th March, 589

According to the *Mishna*,* "On the 1st of Nisan
is a new year for the computation of the reign of
kings, and for festivals." To which the editors of
the English translation add this note : " The reign
of Jewish kings, whatever the period of accession
might be, was always reckoned from the preceding
Nisan ; so that if, for instance, a Jewish king began
to reign in Adar, the following month (Nisan) would
be considered as the commencement of the second
year of his reign. This rule was observed in all
legal contracts, in which the reign of kings was
always mentioned."

2. The years of the different eras are only *in
part* concurrent. For example, the first year of the
desolations dates from the tenth day of Tebeth
(25th December), B.C. 589, and the tenth year of the
captivity begins even later,† while the ninth year
of Zedekiah and seventeenth of Nebuchadnezzar
dates from the 1st Nisan (15th March) B.C. 589.

If these points be kept in view the chronology
of the table will be found to harmonize *every chronological statement* relating to the period embraced in
it, contained in the Books of Kings, Chronicles,
Jeremiah, Ezekiel, and Daniel.

---

* Treatise, *Rosh Hashanah*, I. 1.
† See p. 234, *ante.*

CHRONOLOGICAL TABLE

FROM THE SERVITUDE TO BABYLON TO THE DEDICATION OF THE SECOND TEMPLE

Jewish Year *	Kings of Babylon	Kings of Judah	Era of the Servitude	Era of the Captivity	Era of the Desolations	EVENTS AND REMARKS.
B.C. 606	20th year of Nabo-polassar	3rd year of Jehoiakim (Eliakim)	1			The 3rd year of Jehoiakim, from 1st Nisan, 606, to 1st Nisan, 605. Jerusalem taken by Nebuchadnezzar (Dan. i. 1, 2), see p. 231, *ante*. With this event the servitude to Babylon began, 490 years (or 70 weeks of years) after the establishment of the Kingdom under Saul.
605	Nebuchad nezzar	4	2			"The 4th year of Jehoiakim, that was the 1st year of Nebuchadnezzar," *i.e.*, the year beginning 1st Nisan, 605 (Jer. xxv. 1). Vision of the great image (Dan. ii.)
604	2	5	3			
603	3	6	4			
602	4	7	5			
601	5	8	6			
600	6	9	7			
599	7	10	8			
598	8	11	9	1		This year included the 3 months' reign of Jehoiachin (Jeconiah), whose captivity began in the 8th year of Nebuchadnezzar (2 Kings xxiv. 12, see pp. 234, 236, *ante*). Reigned 11 years (2 Kings xxiv. 18).
597	9	3 months of Jehoiachin / Zedekiah	10	2		
596	10	2	11	3		
595	11	3	12	4		

See explanatory remarks, p. 239, *ante.*

CHRONOLOGICAL TABLE (continued)

Jewish Year B.C.	Kings of Babylon	Kings of Judah	Era of the Servitude	Era of the Captivity	Era of the Desolations	Events and Remarks
594	12	4	13	5		Ezekiel began to prophesy in the 30th year from Josiah's Passover (2 Kings xxiii. 23), and the 5th year of the captivity (Ezek. i. 1, 2.)
593	13	5	14	6		
592	14	6	15	7		
591	15	7	16	8		
590	16	8	17	9		
589	17	9	18	10	1	Jerusalem invested for the third time by Nebuchadnezzar, on the 10th day of Tebeth—"the fast of Tebeth,"—the epoch of the "Desolations" (see pp. 69, 70, *ante*).
588	18	10	19	11	2	"The 10th year of Zedekiah, which was the 18th year of Nebuchadnezzar" (Jer. xxxii. 1).
587	19	11	20	12	3	Jerusalem taken on the 9th day of the 4th month, and burnt on the 7th day of the 5th month in the 11th year of Zedekiah, and the 19th year of Nebuchadnezzar (2 Kings xxv. 2, 3, 8, 9, see p. 234, *ante*), called "The 12th year of our Captivity" in Ezek. xxxiii. 21, the news having reached the exiles on the 5th day of the 10th month.
586	20		21	13	4	
585	21		22	14	5	
584	22		23	15	6	
583	23		24	16	7	
582	24		25	17	8	
581	25		26	18	9	
580	26		27	19	10	

Year				
579	27	28	20	11
578	28	29	21	12
577	29	30	22	13
576	30	31	23	14
575	31	32	24	15
574	32	33	25	16
573	33	34	26	17
572	34	35	27	18
571	35	36	28	19
570	36	37	29	20
569	37	38	30	21
568	38	39	31	22
567	39	40	32	23
566	40	41	33	24
565	41	42	34	25
564	42	43	35	26
563	43	44	36	27
562	44	45	37	28
561	Evil-Mero-dach	46	38	29
560	2 Neriglissar or	47	39	30
559	Nergal-sherezer	48	40	31

The 25th year of the Captivity was the 14th (*inclusive*, as the Jews usually reckoned) from the destruction of Jerusalem (Ezek. xl. 1).

According to the Canon, the accession of Iluoradam (Evil-Merodach) was in the year beginning 1st Thoth (11th Jan.) B.C. 561, (see p. 232, *ante*). But the year 562 in this table is the Jewish year, *i.e.* the year preceding 1st Nisan (or about 5th April 561, and the 37th year of Jehoiachin's captivity was current till towards the close of that year. In this year Jehoiachin was "brought forth out of prison" (Jer. lii. 31).

CHRONOLOGICAL TABLE (continued)

Jewish Year	Kings of Babylon	Era of the Servitude	Era of the Captivity	Era of the Desolations	EVENTS AND REMARKS
B.C.					
558	2	49	41	32	
557	3	50	42	33	
556	4	51	43	34	
555	Nabonidus	52	44	35	The Nabonadius of the Canon is called Nabunnahit in the Inscriptions, and Labynetus by Herodotus.
554	2	53	45	36	
553	3	54	46	37	
552	4	55	47	38	
551	5	56	48	39	
550	6	57	49	40	
549	7	58	50	41	
548	8	59	51	42	
547	9	60	52	43	
546	10	61	53	44	
545	11	62	54	45	
544	12	63	55	46	
543	13	64	56	47	
542	14	65	57	48	
541	15	66	58	49	In or before this year, Belshazzar (the Belsaruzur of the Inscriptions) became regent in the lifetime of his father, Nabonadius. Daniel's vision of the Four Beasts was in the 1st year, and his vision of the Ram and the Goat was in the 3rd year of Belshazzar (Dan. vii., viii.)

B.C.	Reign				Events
540	16	67	59	50	
539	17	68	60	51	
538	Darius (the Mede)	69	61	52	Babylon taken by Cyrus. Daniel's vision of the 70 weeks was in this year.
537	2	70	62	53	
536	Cyrus			54	Decree of Cyrus authorizing the Jews to return to Jerusalem : end of the Servitude. (N.B. The 70th year of the Servitude was current till the 1st Nisan, 536.)
535	2			55	
534	3			56	Year of Daniel's last vision (Dan. x.-xii.)
533	4			57	
532	5			58	
531	6			59	
530	7			60	
529	Cambyses			61	
528	2			62	
527	3			63	
526	4			64	
525	5			65	
524	6			66	
523	7			67	
522	8			68	
521	Darius I			69	
520	2			70	Darius Hystaspes (p. 57, *ante*). End of the Desolations. The foundation of the Second Temple was laid on the 24th day of the 9th month in the 2nd year of Darius (Hag. ii. 18, see p. 70, *ante*).
519	3				
518	4				
517	5				
516	6				
515	7				The Temple was finished on the 3rd day of Adar in the 6th year of Darius (Ezra vi. 15). The Temple was dedicated at the Passover in Nisan 515 (Ezra vi. 15-22), 490 years after the dedication of Solomon's temple (B.C. 1005), and 70 years before the date of the edict to build the *city* (see p. 66, *ante*).

TABLE OF CHRONOLOGICAL PARALLELISMS

SHOWING THAT THE CALL OF ABRAHAM WAS THE CENTRAL POINT BETWEEN
THE CREATION AND THE CRUCIFIXION

B.C.

4141 *	Adam—The Creation	} 1656 years	} 2086 years
2485 *	Noah—The Flood	} 430 years	
2055	Abraham—The Covenant †	} 430 years	} 2086 years
1625	Moses—The Law	} 1656 years	
A.D. 32 ‡	Christ—The Crucifixion		

* These dates differ from Clinton's chronology by three years.   See p. 223, *ante.*

† Gal. iii. 17.

‡ See pp. 97 and 122, *ante.*

CERTAIN LEADING DATES IN HISTORY, SACRED
AND PROFANE.*

B.C.

2055. The Covenant with Abraham.

1625. The Exodus.   The giving of the Law.

1585. The entrance into Canaan under Joshua.

1096. Saul.   The kingdom established.

1056. David.

1016. Solomon

1014. The Temple founded.

1006. The Temple dedicated.

976. Rehoboam.   Israel revolts from Judah, and becomes
         a separate kingdom under Jeroboam.

776. Era of the Olympiads begins.

753. Era of Rome (A. U. C.) begins.

747. Era of Nabonassar begins.

726. Hezekiah king of Judah (reigned 29 years).

721. Israel (the ten tribes) carried captive to Assyria.

697. Manasseh (55 years).

642. Amon (2 years).

640. Josiah (31 years).

627. Jeremiah began to prophesy.

608. Jehoiakim (11 years).

606. BABYLON.—Jerusalem taken   by   Nebuchadnezzar
         The servitude began.

---

* These dates are Clinton's, subject to remarks in App. I., *ante*.
They are selected mainly to throw light on Daniel's visions. The names
of historians, etc., are introduced in the fifth century B.C. to indicate the
character of the age in which the prophetic era of the seventy weeks
began.

B.C.

598. Jerusalem taken the second time by the Babylonians. King Jehoiachin's captivity.

589. Jerusalem besieged the third time by the Babylonians. The Desolations.

587. Jerusalem taken and destroyed.

561. Death of Nebuchadnezzar and accession of Evil-Merodach.

559. Cyrus begins to reign in Persia.

538. PERSIA.—Babylon taken by the Medes and Persians.

536. Cyrus succeeds Darius in the empire. Decree to build the temple.

521. Darius Hystaspes of Persia.

520. The foundation of the second temple. Haggai and Zechariah prophesied.

515. Dedication of the second temple.

490. Battle of Marathon.

485. Xerxes succeeds Darius; the *Ahasuerus* of the book of Esther.

484. Herodotus the historian born.

480. Battles of Thermopylæ and Salamis.

471. Themistocles banished by ostracism. Thucydides the historian born.

468. Socrates born (died 399).

466. Flight of Themistocles to Persia.

465. Artaxerxes Longimanus of Persia.

458. Decree of Artaxerxes to beautify the temple (Ezra vii.)

449. Persians defeated by the Athenians at Salamis in Cyprus.

445. Era of the 70 weeks begins. Twentieth year of Artaxerxes : Jerusalem restored. Herodotus, *æt.* 39, engaged on his history.

B.C.

429. Plato born (died 347).

424. Darius Nothus of Persia (Neh. xii. 22).

405. Artaxerxes Mnemon of Persia.

397. Malachi.   The dispensation of "the Prophets" closes. End of the first week of Daniel's 70 weeks.

359. Ochus of Persia.

336. Darius Codomanus of Persia.

333. GREECE.—Battle of Issus.   (Battle of Granicus, 334 ; and of Arbela, 331.)

323. Death of Alexander the Great.

312. Era of the Seleucidæ begins.

301. Battle of Ipsus.

170. Jerusalem taken by Antiochus Epiphanes.

168. The temple defiled by Antiochus.

165. Jerusalem retaken by Judas Maccabeus.   The temple cleansed, and the Feast of the Dedication appointed. (1 Macc. iv. 52-59 ; John x. 22).

63. ROME.—Pompey takes Jerusalem.

40. Herod the Great appointed king of Judea by the Romans.

37. Herod takes Jerusalem, and is acknowledged as king by the Jews.

31. Battle of Actium.

12. Augustus Emperor of Rome.

4. The Nativity.

3. Death of Herod.   Archelaus made Ethnarch of Judea, and Herod Antipas set over Galilee.

A.D.

14. Tiberius Emperor of Rome (from 19th August).

28. 15th year of Tiberius, from 19th Aug. A.D. 28, to 19th Aug. 29. The Lord's ministry began in this year, Luke iii.

A.D.

32. The crucifixion (at the fourth Passover of the Lord's ministry).

THE JEWISH MONTHS.

Nisan, or Abib	March—April.
Zif, or Iyar	April—May.
Sivan	May—June.
Tammuz	June—July.
Ab	July—Aug.
Elul	Aug.—Sept.
Tisri, or Ethanim	Sept.—Oct.
Bul, or Marchesvan	Oct.—Nov.
Chisleu	Nov.—Dec.
Tebeth	Dec.—Jan.
Sebat	Jan.—Feb.
Adar	Feb.—March.

Ve-Adar (the intercalary month).

Full information on the subject of the present "Hebrew Calendar" will be found in an article so entitled in *Encyc. Brit.* (9th ed.), and also in Lindo's *Jewish Calendar*, a Jewish work. The *Mishna* is the earliest work relating to it.

MISCELLANEOUS: WHO AND WHEN

NOTE A

ARTAXERXES LONGIMANUS AND THE CHRONOLOGY OF HIS REIGN

So thorough is the unanimity with which the Artaxerxes of Nehemiah is now admitted to be Longimanus, that it is no longer necessary to offer proof of it. Josephus indeed attributes these events to Xerxes, but his history of the reigns of Xerxes and Artaxerxes is so hopelessly in error as to be utterly worthless. In fact he transposes the events of these respective reigns (see *Ant.* XI., caps v. and vii.) Nehemiah's master reigned not less than thirty-two years (Neh. xiii. 6) ; and his reign was subsequent to that of Darius Hystaspes (comp. Ezra vi. 1 and vii. 1), and prior to that of Darius Nothus (Neh. xii. 22). He must, therefore, be either Longimanus or Mnemon, for no other king after Darius Hystaspes reigned thirty-two years, and it is certain Nehemiah's mission was not so late as the twentieth of Artaxerxes Mnemon, viz., B.C. 385.

This appears, first, from the general tenor of the history ; second, because this date is later than that of Malachi, whose prophecy must have been considerably later than the time of Nehemiah ; and third, because Eliashib, who was high priest when Nehemiah came to Jerusalem, was grandson

of Jeshua, who was high priest in the first year of Cyrus
(Neh. iii. 1 ; xii. 10; Ezra ii. 2 ; iii. 2) ; and from the first
year of Cyrus (B.C. 536), to the twentieth of Artaxerxes
Longimanus (B.C. 445), was ninety-one years, leaving room
for precisely three generations.*

Moreover, the eleventh chapter of Daniel, if read aright,
affords conclusive proof that the prophetic era dated from
the time of Longimanus. The second verse is generally interpreted as though it were but a disconnected fragment of
history, leaving a gap of over 130 years between it and the
third verse, whereas the chapter is a consecutive prediction
of events *within the period of the seventy weeks.* There were
to be yet (*i.e.,* after the issuing of the decree to build Jerusalem) " three kings in Persia." These were Darius Nothus
(mentioned in Neh. xii. 22), Artaxerxes Mnemon, and
Ochus ; the brief reigns of Xerxes II., Sogdianus, and
Arogus being overlooked as being, what in fact they were,
utterly unimportant, and indeed two of them are omitted in
the Canon of Ptolemy. "The fourth" (and *last*) king was
Darius Codomanus, whose fabulous wealth—the accumu-
lated horde of two centuries—attracted the cupidity of the
Greeks. What sums of money Alexander found in Susa
is unknown, but the silver ingots and Hermione purple
he seized after the battle of Arbela were worth over †
£20,000,000. Verse 2 thus reaches to the close of the
Persian Empire ; verse 3 predicts the rise of Alexander the
Great ; and verse 4 refers to the division of his kingdom
among his four generals.

According to Clinton (*F. H.,* vol. ii., p. 380) the death of

---

* *Encyc. Brit.,* 9th ed., title " Artaxerxes."

† W. K. Loftus, " *Chaldea and Susiana,*" p. 341.

Xerxes was in July B.C. 465, and the accession of Artaxerxes was in February B.C. 464. Artaxerxes of course ignored the usurper's reign, which intervened, and reckoned his own reign from the day of his father's death. Again, of course, Nehemiah, being an officer of the court, followed the same reckoning. Had he computed his master's reign from February 464, Chisleu and Nisan could not have fallen in the same regnal year (Neh. i. 1 ; ii. 1). No more could they, had he, according to the Jewish practice, computed it from Nisan.

Dr. Pusey here remarks,* " The accession of Artaxerxes after the seven months of the assassin Artabanus would fall in the middle of 464. For it is clear from the sequel of the months in Neh. i., ii., and Ezra vii. 7-9, that Chisleu fell earlier in the year of his reign than Nisan, and Nisan than Ab. Then the reign of Artaxerxes must have begun between Ab and Chisleu B.C. 464." This is altogether a mistake. As already mentioned, Chisleu and Nisan fell in the same regnal year ; and so also did Nisan and *the first day* of Ab (Ezra vii. 8, 9). But the 1st Ab of B.C. 459 (the seventh year of Artaxerxes) fell on or about the 16th July, and therefore the passages quoted are perfectly consistent with the received chronology, and serve merely to enable us to fix the dates more accurately still, and to decide that the death of Xerxes and the epoch of the reign of Artaxerxes should be assigned to the *latter* part of July B.C. 465.

Those who are not versed in what writers on prophecy have written on this subject, will be surprised to learn that this date is assailed as being nine years too late. All chronologers are agreed that Xerxes began to reign in

* *Daniel*, p. 160.

B.C. 485, and that the death of Artaxerxes was in B.C. 423; and so far as I know, no writer of repute, unbiassed by prophetic study, assigns as the epoch of the latter king's reign any other date than B.C. 465 * (or 464 ; see *ante*). This is the date according to the Canon of Ptolemy, which has been followed by all historians ; and it is confirmed by the independent testimony of Julius Africanus, who, in his *Chronography*,† describes the twentieth year of Artaxerxes as the 115th year of the Persian Empire [reckoned from Cyrus, B.C. 559] and the fourth year of the eighty-third Olympiad. This fixes B.C. 464 as the first year of that king, as it was in fact the year of his actual accession.

It was Archbishop Ussher who first raised a doubt upon the point. Lecturing on " Daniel's Seventies " ‡ in Trinity College, Dublin, in the year 1613, difficulties connected with his subject suggested an inquiry which led him ultimately to put back the reign of Longimanus to B.C. 474, which is the date given in his *Annales Vet. Test.* The same date was afterwards adopted by Vitringa, and a century later by Krüger. But Hengstenberg is regarded as the champion of this view, and the treatise thereon in his *Christology* § omits nothing that can be urged in its favour.

The objections raised to the received chronology depend

---

* On this point I have consulted the author of *The Five Great Monarchies*, a book to which frequent reference is made in these pages, and I am indebted to Canon Rawlinson's courtesy and kindness for the following reply : " I think you may safely say that chronologers are now agreed that Xerxes died in the year B.C. 465. The Canon of Ptolemy, Thucydides, Diodorus, and Manetho are agreed ; the only counter authority being Ctesias, who is quite untrustworthy."

† *Ante-Nicene Christian Library*, vol. ix., second part, p. 184.

‡ Works, vol. xv., p. 108.

§ Arnold's trans., pp. 443-454.

mainly on the statement of Thucydides, that Artaxerxes was on the throne when Themistocles reached the Persian Court; for it is urged that the flight of Themistocles could not have been so late as B.C. 464.* But, as Dr. Pusey remarks,† "they have not made any impression on our English writers who have treated of Grecian history." ‡ In common with the German writers, Dr. Pusey ignores Ussher altogether in the controversy, though Dr. Tregelles § rightly claims for him the foremost place for scholarship among those who have advocated the earlier date. The apparent difficulty of making the prophecy and the chronology agree has led Dr. Pusey, following Prideaux, in opposition to Scripture, to fix the seventh year of Artaxerxes as the epoch of the seventy weeks, while it induced Dr. Tregelles, ‖ sheltering behind Ussher's name, to adopt the B.C. 455 date for the twentieth year of that king's reign. Bishop Lloyd when affixing Ussher's dates to our English Bible reverted to the received chronology when dealing with the book of Nehemiah.

It is unnecessary to enter here upon a discussion of this question. Nothing short of a reproduction of the entire argument in favour of the new chronology would satisfy its advocates; and for my present purpose it is a sufficient answer to that argument, that although everything has been urged which ingenuity and erudition can suggest in support of it, it has been rejected by all secular writers. Unfulfilled

---

* Krüger's arguments are reviewed by Clinton in *F. H.*, ii., p. 217.

† *Daniel*, p. 171, *note*.

‡ See *ex. gr.* Mitford, ii., 226 ; Thirlwall, ii., 428 ; Grote, v., 379 ; and of Germans *see* Niebuhr, *Lect. Anc. Hist.* (Schmitz ed.), ii., 180-181.

§ *Daniel*, p. 266.

‖ *Ibid.*, p. 99, *note*.

prophecy is only for the believer, but prophecy fulfilled has a voice for all. It is fortunate, therefore, that the proof of the fulfilment of this prophecy of the seventy weeks does not depend on an elaborate disquisition, like that of Hengstenberg's, to disturb the received chronologies.

One point only I will notice. It is urged in favour of limiting the reign of Xerxes to eleven years, that no event is mentioned in connection with his reign after his eleventh year. The answer is obvious : first, that it is to Greek historians, writing after his time, that we are mainly indebted for our knowledge of Persian history ; and secondly, the battles of Thermopylæ and Salamis may well have induced a king of the temperament and character of Xerxes to give himself up to a life of indolent ease and sensual enjoyment.

But further, the twelfth year of Xerxes is expressly mentioned in the book of Esther (iii. 7), and the narrative proves that his reign continued to the twelfth (Jewish) month of his thirteenth year.* Hengstenberg answers this by asserting that it was customary with Hebrew writers to include in a regnal era the years of a co-regency where it existed, and he appeals to the case of Nebuchadnezzar as a

---

* The Feast of Purim derives its name from the fact that when Haman planned the destruction of the people of Mordecai, he cast lots day by day to find "a lucky day" for the execution of his scheme. A whole year—the twelfth year of Xerxes—was thus consumed (Esther iii. 7) ; and the decree for the slaughter of the Jews was made on the 13th Nisan in the following year (*ibid*. iii. 12). The decree in their favour was granted two months later (*ibid*. viii. 9), and the king is mentioned in connection with the execution of that decree in the twelfth month of that year (*ibid*. ix. 1, 13-17). The reign of Xerxes therefore certainly continued to the last month of his thirteenth year. The last chapter of Esther, moreover, clearly shows that his reign did not end with the events recorded in the book, but that his promotion of Mordecai was the beginning of a new era in his career.

proof of such a custom.* If Nebuchadnezzar's reign was in fact reckoned thus, this solitary instance would establish no such custom, for it would prove nothing more than that the Jews in Jerusalem, knowing nothing of the politics or customs of Babylon, reckoned Nebuchadnezzar's reign upon a system of their own. But I believe this theory about Nebuchadnezzar's reign is a thorough blunder. If in the sacred history he is called King of Babylon, in connection with his first invasion of Judea, it is because the writers were his contemporaries. "Lord Beaconsfield was Chancellor of the Exchequer in Lord Derby's administrations" is a statement which will be rightly condemned as an anachronism if made by the historian of the future, but it is precisely the language which would have been used by a contemporary writer acquainted with the living statesman. I have shown elsewhere (App. I., *ante*) that the Jews reckoned Nebuchadnezzar's reign according to their own custom, as dating from the Nisan preceding his accession. Unless, therefore, some entirely new case can be made in support of the co-regency theory of Xerxes's reign, it remains that the book of Esther is absolutely conclusive against Ussher's date, and in favour of the received chronology.

NOTE B

DATE OF THE NATIVITY

In treating of the date of the birth of our Lord, the arguments in favour of an earlier date than that which is here adopted are too well known to be left unnoticed.

---

* *Christology* (Arnold's *trans.*), § 737.

Dr. Farrar states the question thus in his *Life of Christ* (Excursus I.) :—

" Our one most certain datum is obtained from the fact that Christ was born before the death of Herod the Great. The date of that event is known with absolute certainty, for (i) Josephus tells us that he died thirty-seven years after he had been declared king by the Romans. Now it is known that he was declared King A.U.C. 714 ; and, therefore, since Josephus always reckons his years from Nisan to Nisan, and counts the initial and terminal fractions of Nisan as complete years, Herod must have died between Nisan A.U.C. 750, and Nisan A.U.C. 751, *i.e.*, between B.C. 4 and B.C. 3 of our era. (ii.) Josephus says that on the night in which Herod ordered Judas, Matthias, and their abettors to be burnt, there was an eclipse of the moon. Now this eclipse took place on the night of March 12th, B.C. 4, and Herod was dead at least seven days before the Passover, which, if we accept the Jewish reckoning, fell in that year on April 12th. But according to the clear indication of the Gospels, Jesus must have been born at least forty days before Herod's death. It is clear, therefore, that under no circumstances can the nativity have taken place later than February B.C. 4."*

This passage is a typical illustration of the relative value attached to the statements of sacred and profane historians. In the histories of Josephus an incidental mention of an eclipse or of the length of a king's reign suffices to give

---

* Dr. Farrar's book has done much to popularize a controversy which hitherto has interested only the few. It may be well to notice, therefore, that his sweeping statement as to the date of Herod's death is doubtful (*see* Clinton, *Fasti Rom.*, A.D. 29), and that Josephus does *not* always reckon reigns in the manner indicated (*see* p. 262, *post*).

" absolute certainty," before which the clearest and most definite statements of Holy Writ must give place, albeit they relate to matters of such transcendent interest to the writers that even if the Evangelists be dismissed to the category of mere historians, no mistake was possible.

The following is a more temperate statement of the question, by the Archbishop of York, in an article (*Jesus Christ*) contributed to Smith's *Bible Dictionary :*—" Herod the Great died, according to Josephus, in the thirty-seventh year after he was appointed king. His elevation coincides with the consulship of Cn Domitius Calvinus and C. Asinius Pollio, and this determines the date A.U.C. 714. There is reason to think that in such calculations Josephus reckons the years from the month Nisan to the same month, and also that the death of Herod took place in the beginning of the thirty-seventh year, or just before the Passover ; if then thirty-six complete years are added, they give the year of Herod's death, A.U.C. 750."

According to this, the commonly received view, Herod's death took place within the first six days of a Jewish year, and these days are reckoned as a complete year in his regnal era. Now it is admitted that in computing time the Jews generally included both the terminal units of a given period. A signal and well-known instance of this is afforded by the words of the Lord Himself, when He declared He would lie in death for three days and nights. What meaning did these words convey to Jews ? Four-and-twenty hours after His burial they came to Pilate and said, " We remember that that deceiver said, while He was yet alive, ' *After three days* I will rise again ;' command, therefore, that the sepulchre be made sure *until the third* *day."* * Had that Sunday passed leaving the seal upon the tomb unbroken, the Pharisees would boldly have proclaimed their triumph; whereas, by our modes of reckoning, the resurrection ought to have been deferred till Monday night, or Tuesday morning.†

Again, it may be assumed that Herod's accession dated in fact from B.C. 40, and, therefore, that B.C. 4 was the thirty-seventh and last year of his reign. Further it is probable he died *shortly* before a Passover. The question remains whether his death occurred at the beginning or toward the close of the Jewish year.

Josephus relates that when the event took place Archelaus remained in seclusion during seven days, and then presented himself publicly to the people. His first reception was not unfavourable, though he had to yield to many a popular demand then pressed on him; and after the ceremonial, he "went and offered sacrifice to God, and then betook himself to feast with his friends." Soon, however, discontent

---

* Matt. xxvii. 63, 64 ; comp. 2 Chron. x. 5-12. " He said unto them, Come again unto me *after three* days . . . so Jeroboam and all the people came to Rehoboam *on the third day* ? "

† Whether such a system of reckoning appears strange or natural depends on the habit of thought of the individual. A professor of theology might have trouble in defending it in class, but a prison chaplain would have no difficulty in explaining it to his congregation ! Our own civil day is a $\nu\nu\chi\theta\eta\mu\epsilon\rho\sigma\nu$, beginning at midnight, and the law takes no cognizance of a *part* of a day. Therefore in a sentence of three days' imprisonment, the prescribed term is equal to seventy-two hours ; but though the prisoner seldom reaches the gaol till evening, the law holds him to have completed a day's imprisonment the moment midnight strikes, and the gaoler may lawfully release him the moment the prison is opened the second morning after. As a matter of fact a prisoner committed for three days is seldom more than forty hours in gaol. This mode of reckoning and speaking was as familiar to the Jew as it is to the *habitués* of our police courts.

and disaffection began to smoulder and spread, and fresh demands were made upon the king. To these again he yielded, though with less grace, instructing his general to remonstrate with the people, and persuade them to defer their petitions till his return from Rome. These appeals only increased the prevailing dissatisfaction, and a riot ensued. The king still continued to parley with the seditious, but, " upon the approach of the feast of unleavened bread," when the capital became thronged with the Jews from the country, the state of things became so alarming that Archelaus determined to suppress the rioters by force of arms. This was " *upon the approach of* the feast," and the Jews considered the Passover was "nigh at hand " upon the eighth day of Nisan, when they repaired to Jerusalem for the festival.*

The Passover began the 14th Nisan. This final riot took place during the preceding week. The earlier riot occurred before that again, *i.e.*, before the date of the incursion of Jews for the festival, the 8th Nisan. This again was preceded by *some* interval, measured from the day following the court mourning for Herod, which had lasted seven days. The history, therefore, establishes conclusively that Herod's death was more than fourteen days before the Passover, and therefore *at the close and not at the beginning of a Jewish year.*

But which year ? His death must have been *after* the

---

* " When the people were come in great crowds to the feast of un-leavened bread on the eighth day of the month Xanthicus " (*i.e.*, Nisan) (Jos., *Wars*, vi. 5, 3. Comp. John xi. 55 ; xii. 1). " The Jews' Passover was nigh at hand, and many went out of the country up to Jerusalem before the Passover to purify themselves. Then Jesus six days before the Passover came to Bethany."

eclipse of 13th March, B.C. 4 * But the eclipse was only a month before the Passover of that year, and his death was fourteen days at least before the Passover ; could then the events recorded by Josephus as occurring in the interval between the eclipse and the king's death have taken place in a fortnight? Let the reader turn to the *Antiquities* and judge for himself whether it be possible. The natural inference from the history is that the death was not weeks but months after the eclipse, and therefore, again, at the *close* of the year.

The correctness of this conclusion can be established by the application of the strictest of all tests, that of referring to the historian's chronological statements.

In his *Wars* (ii. 7, 3), Josephus assigns the banishment of Archelaus to the *ninth* year of his government; in his later work (*Ant.*, xvii. 13, 3), he states it was in his *tenth* year. And these dates are given with a definiteness and in a manner which preclude the idea of a blunder. They are connected with the narration of a dream in which Archelaus saw a number of ears of corn (nine in the *Wars*, ten in the *Antiquities*), devoured by oxen,—presaging that the years

---

* There was no lunar eclipse visible at Jerusalem between that of the 13th March B.C. 4 and that of 9th January B.C. 1. Many writers take the latter to be the eclipse of Herod, and assign his death to that year. That of B.C. 1 was a fine total eclipse, totality coming on at fifteen minutes past midnight, whereas that of B.C. 4 was but a partial eclipse, and the greatest magnitude was not till 2 h. 34 m. a.m. (Johnson, *Eclipses Past and Future*). But though every consideration of this character points to B.C. 1 as the date of Herod's death, the weight of evidence generally is in favour of B.C. 4. Of recent writers, the former year is adopted by Dr. Geikie (*Life of Christ*, 6th ed., p. 150), and notably by the late Mr. Bosanquet, who argues the question in his *Messiah the Prince*, and more concisely in a paper read before the Society of Biblical Archæology on 6th June, 1871.

of his rule were about to be brought abruptly to an end.
Now whether a ruler be Christian, Jew, or Turk, his ninth
year is the year beginning with the eighth anniversary
of his government, and his tenth year that beginning with
the ninth anniversary ; and it is mere casuistry to pretend
that there is either mystery or difficulty in the matter. It
is evident that the difference between the two statements of
the historian is intentional, and that in his two histories
he computed the Ethnarch's government from two different
epochs. But if Herod died in the first week of the Jewish
year, as these writers maintain, this would be impossible,
for Archelaus's actual accession would have synchronized
with his accession according to Jewish reckoning. Whereas
if his government dated from the *close* of a Jewish year,
A.D. 6 * would be his ninth year in fact, but his tenth year
according to *Mishna* rule of computing reigns from
Nisan.

In numerous treatises on this subject will be found an
argument based on John ii. 20, " Forty and six years was
this temple in building." According to Josephus (it is
urged), " Herod's reconstruction of the temple began in the
eighteenth year of his reign,"† and forty-six years from that
date would fix A.D. 26 as the year in which these words were
spoken, and therefore as the first year of our Lord's ministry.
That writers of repute should have written thus may be described as a literary phenomenon. Not only does Josephus
not say what is thus attributed to him, but his narrative
disproves it. The foundation for the statement is that either

---

* This is the year specified by Dion Cassius for the Ethnarch's
banishment. Clinton, *F. H.*, A.D. 6.

† Farrar, *Life of Christ*, App. Exc. I.

in his eighteenth or nineteenth year * Herod made a speech proposing to rebuild the temple. But the historian adds, that finding his intentions and promises thoroughly distrusted by the people, " the king encouraged them, and told them he would not pull down their temple till all things were gotten ready for building it up entirely again. And as he promised them this beforehand, so he did not break his word with them, but got ready a thousand waggons, that were to bring stones for the building, and chose out ten thousand of the most skilful workmen, and bought a thousand sacerdotal garments for the priests, and *had some of them taught the art of stone-cutters,* and *others of carpenters,* and *then* began to build ; *but this was not till everything was well prepared for the work.*"† What length of time these preparations occupied, it is of course impossible to decide, but if, as Lewin supposes, the work was begun at the Passover of B.C. 18, then forty-six years would bring us exactly to A.D. 29—the first Passover of the Lord's ministry.

NOTE C

CONTINUOUS HISTORICAL SYSTEM OF PROPHETIC INTERPRETATION

THE historical interpreters of prophecy have grasped a principle the importance of which is abundantly proved by the striking parallelisms between the visions of the Apoca-

---

* It depends on the meaning of the word γεγονότος in the passage, whether the eighteenth or nineteenth year be intended. The narrative, as a whole, points to the nineteenth year. *Cf.* Lewin's *Fasti Sacri*, pp. lvi. and 92.

† Josephus, *Ant.*, xv. 11, 27.

lypse and the events of the history of Christendom. But
not content with this, they have on the one hand brought
discredit on prophetic study by wild and arrogant predictions about the end of the world, and on the other, they
have reduced their principle of interpretation to a system,
and then degraded it to a *hobby*. The result is fortunate in
this respect, that the evil cannot fail to cure itself, and the
time cannot be far distant when the "continuous historical
interpretation," in the form and manner in which its cham-
pions have propounded it, will be regarded as a vagary of
the past. The events of the first half of the present century
produced on the minds of Christians such an impression in
its favour, that it bid fair to gain general acceptance. But
the late Mr. Elliott's great work has thoroughly exposed its
weaknesses. A perusal of the first five chapters of the
Horæ Apocalypticæ cannot fail to impress the reader with a
sense of the genuineness and importance of the writer's
scheme, nor will he fail to appreciate the erudition displayed,
and the sobriety with which it is used. But when he passes
from the commentary upon the first five seals, to the account
of the sixth seal, he must experience a revulsion of feeling
which will be strong just in proportion to his apprehension
of the *trueness* and solemnity of Holy Writ. Let any one
read the last six verses of the sixth chapter of Revelation, a
passage the awful solemnity of which has scarcely a parallel
in Scripture, and with what feelings will he turn to Mr.
Elliott's book to find that the words are nothing more than
a prediction of the downfall of paganism in the fourth century ! (*see* p. 138, *ante*).

The words of the Apocalyptic vision in relation to the
great day of Divine wrath (Rev. vi. 17), are the language of
Isaiah (xiii. 9, 10) respecting "the day of the Lord," and

again of Joel's prophecy (Joel ii. 1, 30, 31), quoted by
St. Peter on the day of Pentecost (Acts ii. 16-20). Nor is
this all. The twenty-fourth chapter of St. Matthew is a
Divine commentary upon the visions of the sixth chapter of
Revelation, and each of the seals has its counterpart in the
Lord's predictions of events preceding His second advent,
ending with the mention of these same terrible convulsions
of nature here described. Therefore, even if the mind be
"educated" up to the point of accepting such an interpretation of the vision of the sixth seal, these other Scriptures
remain to be accounted for.

Many other points in Mr. Elliott's scheme might be cited
as equally faulty. Take for example the laboured essay on
the subject of the two witnesses, culminating in the amazing
anti-climax that their ascent to heaven (Rev. xi. 12) was
fulfilled when Protestants obtained "an advancement to
political dignity and power." (*Horæ Ap.*, ii., 410). Still
more wild and reckless is his exposition of Rev. xii. 5. "It
seems clear" (he says) "that whatever the woman's hope in
her travail, the lesser consummation was the one figured in
the man child's birth and assumption, viz., *the elevation of
the Christians, first to recognition as a body politic, then very
quickly to the supremacy of the throne* in the Roman Empire"
(vol. iii., 12). The reference to Wilberforce in connection
with Rev. xv. is almost grotesque (vol. iii., 430). And
finally he drifts upon the rock on which every man who
follows this false system must inevitably be wrecked—the
chronology of prophecy : proving by cumulative evidence
that the year 1865 would usher in the *millennium*, or if not
1865, then 1877 or 1882 (vol. iii., 256-266).

"An apocalyptic commentary which explains everything
is self-convicted of error." This dictum of Dean Alford's

(*Gr. Test.:* Rev. xi. 2) applies with full force to Mr. Elliott's book. Maintaining as he does that these visions have received their absolute and final fulfilment, he is bound " to explain everything ; " and as the result these lucubrations mar a work which if recast by some intelligent student of prophecy would be of the highest value. In days like these, when we have to contend for the very words of Scripture, we cannot afford to dismiss them as harmless puerilities. They have given an impetus to the scepticism of the age, and have encouraged Christian men to treat the most solemn warnings of coming wrath as mere stage thunder.

Mr. Elliott's mantle appears now to have fallen upon the author of the *Approaching End of the Age*. Mr. Grattan Guinness's treatise upon lunisolar cycles and epacts will be deemed by many the most interesting and valuable portion of the work. The study of it has confirmed an impression I have long entertained, that in some mystic interpretation of the prophetic periods of Daniel, the chronology of Gentile supremacy and of the Christian dispensation lies concealed. Professor Birks, however, justly remarks, that it is " very doubtful whether much of the speciality on which Mr. Guinness founds this part of his theory is not due to a partial selection unconsciously made of *some* epact numbers out of many, and that the special relations of the epacts to the numbers 6, 7, 8, 13, would probably disappear on a comprehensive examination of all the epact numbers " (*Thoughts on Sacred Prophecy*, p. 64).

It might also be remarked that with the latitude obtained by reckoning sometimes in lunar years, sometimes in lunisolar years, and sometimes in ordinary Julian years, the list of seeming chronological coincidences and parallelisms might be still further increased. The period from the

Council of Nice (A.D. 325) to the death of Gregory XIII. (1585) was 1,260 years. From the edict of Justinian (533) to the French Revolution was 1,260 years ; and again from A.D. 606, when the Emperor Phocas conferred the title of Pope on Boniface III., to the overthrow of the temporal power (1866-1870), was also 1,260 years. If these facts prove anything, they prove, not that the periods mentioned are the fulfilment of Daniel's visions, for Daniel's visions relate to the history of Judah, with which these events have nothing to do, but that the chronology of such events is marked by cycles composed of multiples of seventy. Therefore, they greatly strengthen the *à priori* presumption that this is a general characteristic of " the times and seasons " as divinely planned, and that the visions will, hereafter, be literally fulfilled. In a word, such proofs prove far too much for the cause they are intended to support.

I have already noticed the transparent fallacy of sup posing that the ten-horned beast and the Babylon of the Apocalypse can *both* be typical of Rome (p. 134, *ante*). In the *Approaching End of the Age* this fallacy is accepted apparently without suspicion or misgiving, for the writer neither adopts nor improves upon the pleasing romance by which Mr. Elliott attempts to conceal the absurdity of such a view.

As the Harlot comes to her doom by the agency of the Beast, it is absolutely certain that they are not identical ; and every proof these writers urge to establish that the Church of Rome is Babylon, is equally conclusive to prove that the Papacy is not the Beast, the Man of Sin. Their whole system is like a house of cards which falls to pieces the moment it is tried. As such books are read by many who are unversed in history it may be well to repeat once

more, that the division of the Roman earth into ten kingdoms has never yet taken place. That it has been partitioned is plain matter of history and of fact : that it has
ever been divided into ten is a mere conceit of writers of
this school.*

Of Dan. ix. 24-27 Mr. Guinness writes, "From the then
approaching command to restore and to build again Jerusalem, to the coming of Messiah the Prince, was to be
seventy weeks " (p. 417). This is a typical instance of the
looseness of the historical school in dealing with Scripture.
The words of the prophecy are, " From the going forth of
the commandment to restore and to build Jerusalem unto
the Messiah the Prince shall be *seven weeks and threescore
and two weeks*." † As this error underlies his entire exposition of the prophecy which forms the special subject of these
pages, it is needless to discuss it. He follows Prideaux in
computing the weeks from the seventh year of Artaxerxes
(*see* p. 62, *ante*).

Again, in common with almost all commentators he confounds the seventy years of Judah's servitude with the
seventy years of the desolations of Jerusalem. The pro-

---

* See p. 39, *ante*. Elliott's list of the ten kingdoms is the following :—
The Anglo-Saxons, Franks, Allmans, Burgundians, Visigoths, Suevi,
Vandals, Ostrogoths, Bavarians, and Lombards. If any one can read
the seventh chapter of Daniel and the thirteenth chapter of Revelation
and accept such an interpretation, there is really no common ground on
which to discuss the matter.

† I deprecate the idea that my object is to review this or any other
book. Were such my intention I could point out other similar errors.
Ex. gr., in Pt. III., chap. 1, the writer enumerates five points of identity
between the Harlot and the Church of Rome, and of these five the two
last are sheer blunders, viz., " The minister of *the harlot* makes fire to
descend from heaven," " And *the harlot* requires all to receive her mark."
(Comp. Rev. xiii. 13, 16)

phecy he quotes from Jer. xxv. (p. 414) was given in the fourth year of Jehoiakim, whereas the servitude began in his third year ; and it foretold a judgment which fell seventeen years later (*see* p. 240, *ante*). It would seem ungracious to notice minor inaccuracies, such as that of confounding Belshazzar with Nabonidus, the last king of Babylon (*see* p. 221, *ante*).

Such a book is useful in so far as it deals positively with the historical fulfilment as a primary and partial realization of the prophecies ; and as a full and fearless indictment of the Church of Rome it is most valuable. But in the dogmatic negation of a literal fulfilment, in the blind and obstinate determination to establish, no matter at what cost to Scripture, that the Apocalypse has been " FULFILLED in the events of the Christian era," such a work cannot fail to be dangerous and mischievous. The real question at issue here is the character and value of the Bible. If the views of these writers be just, the language of Holy Writ in such passages as the close of the sixth chapter of Revelation is the most utter bombast. And if wild exaggeration characterize one portion of the Scriptures, what confidence can we have in any part? If the Great Day of Divine wrath, described in terms of unsurpassed solemnity, were nothing but a brief crisis in the history of a campaign now long past, the words which tell of the joy of the blessed and the doom of the impenitent may after all be mere hyperbole, and the Christian's faith may be mere credulity.

NOTE D

THE TEN KINGDOMS

" PROPHECY is not given to enable us to prophesy," and no one who has worthily pursued the study will fail to feel misgivings at venturing out upon the tempting field of forecasting "things to come." By patient contemplation we may clearly discern the main outlines of the landscape of the future ; but "until the day dawn," our apprehension of distances and details must be inadequate, if not wholly false. The great facts of the future, so plainly revealed in Scripture, have been touched on in preceding pages. For what follows here no deference is claimed save what may be accorded to a " pious opinion " based on earnest and careful inquiry.

Next to the restoration of the Jews, the most prominent political feature of the future, according to Scripture, is the tenfold partition of the Roman earth. The emphasis and definiteness with which *ten* kingdoms are specified, not only in Daniel, but in the Revelation, forbid our interpreting the words as describing merely a division of power such as has existed ever since the disruption of the Roman Empire, though this is undoubtedly a feature of the prophecy. Babylon, Persia, Greece, and Rome in turn sought to grasp universal dominion. That there should be a commonwealth of nations living side by side at peace, was a conception that nothing in the history of the world could have suggested.

The principal clew which Scripture affords upon the subject is the connection between these kingdoms and the

Roman Empire.* But some latitude must probably be allowed as to boundaries, otherwise we should have to choose between two equally improbable alternatives, namely, either that our own nation shall have sunk to the position of a province, not even Ireland remaining under her sway,† or else that the England which is to be numbered among the ten kingdoms will include the vast empire of which this island is the heart and centre. May we not indulge the hope that however far our nation may lapse in evil days to come from the high place which, with all her faults, she has held as the champion of freedom and of truth, she will be saved from the degradation of participating in the vile confederacy of the latter days?

These considerations as to boundaries apply also to Germany, though in a lower degree ; and Russia is clearly out of the reckoning altogether. The special interest and importance of these conclusions depend upon the fact that the antichrist is to be at first a patron and supporter of the religious apostasy of Christendom (see p. 201, *ante*), and that England, Germany, and Russia are precisely the three first-rate Powers who are outside the pale of Rome.

But there is no doubt that Egypt, Turkey, and Greece will be numbered among the ten kingdoms ; ‡ and is it not improbable in the extreme that these nations will ever accept the leadership of a man who is to appear as the champion and patron of the Latin Church? A striking solution of

---

* " The ten horns *out of this kingdom* " (Dan. vii. 24).

† Ireland was entirely, and Scotland was in part, outside the territorial limits of the Roman Empire.

‡ In Dan. xi. 40, Egypt and Turkey (or the Power which shall then possess Asia Minor) are expressly mentioned by their prophetic titles as separate kingdoms at this very time.

this difficulty will probably be found in the definite prediction, that while the ten kingdoms will ultimately own his suzerainty, *three* of the ten will be brought into subjection by force of arms (Dan. vii. 24. *See* p. 214, *ante*).

Turning again to the West, the names of France, Austria, Italy, and Spain present themselves; and seven of the kingdoms are thus accounted for. Can the list be completed? Belgium, Switzerland, and Portugal remain, and these too would claim a place were we dealing with the Europe of to-day; but as it is the future we are treating of, any attempt to press the matter further seems futile. It has been confidently urged by some that as the ten kingdoms were symbolised by the ten toes of Nebuchadnezzar's image, —five on either foot,—five of these kingdoms must be developed in the East, and five in the West. The argument is plausible, and possibly just; but its chief force depends upon forgetting that in the prophet's view the Levant and not the Adriatic, Jerusalem and not Rome, is the centre of the world.

To the scheme here indicated the objection may naturally be raised: Is it possible that the most powerful nations of the world, England, Germany, and Russia, are to have no part in the great drama of the last days? But it must be remembered, first, that the relative importance of the great Powers may be different at the time when these events shall be fulfilled, and secondly, that difficulties of this kind may depend entirely on the *silence* of Scripture, or, in other words, on our own ignorance. I feel bound to notice, however, that doubts which have been raised in my mind regarding the soundness of the received interpretation of the seventh chapter of Daniel point to a more satisfactory answer to the difficulties in question.

As the vision of the second chapter specifies the four empires which were successively to rule the world, and as the seventh chapter also enumerates four " kingdoms," and expressly identifies the fourth of these with the fourth kingdom of the earlier vision, the inference appears legitimate that the scope of both visions is the same throughout. And this conclusion is apparently confirmed by some of the details afforded of the kingdoms typified by the lion, the bear, and the leopard. So strong indeed is the *prima facie* case in support of this view, that I have not felt at liberty to depart from it in the foregoing pages. At the same time I am constrained to own that this case is less complete than it appears to be, and that grave difficulties arise in connection with it ; and the following observations are put forward tentatively to promote inquiry in the matter :—

1st. Daniel ii. and vii. are both in the Chaldee portion of the Book, and are therefore bracketed together, and separated from what follows. This strengthens the presumption, therefore, which would obtain in any case, that the later vision is not a repetition of the earlier one. Repetition is very rare in Scripture.

2nd. The date of the vision of the seventh chapter was the first year of Belshazzar, and therefore only some two or three years before the *fall* of the Babylonian empire.* How then could the *rise* of that empire be the subject of the prophecy ? Verse 17 appears definite that the rise of all these kingdoms was future.

3rd. In the history of Babylonia there is nothing to correspond with the predicted course of the first Beast, for it is scarcely legitimate to suppose that the vision was a pro-

---

* See Chron. Table, App. I , *ante.*

phecy of the career of Nebuchadnezzar, whose death had taken place upwards of twenty years before the vision was given. Moreover, the transition from the lion with eagle's wings to the human condition, though it may betoken decline in power, plainly typifies a signal rise morally and intellectually.

4th. Neither is there in the history of Persia anything answering to the bear-like beast with that precision and fulness which prophecy demands. The language of the English version suggests a reference to Persia and Media ; but the true rendering appears to be : " It made for itself one dominion,"* instead of " It raised up itself on one side."

5th. While the symbolism of the sixth verse seems at first sight to point definitely to the Grecian Empire, it will appear upon a closer examination that *at its advent* the leopard had four wings and four heads. This was its primary and normal condition, and it was in this condition that " dominion was given to it." This surely is very different from what Dan. viii. 8 describes, and what the history of Alexander's Empire realised, viz., the rise of a single power, which in its decadence continued to exist in a divided state.

6th. Each of the three first empires of the second chapter (Babylon, Persia, and Greece) was in turn destroyed and engulphed by its successor ; but the kingdoms of the seventh chapter all continued together upon the scene, though " the dominion," was with the fourth (Dan. vii. 12). Verse 3 seems to imply that the four beasts came up together, and at all events there is nothing to suggest a series of empires, each destroying its predecessor, though the symbolism of

---

* Tregelles, *Daniel*, p. 34.

the vision was (in contrast with that of chap. ii.) admirably adapted to represent this. Compare the language of the next vision (Dan. viii. 3-6).

7th. While the fourth beast is unquestionably Rome, the language of the seventh and twenty-third verses leaves no doubt that it is the Roman Empire in its revived and future phase. Without endorsing the views of Maitland, Browne, etc.,* it must be owned that there was nothing in the history of ancient Rome to correspond with the main characteristic of this beast unless the symbolism used is to be very loosely interpreted. To "devour the earth," "tread it down and break it in pieces," is fairly descriptive of other empires, but Ancient Rome was precisely the one power which added government to conquest, and instead of treading down and breaking in pieces the nations it subdued, sought rather to mould them to its own civilization and polity.

All this—and more might be added †— suggests that the entire vision of the seventh chapter may have a future reference. We have already seen that sovereign power is to be with a confederacy of ten nations ultimately heading up in one great Kaiser, and that several of what are now the first-rate Powers are to be outside that confederacy : it is in the last degree improbable, therefore, that such a supremacy will be attained save after a tremendous struggle. At this moment the international politics of the old world centre in the Eastern Question, which is after all merely a

---

* See p. 38, *ante*.

† The beasts of Dan. vii. are those named in Rev. xiii. 2, to repre-sent the Antichrist. Though this admits of the explanation given at p. 202, *ante*, it may also be used a a strong argument in favour of the view above set forth.

question of the balance of power in the Mediterranean. Now Dan. vii. 2 expressly names the Mediterranean ("the Great Sea") as the scene of the conflict between the four beasts. May not the opening portion of the vision then refer to the gigantic struggle which must come some day for supremacy in the Mediterranean, which will doubtless carry with it the sovereignty of the world? The lion may possibly typify England, whose vast naval power may be symbolized by the eagle's wings. The plucking of the wings may represent the loss of her position as mistress of the seas. And if such should be the result of the impending struggle, we would be eager to believe that her after course shall be characterized by moral and mental pre-eminence : the beast, we read, was " made to stand upon the feet as a man, and a man's heart was given to it."

If the British lion have a place in the vision, the Muscovite bear can scarcely be omitted ; and it may confidently be averred that the bear of the prophecy may represent the Russia of to-day fully as well as the Persia of Cyrus and Darius. The definiteness of the symbolism used in respect of the leopard (or panther) of the vision makes it more difficult to refer this portion of the prophecy to Germany or any other nation in particular. It would be easy to make out an *ad captandum* case in support of such a view, but it may suffice to remark that if the prophecy be still unfulfilled, its meaning will be incontestable when the time arrives.

CHRONOLOGICAL DIAGRAM OF THE HISTORY OF JUDAH

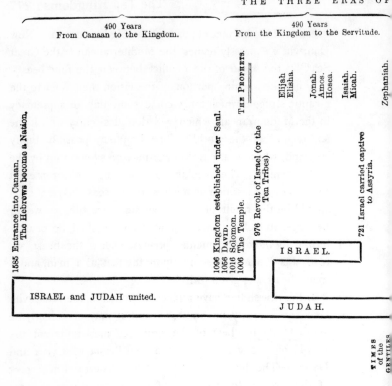

490 Years
From Canaan to the Kingdom.

490 Years
From the Kingdom to the Servitude.

THE PROPHETS.

Elijah
Elisha.

Jonah.
Amos.
Hosea.

Isaiah.
Micah.

Zephaniah.

1585 Entrance into Canaan.
The Hebrews become a Nation.

1096 Kingdom established under Saul.
1056 David.
1016 Solomon.
1006 The Temple.

976 Revolt of Israel (or the Ten Tribes)

721 Israel carried captive to Assyria.

ISRAEL.

ISRAEL and JUDAH united.

JUDAH.

TIMES
of the
GENTILES

B.C.
-1600 -1500 -1400 -1300 -1200 -1100 -1000 -900 -800 -700

OF CENTURIES.

SEVENTY WEEKS

Judah s
National
Existence in
Abeyance

490 Years
Mystic Era of the 70 weeks. (Dan. ix. 25—27.)

Obadiah.
Daniel.

Haggai : Zechariah.

Malachi.

587 Jerusalem destroyed.

515 The Second Temple.

445 Jerusalem restored (Neh. ii.)

397 Era of the Prophets closes.
End of the 7 weeks of Dan. ix. 25.

170 Jerusalem taken by Antiochus Epiphanes.
165 Retaken by Judas Maccabæus.

40 Herod takes Jerusalem and is accepted as King.

A.D. 32, Messiah cut off.

The 70th week. (Dan. ix. 27.)

7 weeks and 62 weeks (Dan ix. 26).

THE GREAT IMAGE. (Dan. ii.)

BABYLON (Gold).	PERSIA (Silver).	GREECE (Brass).	ROME (Iron).

538

333

63
31

The Present Dispensation Intervenes.
The Ten Kingdoms.
THE COMING PRINCE.

THE DAY OF THE LORD.

The Glorious Advent.
Israel and Judah reunited.
THE SABBATIC AGE.

Babylon taken by the Medes and Persians

Battle of Issus

Jerusalem taken by the Romans
Battle of Actium

600
500
400
300
200
100
A.D.
32

SCALE

APPENDIX 3

A RETROSPECT AND A REPLY

"TAKE heed that no man deceive you." Such were the first words of our Lord's reply to the inquiry, "What shall be the sign of Thy coming, and of the end of the age?" And the warning is needed still. "It is not for you to know the times or the seasons," was almost His last utterance on earth, before He was taken up. And if this knowledge was denied to His holy apostles and prophets, we may be sure it has not been disclosed to us to-day. Nor can a secret which, as the Lord declared, "the Father hath put in His own power,"* be discovered by astronomical research or flights of higher mathematics.

But, on the other hand, no thoughtful Christian can ignore the signs and portents which mark the days we live in. I little thought as I penned the introductory chapter of this book that the advance of infidelity would be with such terribly rapid strides. In the few brief years that have since elapsed the growth of scepticism within the Churches has exceeded even the gloomiest forecast. And side by side with this, again, the spread of spiritualism and demon-worship has been appalling. Its votaries are

---

* Acts i. 7.

reckoned by tens of thousands; and in America it has already been systematised into a religion, with a recognised creed and cult.

But these dark features of our times, striking and solemn though they be, are not the most significant. While the warned-against apostasy of the last days thus seems to be drawing near, we are gladdened by signal triumphs of the Cross. It is not merely that at home and abroad the Gospel is being preached by such multitudes with a freedom never known before, but that, in a way unprecedented since the days of the Apostles, the Jews are coming to the faith of Christ. The fact is but little known that during the last few years more than a quarter of a million copies of the New Testament in Hebrew have been circulated among the Jews in Eastern Europe, and the result has been their conversion to Christianity, not by ones and twos, as in the past, but in large and increasing numbers. Entire communities in some places have, through reading the word of God, accepted the despised Nazarene as the true Messiah. This is wholly without parallel since Pentecostal times.

Then again, the return of the Jews to Palestine is one of the strangest facts of the day. There is scarcely a country in the world that does not offer more attractions to the settler, be he agriculturist or trader; and yet, since *The Coming Prince* was written, more Jews have migrated to the land of their fathers than returned with Ezra when the decree of Cyrus brought the servitude to a close. But yesterday the prophecy that Jerusalem should be inhabited "as towns without walls" seemed to belong to a future far remote. The houses beyond the gates were few in number, and no one ventured abroad there after nightfall. To-day the existence of a large and growing Jewish town outside the walls is a fact within the knowledge of every tourist, and year by year the immigration and the building still go on.

If I venture to touch upon the international politics of Europe, it will be but briefly, in connection with the prophecy of the seventh chapter of Daniel. I have given in detail my reasons for suggesting that the "historical" interpretation of that vision does not exhaust its meaning,* and I own to a deepening conviction that every part of it awaits its fulfilment. There, as elsewhere in the Scriptures, "the great sea" must surely mean the Mediterranean; and a terrible struggle for supremacy in the Levant appears to be the burden of the earlier portion of the vision. The nearness of such a struggle is now being anxiously discussed in every capital in Europe, and nowhere more anxiously than here at home. Never indeed since the days of Pitt has there been such cause for national anxiety; and the question of the balance of power in the Mediterranean has recently gained a prominence and interest greater and more acute than ever before attached to it.

I will not notice topics of a more doubtful character, but confine myself to these; nor will I attempt by word-painting to exaggerate their significance. But here we are face to face with great public facts. On the one hand, there is this spread of infidelity and demon-worship, preparing the way for the great infidel and devil-inspired apostasy of the last days; and, on the other hand, there are these spiritual and national movements among the Jews,

---

* *See* pp. 273-277, *ante*. Were I now writing that note in the light of passing events, I should specify France where I have named Germany, and I should allude to the efforts now making by Russia to acquire a naval station in the Mediterranean.

wholly without precedent during all the eighteen centuries which have elapsed since their dispersion. And, finally, the Cabinets of Europe are watching anxiously for the beginning of a struggle such as prophecy warns us will ultimately herald the rise of the last great monarch of Christendom. Is all this to be ignored? Is there not here enough on which to base, I will not say the belief, but an earnest hope, that the end may be drawing near? If its nearness be presented as a hope, I cherish and rejoice in it; if it be urged as a dogma, or an article of faith, I utterly repudiate and condemn it.

As we dwell on these things a double caution will be opportune. These events and movements are not in themselves the fulfilment of the prophecies, but merely indications on which to found the hope that the time for their fulfilment is approaching. Any who searched their Bibles amidst the strange, and startling, and solemn events of a century ago must surely have concluded that the crisis was then at hand; and it may be that once more the tide which now seems so rapidly advancing may again recede, and generations of Christians now unborn may still be waiting and watching upon earth. Who will dare to set a limit to the long-suffering of God? and this is His own explanation of His seeming "slackness."*

We need further to be warned against the error into which the Thessalonian Christians were betrayed. Their conversion was described as a turning from idols to serve the true God and "to wait for His Son from heaven." And the coming of the Lord was presented to them as a practical and present hope, to comfort and gladden them

---

* 2 Peter iii. 9.

as they mourned their dead.* But when the Apostle passed on to speak of " the times and seasons " and " the day of Jehovah," † they misunderstood the teaching ; and, supposing that the coming of the Lord was immediately connected with the day of Jehovah, they concluded that that awful day was breaking. On both points they were wholly wrong. In the Second Epistle the Apostle wrote, " Now we beseech you, brethren, in behalf of the coming of our Lord Jesus Christ and our gathering together unto Him, to the end that ye be not quickly shaken from your mind, nor yet be troubled, either by spirit, or by word, or by epistle as from us [referring of course to the First Epistle], as that the day of the Lord is now present."‡

" The times and seasons " are connected with Israel's hope and the events which will precede the realisation of it.§ The Church's hope is wholly independent of them. And if the Christians of the early days were taught to " live looking for that blessed hope," how much more may we ! Not a line of prophecy must first be fulfilled ; not a single event need intervene. And any system of interpretation or of doctrine which clashes with this, and thus falsifies the teaching of the Apostles of our Lord, stands thereby condemned.‖

---

* I Thess. i. 9, 10, and iv. 13-18.

† I Thess. v. 1-3.

‡ 2 Thess. ii. 1, 2, R.V. " The day of Christ " in A.V. is a wrong reading.

§ Acts i. 6, 7.

‖ *See* I Cor. xi. 26 : "As often as ye eat this bread and drink this cup, ye do show the Lord's death *till He come.*" No past but the Cross ; no future but the Coming. To separate the believer from the Coming is as great an outrage upon Christianity as to separate him from the Cross.

Let us then beware lest we fall into the common error of exaggerating the importance of contemporary movements and events, great and solemn though they be ; and let the Christian take heed lest the contemplation of these things should lead him to forget his heavenly citizenship and his heavenly hope. The realisation of that hope will but clear the stage for the display of the last great drama of earth's history as foretold in prophecy.

If the digression may be pardoned, it may be well to amplify this, and explain my meaning more fully. That Israel will again be restored to the place of privilege and blessing upon earth is not a matter of opinion, but of faith ; and no one who accepts the Scriptures as Divine can question it. Here the language of the Hebrew prophets is unusually explicit. Still more emphatic, by reason of the time when it was given, is the testimony of the Epistle to the Romans. The very position of that Epistle in the sacred Canon gives prominence to the fact that the Jew had then been set aside. The New Testament opens by chronicling the birth of Him who was Son of Abraham and Son of David,* the seed to whom the promises were made and the rightful Heir to the sceptre once entrusted to Judah ; and the Gospels record His death at the hands of the favoured people. Following the Gospels comes the narrative of the renewed offer of mercy to that people, and of their rejection of it. "To the Jew first" is stamped upon every page of the Acts of the Apostles ; and it characterised the transitional Pentecostal dispensation of which that book is the record. The Pentecostal Church was essentially Jewish. Not only were the Gentiles in a minority, but their position was one of comparative tutelage,

---

* Matt. i. 1.

as the record of the Council of Jerusalem gives proof.* Even the Apostle of the Gentiles, in the whole course of his ministry, brought the Gospel first to the Jews. "It was *necessary* that the word of God should first have been spoken to you," he said to them at Antioch. † "The salvation of God is sent unto the Gentiles, and they will hear it," was his final word to them at Rome when they rejected his testimony and " departed." ‡

And *the next book of the Canon is addressed to believing Gentiles.* But in that very Epistle the Gentiles are warned that "God has not cast away His people." Through unbelief the branches are broken off, but the root remains, and " God is able to graft them in again." "And so all Israel shall be saved, as it is written, There shall come out of Sion the Deliverer, and He shall turn away ungodliness from Jacob." § Judgment will in that day mingle with mercy, for He "whose fan is in His hand" will then gather His wheat into the garner, but burn up the chaff with unquenchable fire. The true remnant of the covenant people will become the " all Israel " of days of future blessedness.

That remnant was typified by the " men of Galilee " who stood around Him on the Mount of Olives as " He was taken up, and a cloud received Him out of their

---

* Acts xv. *See also* chap. xi. 19.

† Acts xiii. 46 ; *cf.* xvii. 2, xviii. 4.

‡ Acts xxviii. 29.

§ Rom. xi. ; *see* vv. 1, 2, 11, 12, 15-26. Note that " all Israel " is not = *every Israelite*, for in the Greek there is no such ambiguity as in English ; and the seeming contradictions in the chapter are explained by the fact that the " cast away " of vv. 1, 2, is a wholly different word from the " casting away " of ver. 15, and the " fall " of ver. 11 from the "fall " of ver. 12.

sight." And as with straining eyes they watched Him, two angel messengers appeared to renew the promise which God had given centuries before through Zechariah the prophet: "This same Jesus shall so come in like manner as ye have seen Him go into heaven"; * "His feet shall stand in that day upon the Mount of Olives, which is before Jerusalem on the east." †

A glance at the prophecy will suffice to show that the event it speaks of is wholly different from the Coming of the First Epistle to the Thessalonians. It is the same Lord Jesus, truly, who is coming for His Church of this dispensation and coming to His earthly people gathered in Jerusalem in a dispensation to follow; but otherwise these "Comings" have absolutely nothing in common. The later manifestation — His return to the Mount of Olives — is an event as definitely localised as was His ascension from that same Mount of Olives; and its purpose is declared to be to bring deliverance to His people on earth in the hour of their supreme peril. The earlier Coming will have no relation to locality at all. All the wide world over, wherever His dead have been laid to rest, " the trump of God" shall call them back to life, in "spiritual bodies" like His own; and wherever living "saints" are found, they "will be changed, in a moment, in the twinkling of an eye," and all shall be caught up together to meet Him in the air. While the profane sceptic ridicules all this, and the religious sceptic ignores it, the believer remembers that his Lord was thus caught up to heaven; and as he ponders the promise, his wonder leads to worship, not to unbelief.

---

* Acts i. 1-19.   † Zech. xiv. 4.

And this event, which is the Church's proper hope, is as independent of the chronology, as it is of the geography, of earth. It is with the fulfilment of *Israel's* hope that the "times and seasons" have to do, and the signs and portents that belong to them. The Lord's public manifestation to the world is a further event distinct from both. Our Jehovah-God will come with all His holy ones ; * the Lord Jesus will be revealed in flaming fire, taking vengeance.† What interval of time will separate these successive stages of "the Second Advent," we cannot tell. It is a secret not revealed. All that concerns us is, "rightly dividing the word of truth," to mark that they are in all respects distinct.‡

---

* Zech. xiv. 5.

† 2 Thess. i. 7, 8. The "mighty angels " of the prophecy are, I presume, the " holy ones " of Zech. xiv. 5.

‡ Between the first of these and the second, there will no doubt intervene a period at least as long as that which elapsed between His coming to Bethlehem and His manifestation to Israel at His first advent, and probably a period very much more prolonged. Whether the interval between the second and third will be measured by days or years, we are wholly unable to decide. The only certain indication of its length is that the Antichrist, whose power will be broken by the one, will be actually destroyed by the other.

I am here assuming that all the events which are yet to be fulfilled will occur in a comparatively brief period. But I wish to guard myself against the idea that I *assert* this. I deprecate in the strongest way the idea, now so common, that students of astronomy and mathematics have solved the mystery which God has expressly kept in His own power. Could any student of the Old Testament have dreamed that nearly two thousand years would intervene between the sufferings of Christ and His return in glory? Would the early Christians have tolerated such a suggestion? And if another thousand years should yet run their course before the Church is taken up, or if a thousand years should intervene between that event and the Coming to the Mount of Olives, not a single word of Scripture would be broken. As

I use the expression " Second Advent " merely as a concession to popular theology, for it has no Scriptural warrant. It would be better to discard it altogether, for it is the cause of much confusion of thought and not a little positive error. It is a purely theological term, and it belongs properly to the great and final Coming to judge the world. But while many refuse to believe that there will be any revelation of Christ to His people upon earth until the epoch of that great crisis, the more careful student of Scripture finds there the clearest proof that there will be a " Coming " *before* the era popularly called " the millennium." Here again there are those who, while clearly recognising a " pre-millennial advent," have failed to notice the difference, so plainly marked in Scripture, between the Coming for the Church of the present dispensation, the Coming to the earthly people in Jerusalem, and the Coming to destroy the Lawless One and to set up the kingdom.

But, it may be urged, Is not the expression justified by the closing verse of the ninth chapter of Hebrews ? It is only the superficial reader of the passage, I reply, who can use it thus. " Unto them that look for Him shall He appear the second time," our Authorised Version renders it. And the words are taken as though they were equivalent to " His second appearing," " the Appearing " being a recognised synonym for " the Coming." But this is merely trading on the language of our English version. The word

---

I have said on p. 181, "it is only in so far as prophecy falls within the seventy weeks that it comes within the range of human chronology." (*See also* pp. 153-158, *ante.*) Much is made of supposed eras of 1,260 and 2,520 years. But even if we could certainly fix the epoch of any such era, the question would remain whether they may not be *mystic* periods, like the 480 years of 1 Kings vi. 1. (*See* p. 81, *ante.*)

actually employed is wholly different. It is a general word, and it is the very word used with reference to His manifestation to His disciples after the Resurrection.* And further, the definite article must be omitted : " Insomuch as it is appointed unto men once to die, and after this cometh judgment, so Christ also, having been once [*i.e.,* once for all] offered to bear the sins of many, shall appear a second time, apart from sin, to them that wait for Him, unto salvation." † The statement is not prophetic, but doctrinal ; and the doctrine in question is not the Advent, but the priesthood. It is not the prediction of an event to be realised by those who shall be alive on earth at the time of the end, but the declaration of a truth and a fact to be realised by every believer, no matter in what dispensation his sojourn upon earth may fall.

The passage therefore cannot be appealed to in support of the dogma that never again but *once* will Christ appear to His people upon earth. And as the expression " Second Advent " is so intimately connected with that dogma, it would be well that all intelligent students of Scripture should unite in discarding it. The Coming of Christ is the hope of His people in every age.

The only adverse criticism I have seen of *The Coming Prince* has appeared in later editions of *The Approaching End of the Age.* Feelings of esteem and friendship for the author influenced my notice of that work, but no considerations of this kind have restrained his pen in replying to my strictures ; and the fact that a writer so able and so bitterly hostile has not ventured to question

---

*It occurs four times in I Cor. 15:5-8 † Heb. 9:27, 28.

in a single point the main conclusions here established is a signal proof that they are irrefutable.

Dr. Grattan Guinness complains that I have made no attempt to " reply " to his book. My only reference to it has been made incidentally in an appendix note ; and in so far as it deals with the " primary and partial realisation of the prophecies " I have taken the liberty of praising it. Why then should I " reply " to a treatise in respect of that in it which I value and adopt?   These pages give proof how thoroughly I accept a historical interpretation of prophecy ; * and if any one demands why then I have not given it greater prominence, I recall St. James's answer when the Apostles were accused of neglecting in their teaching the writings of Moses. " Moses," he declared, " hath in every city them that teach him." What was needed, therefore, if the equilibrium of doctrine was to be maintained, was that *they* should teach *grace.*   On similar grounds the task I here set myself was to deal with the *fulfilment* of the prophecies.   But I have no controversy with those who use their every talent in unfolding the " historical " interpretation of them.   My quarrel is only with men who practically deny the Divine authorship of the sacred word, by asserting that their apprehension of it is the limit of its scope, and exhausts its meaning.   And *The Coming Prince* is a crushing reply to the system which dares to write " *Fulfilled*" across the prophetic page.   " The real question at issue here," I again repeat, " is the character and value of the Bible."   Dr. Guinness asserts that the apocalyptic visions have been *fulfilled* in the events of the Christian era.   I hold him to that issue, and I test it by a

---

* *See, e.g.,* Chap. XI. and App., note C.

reference to the vision of the sixth chapter.   Has this been
fulfilled, as in fact he dares to assert it has ?   The question
is vital, for if this vision still awaits fulfilment, so also do all
the prophecies which follow it.   Let the reader decide this
question for himself, after studying the closing verses of the
chapter, ending with the words, " For THE GREAT DAY
OF HIS WRATH IS COME, and who shall be able to stand ? "

The old Hebrew prophets were inspired of God to
describe the terrors of " the great day of His wrath," and
the Holy Spirit has here reproduced their very words.*
The Bible contains no warnings more awful in their
solemnity and definiteness.   But just as the lawyer writes
" Spent " across a statute of which the purpose has been
satisfied, so these men would teach us to write " Fulfilled "
across the sacred page.   They tell us, forsooth, that the
vision meant nothing more than to predict the rout of
pagan hordes by Constantine ! †   To speak thus is to come
perilously near the warned-against sin of those who "take
away from the words of the book of this prophecy."   But
when our thoughts turn to these teachers themselves we
are restrained by remembering their piety and zeal, for
"their praise is in all the Churches."   Let us then banish
from our minds all thoughts of the *men*, and seize upon the
system which they advocate and support.   No appeal to
honoured names should here be listened to.   Names as
honourable, and a hundred times more numerous, can be
cited in defence of some of the crassest errors which corrupt
the faith of Christendom.   What then, I ask, shall be
our judgment on a system of interpretation which thus

---

* *Cf.* Isa. xiii. 9, 10, and Joel ii. 31, iii. 15 ; *see also* Zeph. i. 14, 15.
† *See* pp. 138-141, *ante*, and especially the quotation from Dean
Alford.

blasphemes the God of truth by representing the most awful warnings of Scripture as wild exaggeration of a sort but little removed from falsehood?

If it be urged that the events of fifteen centuries ago, or of some other epoch in the Christian dispensation, were within the scope of the prophecy, we can consider the suggestion on its merits; but when we are told that the prophecy was thus *fulfilled*, we can hold no parley with the teaching. It is the merest trifling with Scripture. And more than this, it clashes with the great charter truth of Christianity. If the day of wrath has come, the day of grace is past, and the Gospel of grace is no longer a Divine message to mankind. To suppose that the day of wrath can be an episode in the dispensation of grace is to betray ignorance of grace and to bring Divine wrath into contempt. The grace of God in this day of grace surpasses human thought; His wrath in the day of wrath will be no less Divine. The breaking of the sixth seal heralds the dawning of that awful day; the visions of the seventh seal unfold its unutterable terrors. But, we are told, the pouring out of the vials, the "seven plagues which are the last, *for in them is finished the wrath of God*," * is being now accomplished. The sinner, therefore, may comfort himself with the knowledge that Divine wrath is but stage thunder, which, in a practical and busy world, may safely be ignored! †

I called attention to Dr. Guinness's statement that "from the then approaching command to restore and to build again Jerusalem to the coming of Messiah the Prince was to

---

* Rev. xv. 1, R.V.

† It is only by reason of its almost inconceivable silliness that such teaching can escape the charge of profanity.

be *seventy* weeks " ; and I added, " This is a typical instance of the looseness of the historical school in dealing with Scripture." Of this, and of some other errors which I noticed, the only defence he offers is that "expressions not strictly correct, yet perfectly legitimate, because evidently elliptical, are *for brevity's sake* employed." How brevity is attained by writing " seventy " instead of " sixty-nine " I cannot conceive. The statement is a sheer perversion of Scripture, unconsciously made, no doubt, to suit the exigencies of a false system of interpretation. The prophecy plainly declares the period " unto Messiah the Prince " to be *sixty-nine weeks*, leaving the seventieth week to be accounted for *after* the specified epoch ; but Dr. Guinness's system can give no reasonable account of the seventieth week, and so, unconsciously, I repeat, he shirks the difficulty by misreading the passage. Insist on his reading it aright and accounting for the last seven years of the prophetic period, and his interpretation of the vision at once stands refuted and exposed.

When the language of Scripture is treated so loosely by this writer, no one need be surprised if *my* words fare badly at his hands. He is wholly incapable of deliberate misrepresentation, and yet his inveterate habit of inaccuracy has led him to misread *The Coming Prince* on almost every point on which he refers to it.*

---

* For instance, he becomes vehement in denouncing my statement that " all Christian interpreters are agreed " in recognising a parenthesis in Daniel's prophetic vision of the beasts. No doubt he read the passage as though I had there spoken of the *fall* of the Roman empire, and not its " rise " ; for the statement is indisputably true, and he himself is numbered among the " Christian interpreters " who endorse it.

Here is another specimen. With reference to the question of the

The fact is, he only knows two schools of prophetic interpretation, the Futurist and his own ; and therefore he seems unable even to understand a book which is throughout a protest against the narrowness of the one and the mingled narrowness and wildness of the other. But his

---

ten kingdoms, he says, "Dr. Anderson and other Futurist writers . . . teach—(1) that the ten horns are not yet risen ; (2) that when they do rise five will be found in Greek territory, and five only in Roman ; and that when at last developed, (3) after a gap of 1,400 years of which the prophecy takes no notice at all, (4) they will last for three and a half years" (p. 737).

I have numbered these sentences to enable me briefly to remind the intelligent reader that, excepting No. 1, everything here attributed to me is in flat opposition to some of the plainest statements in my book. In the same way he attributes to me the figment that the career of Antichrist will be limited to three and a half years. I have sometimes wondered whether he ever read *The Coming Prince* at all !

A word as to his strictures on my title. I am aware of course that in the Hebrew of Dan. ix. 26, there is not the article, but I am not misled by the inference he draws from its omission. Had the article been used, the prince intended would clearly have been "Messiah the Prince" of ver. 25. In English the article has not this force, and therefore it is rightly inserted, as both the Translators and the Revisers have recognised. Dr. Tregelles here remarks, "This destruction is here said to be wrought by a certain people, not by the prince who shall come, but by his people : this refers us, I believe, to the Romans as the last holders of undivided Gentile power ; they wrought the destruction long ages ago. The prince who shall come is the last head of the Roman power, the person concerning whom Daniel had received so much previous instruction." Such is the pre-eminence of this great leader that he is bracketed with our Lord Himself in this prophecy, and the people of the Roman empire are described as being *his* people. Yet Mr. Guinness believes that Titus is referred to ! Really the day is past for discussing such a suggestion.

I may here remark that the rendering of Dan. ix. 27 in the Revised Version disposes of the figment that it was Messiah who made a seven years' covenant with the Jews. The causing the sacrifice to cease is not an incident in the midst of the "week," but a violation of the treaty "*for half of the week.*"

personal references are unworthy of the writer and of the subject. I pass on to deal with the only points on which his criticisms are of any general interest or importance; I mean the predicted division of the Roman earth, and the relations between Antichrist and the apostate Church.

My statement was : " The division of the Roman earth into ten kingdoms has never yet taken place. That it has been partitioned is plain matter of history and of fact ; that it has ever been divided into ten is a mere conceit of writers of this school."

" An astonishingly reckless assertion " Dr. Guinness declares this to be; and yet we have but to turn the page to obtain from his own pen the plainest admission of its truth. It must be borne in mind, he says, that the ten kingdoms are to be sought " *only in the territory west of Greece.*" And if we are prepared to accept this theory, we shall find, after making large allowances as to boundaries, that in this, which is prophetically *the least important moiety of the Roman earth,* "the number of the kingdoms of the European commonwealth has, as a rule, averaged ten." Mr. Guinness gives a dozen lists—and he tells us he has a hundred more in reserve—to prove that, with kaleidoscopic instability and vagueness, or, to quote his words, "amidst increasing and almost countless fluctuations, the kingdoms of modern Europe have from their birth to the present day always averaged about ten in number." " *Averaged about ten,*" mark, though the prophecy specifies *ten* with a definiteness which becomes absolute by its mention of an eleventh rising up and subduing three of them. And "modern Europe," too ! Zeal for the Protestant cause seems to blind these men to the plainest teaching of Scripture. Jerusalem, and not Rome, is the centre of the Divine prophecies and of God's dealings with His people ; and the attempt to explain Daniel's visions upon a system which ignores Daniel's city and people does violence to the very rudiments of prophetic teaching.   This vaunted canon of interpretation, which reads "modern Europe" instead of the prophetic earth, is, I repeat, "a mere conceit of writers of this school." First they minimise and tamper with the language of prophecy, and then they exaggerate and distort the facts of history to suit their garbled reading of it. "Can they," Dr. Guinness demands of us, "alter or add to this tenfold list of the great kingdoms now occupying the sphere of old Rome?—Italy, Austria, Switzerland, France, Germany, England, Holland, Belgium, Spain, and Portugal. Ten, and no more ! ten, and no less !" I answer, Yes, we can both alter it and add to it.   The list includes territory which was never within "the sphere of old Rome " at all, and it omits altogether nearly half of the Roman earth.

This is bad enough, but it is not all.   For if we accept his statements, and seek to interpret the thirteenth chapter of Revelation by them, he at once changes his ground and protests against our numbering " Protestant nations " among the ten horns at all.   They are " chronologically out of the question," he tells us.   Here is the language of this vision about Antichrist : "And there was given to him authority over every tribe, and people, and tongue, and nation.   And all that dwell on the earth shall worship him, every one whose name hath not been written in the book of life." *
What mean these most definite and solemn words ?
Nothing, he tells us, but that " throughout the Dark Ages,"

---

* Rev. xiii., 7, 8, R.V.

and "prior to the rise of Protestantism," the Roman Catholic religion should prevail in the western moiety of the Roman earth. This, he declares, is "the fulfilment of the prediction." He calls this "explaining" Scripture. Most people would call it *explaining it away*!

I now come to the last point. "Our critics maintain," Dr. Guinness writes, "that Babylon runs her career, and is destroyed by the ten horns, who then agree and give their power to Antichrist, or the Beast. That is, they hold that the reign of Antichrist *follows* the destruction of Babylon by the ten horns."

The foundation of this statement must be sought in the author's own lucubrations, for nothing to account for it will be found in the pages he criticises; and a similar remark applies to his references to *The Coming Prince* in the paragraphs which follow. I will not allude to them in detail, but in a few sentences dispose of the position he is seeking to defend.

We have now got to the seventeenth chapter of Revelation. His argument is this : The eighth head of the Beast must be a dynasty; the Beast carries the Woman; the Woman is the Church of Rome. Therefore the dynasty symbolised by the eighth head must have lasted as long as the Church of Rome; and thus the Protestant interpretation is settled "on a foundation not to be removed."

It is not really worth while pausing to show how gratuitous are some of the assumptions here implied. Let us, for the sake of argument, accept them all, and what comes of it ? In the first place, Dr. Guinness is hopelessly involved in the transparent fallacy I warned him against on p. 268 of this volume. The Woman is destroyed by the agency of the Beast. How then is he going to separate the Pope from the apostate Church of which he is the head, and which, according to the "Protestant interpretation," would cease to be the apostate Church if he were no longer owned as head?

The historicist must here make choice between the Woman and the Beast. They are distinct throughout the vision, and in direct antagonism at the close. If the Harlot represents the Church of Rome, his system gives no account whatever of the Beast; it ignores altogether the foremost figure in the prophecy, and the vaunted "foundation" of the so-called "Protestant interpretation" vanishes into air. Or if he takes refuge upon the other horn of the dilemma, and maintains that the Beast symbolises the apostate Church, the Harlot remains to be accounted for. He forgets, moreover, that the Beast appears in Daniel's visions in relation to Jerusalem and Judah. Suppose, therefore, we should admit everything he says, what would it amount to? Merely a contention that "the springing and germinant accomplishment" of these prophecies "throughout many ages" (I quote Lord Bacon's words once more) is fuller and clearer than his critics can admit, or the facts of history will warrant. The truth still stands out plainly that "the height or fulness of them" belongs to an age to come, when Judah shall once more be gathered in the Promised Land, and the light of prophecy which now rests dimly upon Rome shall again be focussed on Jerusalem.

The popularity of the historical system lies no doubt in the appeal it makes to the "Protestant spirit." But surely we can afford to be sensible and fair in our denunciation of the Church of Rome. Who can fail to perceive the growth of an antichristian movement that may soon lead us to hail the devout Romanist as an ally? With such, the Bible, neglected though it be, is still held sacred as the inspired word of God ; and our Divine Lord is reverenced and worshipped, albeit the truth of His Divinity is obscured by error and superstition. I appeal here to the Pope's Encyclical Letter of the 18th November, 1893, on the study of the Holy Scriptures. The following is an extract from it :—

" We fervently desire that a greater number of the faithful should undertake the defence of the holy writings, and attach themselves to it with constancy ; and, above all, we desire that those who have been admitted to Holy Orders by the grace of God should daily apply themselves more strictly and zealously to read, meditate upon, and explain the Scriptures. Nothing can be better suited to their state. In addition to the excellence of such knowledge and the obedience due to the word of God, another motive impels us to believe that the study of the Scriptures should be counselled. That motive is the abundance of advantages which follow from it, and of which we have the guarantee in the words of Holy Writ : ' All Scripture is given by inspiration of God, and is profitable for doctrine, for reproof, for correction, for instruction in righteousness, that the man of God may be perfect, thoroughly furnished unto all good works. [13] It is with this design that God gave man the Scriptures ; the examples of our Lord Jesus Christ and His apostles show it. Jesus Himself was accustomed to appeal to the holy writings in testimony of His Divine mission."

There is here surely, in some sense at least, the ground for a common faith, which might, as regards individual Christians, be owned as a bond of brotherhood ; but an impassable gulf divides us from the ever-increasing host of so-called Protestants who deny the Divinity of Christ and the inspiration of the Scriptures. These have their true place in the great army of infidelity which will muster at last around the banner of the Antichrist.

---

[13] See Appendix 4, p. 307 note 13.

My protest is made, not in defence of the Papacy, but of the Bible. If any one can point to *a single passage of Scripture* relating to Antichrist, whether in the Old Testament or in the New, which can, without whittling it down, and frittering away the meaning of the words, find its *fulfilment* in Popery, I will publicly retract, and confess my error. Take 2 Thessalonians ii. 4 as a sample of the rest. The " man of sin " " opposeth and exalteth himself against all that is called God or that is worshipped [*Greek*, that is an object of worship], so that he sitteth in the temple of God, setting himself forth as God." This means merely, forsooth, that on certain occasions the Pope's seat in St. Peter's is raised above the level of the altar on which the " consecrated wafer " lies ! Such statements—I care not what names may be cited in support of them—are an insult to our intelligence and an outrage upon the word of God.*

---

* The reference to the Temple is explained by Dan. ix. 27, xii. 11, and Matt. xxiv. 15. See p. 84, *ante.* These teachers ask us to believe that while the Church of Rome is the Beast and the Harlot and everything that is corrupt and infamous in apostate Christianity, yet St. Peter's, the great central shrine of this apostasy, is owned by God as being *the Temple of God.* The sacrifice of the Mass they denounce as idolatrous and blasphemous, and yet we are tò suppose that Holy Scripture refers to it as representing all that is Divine on earth ! The sacred words admit of only one meaning, viz., that the Antichrist, claiming to be himself Divine, will suppress all worship rendered to any other god.

Such are the wild extravagances and puerilities of interpretation and of forecast which mar the writings of these interpreters, that men have come to regard these visions, which ought to inspire reverence and awe, as "principal subjects of ridicule "—the speciality of mystics and faddists. How great the need, then, for a united and sustained effort to rescue the study from the contempt into which it has fallen !

Each of the recognised schools of interpretation has truth which the rival schools deny. A new era would begin if Christians would turn

Then, again, in the ninth verse, the coming of the " Law-less One " is said to be " according to the working of Satan, with all power and signs and lying wonders." These words are explained by the vision of the Beast in the thirteenth chapter of the Revelation, which declares that " the Dragon gave him his power, and his throne, and great authority." And we have from the lips of our blessed Lord Himself the warning, that the " great signs and wonders," thus to be wrought by Satanic power, shall be such that, " if it were possible, they shall deceive the very elect." * In a word, the awful and mysterious power of Satan will be brought to bear upon Christendom with such terrible effect, that human intellect will be utterly confounded. Agnosticism and infidelity will capitulate in presence of overwhelming proof that supernatural agencies are at work. And if faith itself, divinely given, shall stand the test, it is only because it is impossible for God to allow His own elect to perish.

When we demand the meaning of all this, we get answer " Popery." But where, we ask, are the "great signs and wonders" of the Popish system? And, in reply, we are told of its millinery, and its mummery, and all the well-known artifices of priestcraft, which constitute its special stock-in-trade. As though there were anything in *these* to deceive the elect of God ! To take the low ground of mere Protestantism, it is notorious that here in England none become entangled in the toils of Rome save such as have already become enervated and corrupted by sacerdo-

from all these schools—Preterist, Historical, and Futurist—and learn to read the prophecies as they read the other Scriptures : as being the word of Him who is, and was, and is to come, our Jehovah-God, with whom present, past, and future are but one "eternal now,"

* Matt. xxiv. 24.

talism and superstition within the communion they abandon. And it is no less notorious that, in Roman Catholic countries, the majority of men maintain towards it an attitude of either benevolent or contemptuous indifference. Remembering, moreover, that the followers of the Beast are doomed to endless and hopeless destruction, we go on to inquire whether this is to be the fate of every Roman Catholic. By no means, we are assured; for, in spite of the evils and errors of the Romish Church, some within its pale are reckoned among the number of "God's elect."

What conclusion, then, are we to come to? Are we to accept it as a canon of interpretation that Scripture never means what it says? Are we to hold that its language is so loose and unreliable as to be practically false? We repudiate the profane suggestion; and, adopting the only possible alternative, we boldly assert that all these solemn words still await their fulfilment. In a word, we are shut up to the conclusion that THE ANTICHRIST IS YET TO COME.

APPENDIX 4

UP-DATED INFORMATION 1983

Page viii
 1. The author here refers to World War 1.

Page xiv
 2. That is, the eighteenth century for this work was writ-
    ten near the end of the nineteenth century.

Page xxii
 3. For the solution of the problem, we refer you to page
    xv (Preface to the Tenth Edition) and also to the ex-
    haustive study of J.C. Whitcomb, *Darius the Mede*.

Page xxxiv
 4. It is interesting to note, in this connection, that the
    author, Sir Robert Anderson, was a lawyer and that he
    served many years as Director of England's Crime In-
    vestigative unit - Scotland Yard.

Page 27
 5. Written about 64 years before the establishment of
    the new Sate of Israel.

Page 76
 6. This work was written near the end of the nineteenth
    century. The State of Israel was proclaimed by Ben
    Gurion in May, 1948.

Page 128

7. Based on a subsequent work of Harold W. Hoehner, "Daniel's Seventy Weeks and New Testament Chronology" - *Bibliothca Sacra*, Jan.-Mar. 1975, a discrepancy of ten days was found in the chronology with respect to the beginning of the 70th week.

Page 129

8. The author is speaking here of England with regards to the late correction of the calendar. Since this work was written the Soviet Union calendar has been corrected.

Page 129

9. Again, we remind the reader that, since the author wrote this work, the restoration of Judah in Palestine took place with the founding of the State of Israel in May, 1948.

Page 150

10. At the time this book was written, the Turkish Empire was Lord and owner of the Promised Land.

Page 168

11. It is worthy of note that Sir Robert Anderson distinguishes between mere *probabilities* and the brilliant exposition of the *Scriptures* themselves. It is curious to see that finally the Jewish immigration to Palestine took place against much opposition, even the very same country of Sir Robert Anderson (England) which did not want to take away the Arabs and their influence in the region. Certainly, the Jews were led to Israel, not under favorable circumstances, but in spite of all the impossibilities.

Page 168

12. Here, unfortunately, National independence is confused with sovereignty over Jerusalem. In 1948, the Jews obtained the first (National independence) but not sovereignty over Jerusalem itself, the city of David, into a large portion of which they entered in 1967. In effect, from the viewpoint of God, Jerusalem "the place which the Lord your God shall choose out... to put His name there," is Mount Zion and particularly the threshing place of Arumah, the Jebusite, the place of the Temple, which has in its center the Mosque of Omar, a sacred place of Islam, and in other corners the *Mosque of ElAgsa* and the *House of the Treasury* or *Qubbet Es Silsile*. These places, *precisely in the area of the Temple*, are still under the sovereignty and protection of Islam and, from an objective viewpoint, Jerusalem *continues to be trodden under by the Gentiles*. Thus, even though the Jews are already back in Israel, and possess the *city of Jerusalem*, the definite element of the city and that which really defines Judaism as such—the Jewish worship in the Temple—is still not in their reach and is awaiting the time that God has earmarked.

Page 301
13. 2 Timothy 3:16,17

INDEX

310 / Index

BIOGRAPHICAL SKETCH

Sir Robert Anderson described himself as "an anglicized Irishman of Scottish extraction." Before his death in 1918, he was widely recognized as a popular lay-preacher, an author of best-selling books on Biblical subjects, and one of the most capable "defenders of the faith" at a time when the "higher criticism" was threatening the church.

Robert Anderson was born in 1841 in Dublin, where his father, Matthew Anderson, served as Crown Solicitor for the city. His father was also a distinguished elder in the Irish Presbyterian Church. Robert was educated privately in Dublin, Paris, and Boulogne; and in 1859 he entered Trinity College, Dublin, graduating in 1862.

Brought up in a devout Christian home, Anderson in his late teens had serious doubts about his own conversion. About that time (1859-60) the Irish Revival was touching and changing the lives of many, including Robert's sister. She persuaded her brother to attend one of the services, but the popular hymns disturbed him and he got very little out of the message. The following Sunday, he attended church and heard Dr. John Hall preach at the evening service. The message so disturbed him that he remained to argue with the preacher.

In telling of the experience, Anderson wrote: "...facing me as we stood upon the pavement, he repeated with great solemnity his message and appeal: 'I tell you as a minister of Christ and in His name that there is life for you here and now, if you will accept Him. Will you accept Christ or will you reject Him?' After a pause — how prolonged I know not — I exclaimed, 'In God's name I will accept Christ.' ...And I turned homeward with the peace of God filling my heart."

Two years later, Anderson was active as a lay-preacher and was greatly used to win many to Christ. In 1863 he was made a member of the Irish Bar and served on the legal circuit. About this time, the Fenians were at work (a secret society attempting to overthrow British rule in Ireland), and he became involved interrogating prisoners and preparing legal briefs. This was his introduction into police work.

He was married in 1873 and four years later moved to London as a member of the Home Office staff. He had access to the detective department and made good use of it. In 1888, while Jack the Ripper was terrorizing London, Anderson moved into Scotland Yard as Assistant Commissioner of Metropolitan Police and Chief of the Criminal Investigation Department. He served his country well until his retirement in 1901, and the records show that crime decreased in London during that period. Conan Doyle was entertaining London at that time with his Sherlock Holmes stories, but it was

Anderson and his staff who were ridding the city of crime and criminals.

Anderson had a large circle of friends, not only politicians but especially preachers: Dr. Handley G. Moule, J. Stuart Holden, Henry Drummond, James M. Gray, C.I. Scofield, A.C. Dixon, and E.W. Bullinger, whose views on Israel and the church greatly influenced Anderson. It was Horatius Bonar who first taught Anderson the great truths concerning the second coming of Christ, and "the blessed hope" was a precious doctrine to him, especially during the dark days of the first war.

He authored seventeen major books on Biblical themes, and it is good to see them coming back into print. Charles H. Spurgeon said that Anderson's book *Human Destiny* was "the most valuable contribution on the subject" that he had ever seen. His last book, *Unfulfilled Prophecy and the Hope of the Church*, was published in 1917. These books underscore the inspiration and dependable authority of the Bible, the deity of Jesus Christ, and the necessity of new birth. He tracked down myths and religious error, arrested and exposed it, with the same skill and courage that he displayed when he tracked down criminals. If you have never met Sir Robert Anderson, then you are about to embark on a thrilling voyage of discovery. If he is already one of your friends, then finding a new Anderson title, or meeting an old one, will bring joy to your heart and enlightenment to your mind. Happy reading!

WARREN W. WIERSBE

**SIR ROBERT ANDERSON
LIBRARY SERIES**

THE COMING PRINCE
This is the standard work on the marvelous prophecy of Daniel about the AntiChrist and the Seventy Weeks. It deals fully with the details of the chronology and with the vexing questions of the last of the Seventy Sevens.

FORGOTTEN TRUTHS
The author shares valuable insight into the difficulty for some people caused by the delay of our Lord's return, as well as other truths seemingly irreconcilable because of finite human minds.

THE GOSPEL AND ITS MINISTRY
A study of such basic Christian truths as Grace, Reconcilation, Justification and Sanctification. In the author's own direct, yet devotional, style these truths are stated, then emphasized; so that the skeptic becomes convinced and the believer is blessed.

THE LORD FROM HEAVEN
A devotional treatment of the doctrine of the Deity of Christ. This differs from other works in that it offers indirect testimony of the Scriptures as to the validity of this doctrine. This book is not written to settle doctrinal controversy, but rather it is a Bible study that will deepen the student's conviction, while giving a warm devotional approach.

REDEMPTION TRUTHS

The author presents unique insights on the gift offer of salvation, the glory of Sonship and the grandeur of eternity's splendor.

THE SILENCE OF GOD

If God really cares, why has He let millions on earth suffer, starve and fall prey to the ravages of nature? Why has He been silent for nearly two millennia? The author gives a thorough and Scriptural answer. He also discusses the subject of miracles today with excellent answers. Here is a "must" for serious Bible students.

TYPES IN HEBREWS

A study of the types found in the book of Hebrews. Anderson ties the revelation of God to the Hebrew nation to the full revelation of the Church of Jesus Christ, with the premise that God's provision for the Jew was a forerunner of the blessings for the Christian. The author moves from type to type with his own pithy comments and then augments them with the comments of his nineteenth century contemporaries.